CREAD

THE COARSE
FISHERMAN'S
COMPANION

THE COARSE
FISHERMAN'S
COMPANION

Foreword by Bob Nudd

B🌿XTREE

First published in the UK 1994
by Boxtree Limited
Broadwall House
21 Broadwall
London SE1 9PL

1 3 5 7 9 10 8 6 4 2

© (text and photographs) Emap Pursuit Publishing Ltd,
with the exception of 'Section Four – Baits'
© (text and photographs) John Wilson

Cover design by Millions Design
Text design by Anita Ruddell
Edited by Neil Pope

Colour origination by Typongraph, Verona, Italy
Printed in England by New Interlitho, Milan, Italy

A catalogue record for this book is available from the British Library.

ISBN: 1 85283 476 5

Contents

ACKNOWLEDGEMENTS

The editor and publishers would like to thank the following:

Kevin Wilmot for editing the original editions of *Pole Fishing* and *Match Fishing*,
and Mac Campbell for editing the original edition of *Legering*

Malcolm Lane and Dave Batten for the use of their illustrations

Bob Atkins, Phil Bagnall, Angus Murray, Matthew Roberts and John Wilson
for use of their photographs

Thanks also to all of the anglers, especially Len Arbery, Bob James, Matt Hayes, Lee Jackson
and Mick Brown, who have helped to contribute to *Improve Your Coarse Fishing* magazine
since its launch in 1991.

Foreword

My love of fishing comes from a combination of factors but it all centres around the actual catching of fish: the unknown! Will I catch today? How many? What species? What size? The real excitement is when the float dips, you strike and the fish is on, the playing and the landing, and then just simply looking at the fish you have just managed to outwit.

When I was a very young boy, my two elder sisters used to take me fishing. Although I did not take it up seriously until I was about twenty-four, my first really major match win came ten years later in 1978 when I won the first day of the Benson & Hedges Classic on the river Erne in Northern Ireland, with a weight of 166 lb 9 oz – at the time only 2 oz short of the world record set by Ian Heaps the previous year.

In my early days as a match angler, pole fishing had not really arrived in this country so most of my fishing was done with a waggler and leger and concentrated on a prolific carp water – the layer pits near Colchester. Weights of between 50 lb and 100 lb were frequently recorded there. This gave me a thorough grounding in long range leger and float tactics and also taught me how to handle large fish.

Once I realized that pole fishing was going to form a major part of our match angling tactics in this country, I decided to travel abroad to Italy and France to learn all I could about this new technique. There weren't magazines like *Improve Your Coarse Fishing* about in those days, but we had our national weekly, *Angling Times*.

I rarely went to watch other anglers: I loved catching fish so much, I didn't want to waste a minute. While fishing in Ireland, I managed to get to know Kevin Ashurst, Ivan Marks and Ian Heaps, plus many other notable anglers, all from whom I gleaned lots of information.

Although I have won the World Championships twice, I still have a thirst for knowledge. Once you stop learning, then there is only one way to go: downhill. Technology, tactics and techniques are forever changing and you must always be aware of the current trends. If you wish to improve as an angler, you have to work very hard, reading, mixing with other anglers, watching videos and going to watch top team and international matches.

Anglers are great conservationists, ever mindful of polution and on many occasions, because of their care and knowledge of these things, have managed to avoid major fish kills. Litter can be a problem and if we wish to protect our sport then we should be seen at all times respecting the countryside, wildlife and riverlife.

The real pleasure of angling comes from catching fish. Look, listen and learn, improve your skills and you will become better anglers and enjoy your sport so much more.

Tight lines

Bob Nudd
Twice-winner of the World
Championships, in 1990 and 1991

The master at work: top floatfisherman Dave Harrell shows how it is done.

FLOAT FISHING

There is something special about watching a carefully-shotted float disappear beneath the surface of the water as a fish takes the bait. Whether it is the uncertainty of not knowing what has taken the bait I find so exciting, I'm not sure, but this type of fishing holds a special attraction for me. These days, with so many varied methods available to the angler, a newcomer could quite easily overlook this branch of the sport. I can accept the fact there are easier ways for a beginner to get started but nothing can match the sheer thrill of a bite on the float.

I started fishing at the age of five with my father and grandfather. Each weekend we would go out fishing, mostly on canals. Occasionally, however, we would venture on to a river. I could handle canals quite easily as, for most of the time, the water was still. Rivers were a different proposition and it took me a long time to get to grips with them. For a start I was using the wrong floats, although I didn't realise it at the time. In those days float choice was very limited compared to today's vast array of purpose-made works of art. Quite often the angler had to make his own floats to cope

with the various conditions, and as I got older I used to spend hours developing a new pattern. This, in turn, led to a floatfishing love affair which still exists today.

As the years passed I gradually improved. I used to read many articles by the top anglers and try to adapt their methods for my own fishing. Some worked, some didn't, it was a process of elimination. I still read a lot of articles and books to find out if I'm missing out on something.

I'm often asked how an angler can become successful. The answer is sheer hard work. There is no real short-cut to gaining the experience which is needed to make you a top angler. It can, though, be an extremely rewarding and satisfying learning curve. Having read this book, no angler can fail to benefit from its contents.

When I was five years old I used to get a thrill watching the float go under. These days, if anything, it is even more exciting. Long may it continue!

Dave Harrell
Matchman of the Year 1989, 1992.

CHAPTER ONE

Types of Float

Floatfishing is undoubtedly the most enjoyable and successful way of catching fish. There can be no better feeling than to cast out a float, watch it travel the length of a swim and see it suddenly disappear underwater as a fish takes the bait.

For most anglers, their first introduction to fishing is with the float, and it is such an enjoyable experience that they become hooked on the sport for life. Few ever forget this early-learning stage because of the beauty of the method. However, if you fail to master the art of floatfishing you can easily get disillusioned and walk away from angling. For the inexperienced there is so much that can go wrong.

Where do you start? Walk into any tackle shop today and you will be confronted by a mass of floats in different colours, sizes and shapes, and it can prove a minefield for anglers unsure about which type will best suit their needs. Float choice, and knowing when and where to use each, is very important to success. Do not get carried away with fancy colours and shapes. In the early days it is far better to stick to a small number of floats and follow a few basic rules.

STRAIGHT WAGGLER

Perhaps the most basic of all floats is the straight waggler. This is simply a straight piece of buoyant material, sealed to make it waterproof. It has a ring attached at the bottom through which the line is threaded. The float is secured by the bottom end only, usually by placing two or more 'locking shot' on the line either side of the bottom eye.

The waggler's main advantage is that once it has been cast out into the water, the line can be sunk out of harm's way. Bites will be few and far between with a waggler in most conditions if the line is left on the surface.

Instead, after casting, plunge the top 2 ft of your rod under the surface and make a couple of quick turns of the reel handle to sink the line. Usually you will be able to see when the line is sunk completely. A couple of sharp flicks of the rod-tip will have the same result – in fact, this line-sinking method can often be more desirable as it will not tend to pull the float as far towards you as when the line is sunk by the reel-turning method.

If the line is sunk, it will not be dragged along by the force of the wind on the surface of the water. Whenever there is any wind blowing, the top part of the water moves at a different rate from the lower layers – and this looks unnatural to the fish. Generally speaking, the stronger the wind, the greater the depth of water that will be moving unnaturally. So it follows that the stronger the wind, the longer the float you should use, so that your line will not be affected by it. This applies just as much on lakes as it does on rivers.

Materials for straight wagglers vary enormously, but the best is probably peacock quill. This natural material has never been

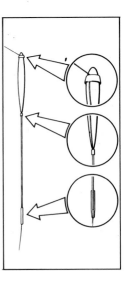

Three float rubbers are better than one for attaching a stick float to the line.

bettered by anything man-made. It is very buoyant, comes in many varying thicknesses, and can be cut to any length from 1 in to 2 ft. Straight peacock wagglers are available in just about every tackle shop in the country. A good float is quite expensive but that expense is more than made up for by the float's effectiveness in just about every condition.

A straight peacock waggler is often the float to choose on a river with little or moderate flow if the wind is blowing in a downstream direction. An insert waggler (see below) is sometimes too sensitive for this type of fishing, but a straight waggler will allow you to fish a little overdepth, or to hold back very slightly against the float if you desire. Holding back makes the bait rise attractively from the river bed before settling again as the float is allowed to continue its course. A waggler with a thin insert would be dragged

under as it is held back, but the extra buoyancy in a thicker piece of peacock quill will allow you to do this without too much difficulty. As a general rule, the faster the river, the thicker should be the peacock quill from which the float is made.

However, straight wagglers are not used only on rivers. Many anglers like them for lake-fishing too, because they can be seen better at long range. And don't forget that although many peacock wagglers are quite thick, they are also available made from the tips of peacock quills. These are very thin indeed and are ideal for shy-biting fish on lakes, rivers and even canals. They are very sensitive, and good for fish feeding as the bait sinks and before it reaches the bottom.

So, as you can see, the straight waggler is a truly versatile float. You can even use it in water of only 1 ft or so deep. A tiny, dumpy

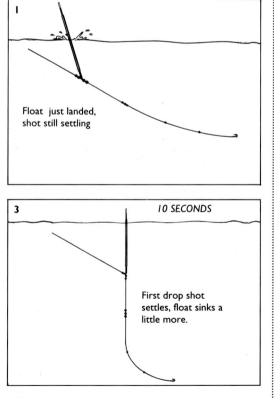

Float just landed, shot still settling

First drop shot settles, float sinks a little more.

After casting a waggler it pays to count the time it takes the float to settle. If the float hasn't settled in the allotted time then a fish has probably snatched the bait on its way down, and the angler should strike.

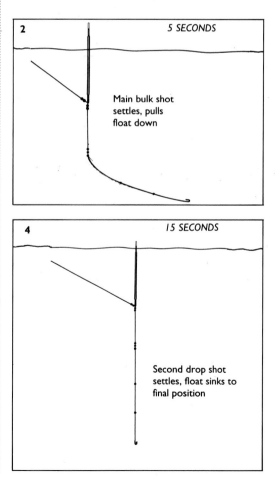

5 SECONDS

Main bulk shot settles, pulls float down

10 SECONDS

15 SECONDS

Second drop shot settles, float sinks to final position

A fish is hooked and an angler takes up the challenge. This is what floatfishing is all about.

piece of thick peacock quill has taken many a good catch of chub or dace in shallow water.

If the line has to be sunk out of the way of the wind, use a waggler. There are times, however, when the line does not need to be sunk. When there is no wind on a river or lake, for example, bites can be hit much more quickly if the line is left on the surface. In addition, if the wind is blowing in an upstream direction on a river, against the flow, it's surprising how many fish you will catch by leaving the line on the surface and using the wind to slow down the passage of the float through the swim. As a bow forms in the line, 'feed' it by allowing a little line to leave your reel. This will allow the float to trot through, but much slower than the current.

You can also feed the bow when the wind is blowing downstream, but for a different purpose. When the wind is quite strong and blowing downstream, it will stop the float being dragged along faster than the current. There will be a lot of line between rod and float when you do get a bite, so the strike

should be a sweeping arc of the rod, feeling all the time for that point where contact is made with the fish.

Other materials for straight wagglers include sarcandas reed, balsa and clear plastic, a type of float that has become extremely popular for clear water. Many anglers have more straight wagglers in their float boxes than any other type of float. They can take from around three No.4 shot to as much as four SSG.

The size of float you choose depends not only on the conditions, but also on the fish you are expecting to catch. For shallow-water fishing for dace and roach, for example, your float should take only around two AAA shot – as long as big casts are not required. By far the majority of the float's shotting capacity is placed immediately either side, with just a couple of No.8s and a No.10 'down the line' to give the bait a slow fall through the water. Coupled with heavy loose-feed of maggots, this float has accounted for some large bags of dace and roach on rivers like the Warwickshire Avon.

For swims over 5 ft deep, however, you should go for a larger float taking, say, three or four AAA, with more shot between float and hook, or the bait will take too long to fall

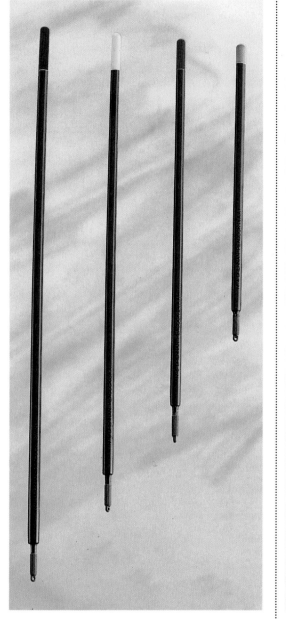

Two types of waggler float: (left) a straight peacock waggler; (right) an insert peacock waggler.

through the water. Sometimes in these swims, you will find the fish feeding in the bottom 3 ft or so. Then is the time to place a small 'bulk' of, say, three No.8s, at about 4 ft from the hook to get the bait down quickly, with another No.8 and a No.10 shot below. Here

you get the best of both worlds. The small bulk sinks quickly, but thereafter the rest settle very slowly, allowing you to pick up those fish.

One rule to remember when waggler fishing is that whenever you feel you are not in total control of the float, change it for a larger one. Shotted correctly, a straight waggler taking three SSG shot can be just as sensitive as one taking three No.4s.

INSERT WAGGLER

An insert waggler is exactly as its name suggests – a straight piece of buoyant material with a thinner insert glued into the top. Again, the best material is peacock quill for both main float stem and insert, and the insert should err towards the long side – 2 to 3 in is best, depending on the size of your float.

Insert wagglers are more sensitive than straight wagglers, and are used much more for lakes and slow-moving rivers. They are ideal for fishing at distances of up to seven or eight rod-lengths and are perfect for catching fish feeding on the drop. That is because the thin insert on the float is highly sensitive and it will be easy to see each shot register as it settles. After a few casts, make a picture in your mind's eye of what is happening beneath the water. Each shot settles and registers by sinking the float a little more. If one shot fails to settle properly, this will be recognisable by the float taking more time than usual to settle, and means that a fish has intercepted the bait on its way through the water.

Inserts can be used in windy conditions, but they should be longer than used in calm conditions. They are shotted much the same as their all-straight cousins.

BODIED WAGGLER

When really long casts are required, or when you want to place a lot of shot 'down the line'– when bream fishing for example – then is the time to use a bodied waggler. They take a lot of shot for their size and are best made from peacock quill with either a balsa or polystyrene body.

They should not really be used for shallow water as they tend to plunge well beneath the surface on hitting the water. However, the body adds a lot of stability to the float, so if conditions are really windy, it can sometimes pay to use this float.

LOADED WAGGLER

Since the arrival of non-toxic shot, many float manufacturers have taken to producing more loaded floats than ever before. Prompted by the unsuitability of the new shot in larger sizes as float locking-shot, the manufacturers decided to incorporate a brass loading in the base of the float. Only a couple of small shot are then needed to 'lock' the float in position.

Loaded wagglers undoubtedly work well, although it has to be said that there are now several lead substitutes on the market as good as lead for locking shot. Where loaded wagglers score is in their casting. There are no large shot around the float to create wind resistance when casting, so greater distances can be achieved. Don't use them, however, when you want to fish a large 'bulk' near to the hook, as the floats don't take enough shot to allow you to do this.

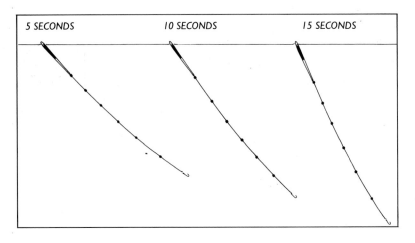

| 5 SECONDS | 10 SECONDS | 15 SECONDS |

A cane-stemmed stick float gives the hookbait a slow fall through the water – ideal for fish feeding on the drop.

SLIDING FLOAT

Many anglers, even experienced ones, don't know how to use a sliding float properly, and those who do often imagine this float should only be used in depths greater than the length of your rod. However, the sliding float is much more versatile than that. Excessive depth obviously requires a slider, but what about when bankside vegetation doesn't allow you to cast a full depth properly? Even depths of 7 or 8 ft can pose all sorts of problems if the bankside vegetation doesn't allow you to cast. So instead of struggling away getting into tangles, use a slider.

There are two ways of using a sliding float. The method that most people associate with it involves using a heavy, loaded float with a body. The float rests on a No.4 shot, while a 'bulk' of, say, three AAAs is placed at around 4 ft from the hook with a BB and a No.4 beneath it. When it is cast, the loading in the float makes it 'hug' the No.4 until it hits the water, after which the float slides up the line until it reaches the special sliding stop knot you have tied at the required distance from the hook – usually a little more than the depth of the water. This is the sliding-float method to use for catching large, bottom-feeding fish in water that is very deep, but there is another, much more delicate way of fishing the slider.

This involves using a float that is again loaded, but has no body and takes less shot than the bodied slider. Again, the float rests on a No.4, but below this are placed one BB, one No.4 and a No.8, almost like a normal 'fixed' waggler. In fact, any of your ordinary loaded wagglers, as long as their eye is small, can act as a sliding float. This sliding-float method really comes into its own when casting is made difficult by trees or whatever is behind you, and can be used even in quite shallow water – say, 6 ft deep – if need be.

Shotted correctly, sliders are a joy to use, and they won't tangle. Remember to use a loaded float and you can tell everything is working correctly when the float 'waggles' as line is pulled through it, and by the line snaking away from your rod-tip until the float hits the sliding stop knot.

CANAL FLOATS

Not all canal fishing is about using tiny floats attached top and bottom. Many fine catches on canals, and all small, narrow waters for that matter, are made every season by using floats attached by the bottom end only. The reason for using a miniature waggler on a canal is the same as before – to beat the wind. For while a waggler cannot quite match the presentation offered by a tiny, delicately shotted pole float in many conditions, there are days when it will outfish the pole every time.

Canal and small-water wagglers have developed a lot in recent years. No longer will a smaller version of their larger river cousins suffice. Instead, most canal wagglers are now made from balsa, or balsa with a tiny plastic body at the base. The lighter the balsa, the

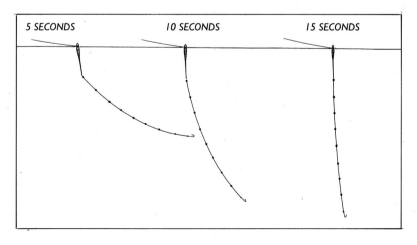

This shows the action of a wire-stemmed stick float after it is cast into the water. The hookbait sinks quicker than when using a cane-stemmed float.

5 SECONDS   10 SECONDS   15 SECONDS

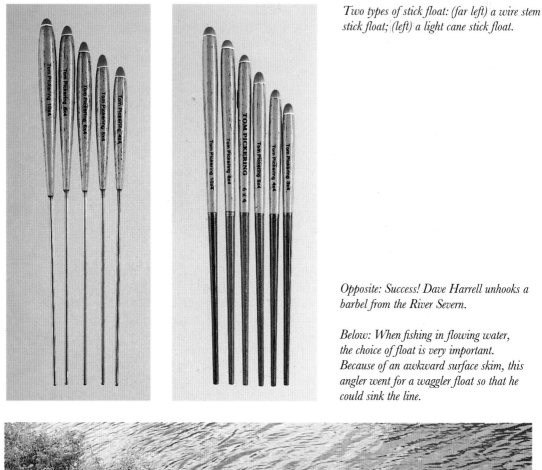

Two types of stick float: (far left) a wire stem stick float; (left) a light cane stick float.

Opposite: Success! Dave Harrell unhooks a barbel from the River Severn.

Below: When fishing in flowing water, the choice of float is very important. Because of an awkward surface skim, this angler went for a waggler float so that he could sink the line.

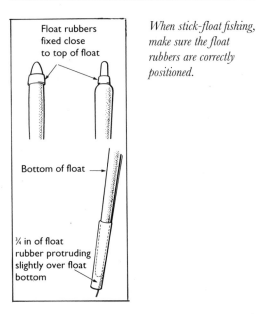

Float rubbers
fixed close
to top of float

Bottom of float

¼ in of float
rubber protruding
slightly over float
bottom

When stick-float fishing, make sure the float rubbers are correctly positioned.

better the float, as light balsa will produce a smaller float for the shotting capacity required.

STICK FLOATS

Stick floats come in many varied shapes and sizes, but they all have one thing in common – they are attached to the line at top and bottom. Although originally designed as a float to beat awkward wind on canals, the trusty 'stick' has developed over the years into the best float there is for running water.

Things can be done with a stick float, that you could never do with a waggler, and when some anglers say they can make their stick floats talk they are only exaggerating slightly! In a nutshell, the stick float is a subtle combination of light and heavy.

In order to select the right type of stick float it is vital to understand the principle of a stick float's construction, which combines light and dense materials. Traditionally, the upper third was made of balsa wood, fitted to a stem of heavy cane. These two materials combined well: balsa to provide buoyancy, which is needed to prevent the float being pulled beneath the surface by the flow, and a heavy cane stem to give stability. This allows the float to be held back against the flow without it riding up (out of the water. Many

other materials have been used to replace these two, but all are incorporated with the same combination in mind. Stems made from wire, glass fibre, lignum and alloys have appeared in recent years, and the balsa has been replaced in some cases by various foams, hollow plastics and man-made materials. All work well, but as a general guide check that your float does have the light and heavy combination. Unfortunately, some cheap floats are not what they appear to be. A stick float that does not have a dense stem is next to useless.

The beginner to stick-float fishing should stick to just a few types, and a selection of floats carrying from two No.4 shot to seven No.4s should see you through most conditions. It may also be worthwhile considering a wire-stem pattern as a good choice with which to start. The reasoning behind such a choice is that the wire stem makes for a very stable float and one which will be easy to control, even in difficult situations and poor wind conditions. On a river with a nice, steady flow and in perfect conditions it may not be so effective as a model with a cane or lignum stem, but overall a wire stem will cater for every situation and get you fishing effectively.

Once you become familiar with the general fishing procedure, apply the rule that a wire stem is the choice when conditions are difficult, and a cane of lignum pattern is right for good conditions or when you are catching on the drop.

In most conditions, the stick float is fished with the line from rod-tip to float on the surface, and here is where the skill of this delightful method is employed. With your line on the surface, it obviously can be blown about by the wind, unlike using a waggler, when the line is sunk and tackle control is near perfect. When there is little or no wind, or when the wind is blowing in the opposite direction from the river current, this poses few problems. However, in a downstream wind, stick-float fishing can be difficult.

The amount of line between rod-tip and float is vitally important when stick-float fishing – you want neither too much nor too little. Many top anglers prefer to use a closed-

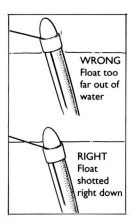

Stick floats should be shotted right down in the water, so tip colour selection is important.

WRONG Float too far out of water

RIGHT Float shotted right down

face reel for this type of fishing, tucking the reel into their body and 'feeding' line out by hand as the float travels the swim. By doing this, they can have perfect control over their tackle. Feed less line, and the float will be held back slightly against the current. More line, and the float can be made to travel at the same rate as the current. However, always make sure you don't feed too much line, or a bow will be formed on the surface and the float and bait will be dragged off line.

As use of the stick float has developed into an art form, numerous different varieties have been devised to deal with certain conditions. While conventional stick floats will work, and work well, under most conditions, turbulent water is best handled with a stick float with a wire stem. This stem is both heavy and narrow, creating less resistance as the erratic water hits it to drag it off line.

Similarly, special floats have been developed to enable you to cast further than normal with a stick float. These floats have very heavy stems made from either lignum wood or plastic, with bulbous ends. They cast and ride the water very well.

Casting a stick float requires care. Ideally, the float should land upstream of the hook, with the tackle in a straight line parallel to the bank. Remember to shot it so that only the very tip of the float is showing on the surface. You will see every tiny bite, and when you hold the float back it won't rise too far out of the water.

TIP COLOURS

There's nothing worse than tackling up, only to discover that you're using a float with a tip that you can't see against the reflection formed on the water. A few minutes spent surveying the scene before fishing could save valuable time changing your float because cannot see it.

Most floats sold in the shops have tips painted either red, yellow or sometimes black. If you're fishing against a dark reflection of, say, trees or bushes on the far bank, a red- or yellow-tipped float is the best type to use. If, however, the background is very light, such as the sky, then a black-tipped float is best. Mistakes are often made even by the best anglers, so it's always worth carrying a bottle of typewriter correcting fluid and a permanent black marker in your tackle-box. Then you can change your float colour in seconds if you want to. Alternatively, of course, use a float with an interchangeable tip, or a float adaptor, allowing you to change the whole float in seconds.

CHAPTER TWO

....

The Rigs to Use

One of the main areas in which inexperienced anglers struggle is shotting their wagglers and stick floats. If you take a walk along a riverbank in summer, you will find many anglers having trouble in catching fish, and the main reason is that they have failed to shot their float properly.

Confusion reigns over shotting patterns, but in truth you can stick to just a few basics to cover the whole of your floatfishing needs. Once your confidence and experience have grown, then by all means experiment with different shotting patterns, but at the outset don't get too ambitious. Choose the size of float according to how far you want to cast it, and also take the wind conditions into account. Obviously, the further you want to cast and the stronger the wind, the heavier the float should be.

If there were one waggler float that could handle most situations, it would be a float taking three AAA shot. If you decide to increase the size of the float, the extra weight should be added to the locking shot, with the 'down-the-line' shotting patterns remaining the same.

To help you with the different sizes of shot available there is a useful guide at the end of this chapter. Don't try to memorize the exact weights. Just keep a rough idea of their relative sizes; so you know, for example, how many BBs are equivalent to one AAA. It may pay you to write the shot sizes and their weights down on a piece of paper, which you can take along with you to the riverbank.

WAGGLER PATTERNS

Just because a float's markings tell you it takes three AAAs, that doesn't mean you have to fix three AAAs on the line and nothing more. For a typical summer shotting pattern, all you need between float and hook are a few small

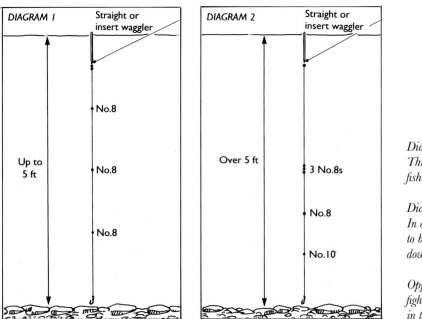

Diagram 1:
This rig is ideal for fishing depths up to 5 ft.

Diagram 2:
In deeper water there needs to be more shot placed down the line.

Opposite: After a spirited fight, a plump carp is safely in the angler's net.

shot like No.8s. So if you lock the float on the line with two AAAs and a BB, that leaves you with the equivalent of one BB to be placed between float and hook. A quick calculation will reveal that roughly six No.8s will suffice. Of course, you can go further still by splitting the No.8s up into No.10s or even smaller.

You don't have to make these calculations every time you fish. Experience will soon teach you how shot can be separated into smaller ones. Use the float's markings as a guide only.

Let us start by looking at a fairly simple rig for fishing a waggler in depths of water up to about 5 ft. The rig shown in *diagram 1* is ideal for catching roach, dace and chub in rivers, and carp in lakes. After placing the locking shot around the float, there are two No.8s

and one No.10 down the line. The No.10 is placed about 10 in from the hook, with the No.8s equally spaced between here and the float. For fast water it would be best to use a straight waggler, while for slow or still water an insert float would be the choice.

In deeper water, say from 5 ft to 13 ft, there needs to be more shot down the line to take the bait down to the bottom. *Diagram 2* shows a rig where three No.8s are grouped together just below half-depth, with another No.8 and one No.10 spaced out below. This rig is particularly good for roach and bream in summer, using a straight waggler for fast water and an insert for slow and still water. If you need to cast long distances then you may need to use a loaded float.

If there is a strong upstream wind on a slow-flowing river, you require more shot down the line, as in *diagram 3*. A bulk of six No.8s is placed just below half depth to pick up the true flow of the river, otherwise the float would travel backwards with the upstream wind, ruining bait presentation. A No.10 shot is fixed 10 in from the hook, with a No.8 and two No.8s between this and the main bulk. Again, this pattern, using either a straight or insert waggler, is ideal for catching roach and bream.

The three rigs mentioned are ideal for fish feeding on the bottom, but what about those species that feed higher up in the water, like dace, bleak, chub and carp? Obviously, you'll need a smaller float to create less disturbance on the cast, and an all-balsa or a tiny insert waggler are ideal. The float is set shallow (as in *diagram 4*), up to 2 ft below the surface, and all that is needed down the line are three No.10s equally spaced out between float and hook; the rest of the float's shotting capacity is locking shot. If conditions are ideal rise the all-balsa float, but if strong winds are affecting the water then a small peacock insert waggler will handle the conditions better.

Bottom-feeding bream need a static bait and as a result most anglers use leger tactics for this species. However, they can still be tempted on the float as long as there is a shot about 8 in from the hook resting on the bottom. A straight waggler is best because its buoyancy prevents it being pulled under on a flowing river, and a similar float will also combat surface drag on lakes. *Diagram 5* shows a heavy bulk of between three BBs and three AAAs placed just off the bottom, and that all important bottom shot, a No.4, beneath. The rest of

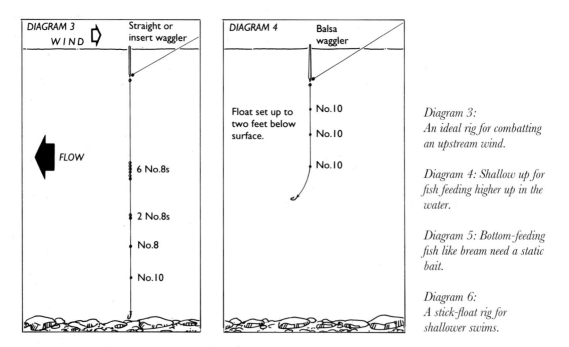

Diagram 3:
An ideal rig for combatting an upstream wind.

Diagram 4: Shallow up for fish feeding higher up in the water.

Diagram 5: Bottom-feeding fish like bream need a static bait.

Diagram 6:
A stick-float rig for shallower swims.

the float's shotting capacity is used as locking shot.

One final point on waggler-float patterns, and that is timing. Often a fish will bite as the hookbait is falling through the water, and this will be shown by the float not settling into its normal position at the surface. This is caused by the fish taking the bait and preventing a shot sinking to its normal position. After casting, try to get a good idea of how long the interval is between each shot or group of shot settling. Any change to this time-span signals that a fish has intercepted the bait on the way down.

Always make sure that you shot your float down in the water to the very tip; then, on-the-drop and proper bites will be easier to spot.

STICK-FLOAT PATTERNS

The big difference between stick floats and wagglers is that stick floats are attached to the line at both the top and bottom with float rubbers, while wagglers are fixed by the bottom end only. Attached top and bottom, stick floats present your line from float to rod-tip actually on the surface. If conditions are favourable with little wind, you will encounter few problems. Line is left on the surface and the float travels through the swim as you release line from the reel. In awkward wind conditions, however, line can soon be dragged round the front of the float, pulling your hookbait off the correct line. No self-respecting fish will look at a bait presented in this fashion.

To attach a stick float to the line, it is best to use three thin float rubbers instead of two. Place one about a ¼ in from the top of the float, one in the middle, and one at the bottom. The rubber at the top of the float should have a wider diameter than the other two, and you should make sure that the rubber at the base overlaps the float slightly to help reduce tangles on the cast and produce a more streamlined rig. Don't use big, bulky float rubbers because they will ruin the sensitivity of the float.

There are various devices open to the angler to improve bait presentation in awkward conditions. A heavier float can be used, with more shot fixed nearer to the hook than to the float. This increases the stability of the lower half of the rig. Backshotting is another way of improving bait presentation. A No.8 shot is placed around 6 in above the float to sink the line in this area. Although

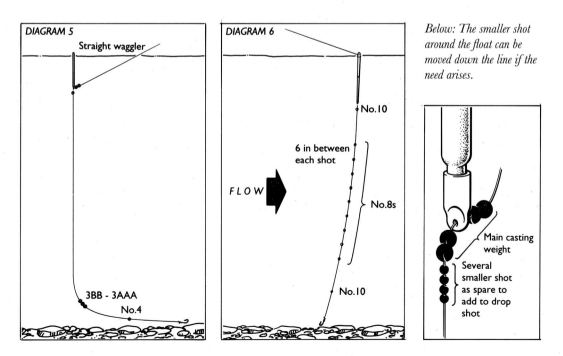

Below: The smaller shot around the float can be moved down the line if the need arises.

this results in better bait presentation, it can make effective striking difficult, as it puts an extra obstacle between angler and fish.

A stick float can present the bait with more versatility than a waggler. It can be stopped, slowed down, run through at the same speed as the current, or even run through so the float stops and starts again several times as it makes its progress along the swim. This just isn't possible with a waggler, which gets pulled under easily when checked.

In the shallower swims – up to 6 ft deep – the rig shown in *diagram 6* is a successful pattern. Any type of stick float can be used here; a light-cane base in the really shallow swims to heavier cane or wire-stem in deeper water. Place a string of No.8 shot at 6-in intervals between a No.10 depth marker and another No.10 on the hooklength. This is a good rig for roach, dace, chub and barbel.

Much deeper swims, between 6 and 9 ft, require a heavier float. *Diagram 7* shows the pattern clearly, groups of two No.8s being placed on the line at 6-in intervals, and three single-dropper shot below. For the deepest swims, you will need a four-BB heavy wood-and-balsa float.

For fish like dace, chub and bleak feeding close to the surface use a pattern shown in *diagram 8*. Shot a light cane or balsa waggler with No.10 shot at 6-in intervals. It can be fished at full depth as long as the water is under 5 ft.

In the deepest swims where roach, chub and bream are the quarry, start your string of shot from mid-depth (*diagram 9*), otherwise too much time will be wasted as the bait falls. If the shot starts at mid-depth, this will ensure that the bait falls quickly. You must use a heavy wood and balsa stick or a heavy wire-stem float in these circumstances. Make sure you always shot your stick float so that you can just see its top at the surface. Bites can sometimes be hard to spot with a stick float, but the job will be made easier as long as the float is shotted right down. This is also important when holding the float back. It will want to rise out from the water as it tilts, but with a float shotted right down, you will still see bites.

Always fix a No.10 shot directly underneath the float and once you have plumbed the depth, keep the shot next to it. If you try going deeper, keep the shot where you put it so it acts as a depth marker. Once you have plumbed the depth, it often pays to move the float 6 in or more up the line so that the bait is presented trundling along the bottom.

Diagram 7:
A heavier float is needed in deeper water. Most of the shotting is in blocks of 2 No.8s.

Diagram 8:
For a slower fall of bait when fish are feeding close to the surface, use No. 10 shot.

Opposite: Dave Harrell used floatfished tactics to catch this superb net of barbel and chub from the River Severn.

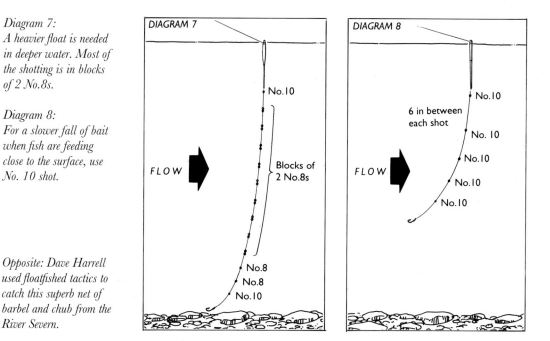

CHAPTER THREE

The Right Tackle

One of the most important aspects of fishing is to make sure you have the right rod and reel, because good, balanced tackle can prove decisive. There is no point in having the best floats on the market if you're not comfortable with the 'engine room'. For a start always buy your tackle from a specialist dealer. There is no substitute for the help and advice he can offer. He should know his tackle, and your continued custom will be valued so there is little chance he will try to sell you a 'dud'.

With all tackle, the price is a good guide to quality. The tackle industry is too well stocked for the rubbish to survive. However, it is still possible to find a reasonable rod and reel that have sensible price-tags. Such products will last the casual angler several seasons, but don't expect cheap tackle to run like a ball of silk forever. Strange names are also to be looked upon with some doubt. If the make is not known to you, it is probably from a back-street factory in the middle of a far-off country.

When it comes to reels, check that spares are available, and even ask if they are in stock. If they are, you won't have to wait weeks for a replacement balearm spring to be sent from the factory. Ask if a spare spool – or two – is included in the price. If not, be sure you can buy one, and remember to take the extra cost into account. Next, decide exactly what you intend to use the reel for. If you are planning to floatfish for roach there is no reason to buy a reel capable of holding 300 yd of 10 lb line. Above all, always try to match rod, reel and terminal tackle.

RODS

Long gone are the days when most rods were made out of split cane, or even glass-fibre. Now, carbon rules. You can buy a reel made from this material for as little as £20 to £30, or as much as £150; the price depends on the grade. Cheap carbon is made from a much coarser grade than expensive carbon. A coarse-grade carbon rod is likely to be weak and have little action. That's why some manufacturers add glass-fibre to their cheap carbon rods, making it 'composite' and stronger into the bargain. Boron and kevlar are used in the more expensive rods to give a better action and reduced reel diameter, along with greater resistance to distortion when under pressure.

The most important feature of any rod is its action and balance. If either of these are wrong, you will not fish well and sooner or later your attention will turn towards yet another purchase.

Rod action is something of a personal judgement, but if you spend most of your time stick-float fishing you will be looking for a sharp-action rod, which is very stiff except for the first 18 in or so. Such a rod is likely to have a splice in the top section. For long-range fishing or for use with big waggler floats, a slightly softer action will be best. It should not be sloppy, but when pressure is applied to the tip there should be action running well into the second joint. Get someone to hold the tip so that you can pull hard to form the rod into a steep curve. Don't be afraid of it. Give it a bit of stick and watch for the way the curve develops. There should be no signs of 'flat spots'. The curve in a good rod will be a gradual progression of the curve, which tightens towards the tip. If it looks like a series of flats, leave it in the shop.

It pays to take your reel along when buying a rod, as a rod that feels strange without a reel may be just right with one in place. Position the reel well up the handle, which if everything is right should extend by about 4 in beyond your elbow. Watch out for cheap rods that feel good. It's an old trick to balance them with a weight inside the butt.

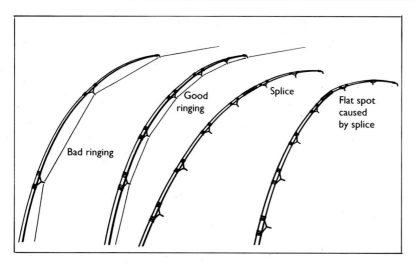

Bad ringing

Good ringing

Splice

Flat spot caused by splice

Make sure your rod is properly ringed, and that there are no flat spots caused by a splice in the rod.

The handle should feel comfortable too. If it is too small or too large in diameter, sooner or later it will give you cramp in your fingers.

Another important factor to look for is how the rod is ringed. Even the best blank can be ruined if it is badly ringed. Too many rings and the rod will become tip heavy. If there are too few, line will not flow in the correct path along the bank. In wet weather, big gaps between rings will encourage line to stick to the rod, making casting difficult; and large bows will form in windy weather, maybe causing tangles or even slowing down the strike.

To check good ringing it is best to thread up a line through the rings and pull hard to form the rod into a very steep curve. Check that the line forms a series of small, straight sections, following the curve as closely as possible. If the straights form angles at each ring the rings are wrongly or too widely spaced.

On rods that have not been painted, look for a straight seam running along the entire length of the sections. This is called the 'spine' and is where the carbon cloth that makes up the blank tube is joined. This is the most rigid area of the blank and the rings should run either along it or directly opposite it. It is often possible to find it by holding the joints up to the light and looking down the inside of the blank.

Even if the rings are correctly spaced and situated in the right relationship to the spine, they can still ruin an otherwise good rod.

Rings that are too heavy will soften the rod's action, cause the tip to sag and spoil the overall balance. It pays to check the tip-ring too. Those with threaded tubes on them are intended for leger rods and have no place on a float rod. A good set of rings will reduce in size towards the tip. There is a trend towards very small rings throughout the rod's length, but this has no real value and does in fact slightly reduce the casting potential of the rod. The rings nearest the reel should be just large enough to allow the line to spiral as it comes off the spool.

Good-quality, lined rings, it is claimed, reduce line wear. While this may be true, you have to decide if the extra cost – and weight – is what you want. If you go for the lined rings take care to check them over – there are many cheap copies around. Names such as Fuji and Seymo have stood the test of time and are now available in very small sizes that match modern, low-diameter blanks.

Too much varnish on the whippings of a rod can add unwanted weight, and you should avoid rods on which the varnish has been allowed to form unsightly blobs. The whippings should be neatly finished with a minimum of varnish: just enough to make a smooth surface on the thread and to fill up the tiny gap between whipping and rod at the foot of each ring.

Several different types of ferrule – where the sections of a rod meet – are available. Whichever you choose, make sure they fit well together: tight but easy to pull apart.

Ferrules on some cheap rods lock together by means of a taper towards the back of the joint that fits inside. This will cause stress on the rod, and this type of joint should be avoided. Spigoted ferrules, where an extra piece of carbon is built into the blank, should be checked for a close fit. When you have assembled a rod, waggle it around and listen and feel for any 'knocking'. This is a sure sign of a loose-fitting joint. Check that they have been tightened. If they have and the rod still knocks, the rod is no good.

The length of a rod is another consideration. The most popular length for a float rod is 13 ft although some anglers, particularly in the south, prefer 12-ft versions. The choice is yours, but you must pick a length that is both comfortable and effective. You can buy rods today that are adjustable, and will extend if conditions change during the fishing session. However, these are obviously more expensive and are perhaps aimed at the experienced angler.

Choosing good quality tackle will pay dividends in the future. Spend some time in a well-stocked tackle shop.

REELS

Three types of reel are generally used for floatfishing: open-face, closed-face (both fixed-spool reels) and centre-pins. By far the most popular are open-face reels, but the other two are still very effective.

The design of open-face reels has come on in leaps and bounds, and one of the most positive steps forward is the introduction of the skirted spool. The 'skirt' carries the spool rim over the main bale-arm housing and thus reduces the chances of line getting inside the works and around the main spindle. It is a design feature that makes fishing into a head wind much easier – definitely well worth thinking about when buying a fixed-spool reel. A good model will have a 'skirt' that runs closely over the housing – the smaller the gap, the less the danger of tangles.

Perhaps the greatest benefit of an open-face reel is that it will cast your float a lot

Above: Dave Harrell is an advocate of the closed-face reel, especially for trotting a stick-float on a pacey river.

Left: An open-faced reel is the most popular choice for anglers nowadays. When buying a new reel make sure it comes complete with a spare spool.

further than a closed-face or centre-pin, and this is particularly useful when you are fishing stillwaters. However, don't make things difficult for yourself by underfilling your reel spool. As a general rule, your line should reach up $\frac{1}{16}$ in from the spool lip. Casting will then be easy, with less resistance between line and spool edge.

Many modern reels are sold with a match spool, which holds 100 m of 3 lb line. If the reel spool is too deep, simply wind some backing – such as tightly wound wool or cotton – on to it before filling it with line.

There have been many attempts to produce a good closed-face reel. Unfortunately, most have fallen by the wayside. However, in recent seasons a number of better models have been finding

To help line sink fast, store your reel spool in a mild detergent solution.

favour with anglers. Older models have very narrow spools, which tend to cause line to 'bed down'. They work well for an hour or so, but once a few fish have been landed, casting becomes more difficult as a result of the line jamming down. Look for a wide, larger-diameter spool. To work well, these reels need to hold a very small amount of line. The more you put on, the more bedding-in will occur, even on the best reels. Before using a closed-face, be sure you can reach the release button with your index finger – you'll need to try it on a rod to be sure.

Take the spool housing off a close&faced reel and remove the spool a couple of times. Some tend to jam or may even require the removal of a screw, which can easily be lost. One vital tip is to oil your reel regularly. Some anglers prefer to remove all the grease from the inside of the reel before spraying it with WD40 lubricating spray.

On closed-face reels line is carried over the bell-housing by means of a small pin, which pops up when the handle is turned. Examine it carefully to see that it operates through a hole just large enough. A slack fit here will result in line getting caught.

Do not overload a closed-face reel with line. This will cause 'bedding-in' on the cast, reducing distance considerably. Go for around 75 turns of the reel handle, and remember to change the line regularly. Line stronger than 3 lb breaking strain is not really suitable for closed-face reels. It's better to use an open-face if heavier line is required.

One-handed casts are easy with closed-face reels as the line-release mechanism can be operated with the casting hand, unlike most open-face reels whose bale arms have to be operated by the non-casting hand.

Centre-pins have fallen from favour with all but the match anglers and the purists. However, a good centre-pin can open up a whole new way of fishing. For close-in work with a stick float on a running river they are a pleasure to use. The main advantage of the centre-pin is its simplicity. There is no winding through gears like a fixed-spool reel, the angler having direct contact with the line. You know exactly what the line is doing at all times, particularly important when casting, feeling for bites and playing fish. During the cast, the angler has total control over how much line is released, and this results in more accurate casting.

Trotting a stick float on rivers and streams is also much easier using a centre-pin, the power of the current pulling line off the revolving drum much more smoothly than off a fixed-spool. The angler can hold back a float better by just trapping the thumb on the lip of the drum to prevent it turning; and can strike a bite immediately with similar but firmer pressure. The main disadvantage, of course, is that it cannot cast tackle as far as a fixed spool reel.

A good centre-pin will be light, free running, have a large drum diameter, and be wide enough to allow line to spread thinly.

HOOKS

Choosing the right hook for the job is a problem faced by coarse anglers every time they go fishing. However, with a little thought and practice, you should soon be able to pick the right size and pattern.

When considering the size of hook to use, three factors should govern your decision. First, how large is the bait you are using? Obviously, the larger the bait, the larger the hook. Small baits like maggot and caster should be fished in singles on hooks ranging from size 22 to 18 and in doubles from size 20 to 14 – as a guide, the smaller the hook, the higher the number. Tiny baits like pinkies, squatts and bloodworm should not be attached to anything larger than a size 22 in ones and 20 in twos. Conversely, bigger baits like bread, sweetcorn and luncheon meat must be fished on much larger hooks. For breadflake, go for a size 12 or larger. Sweetcorn can be used on a size 14 and a small piece of meat on a 12. Don't be afraid to use larger pieces on a size 8 or even 6, but these baits will probably be better used in conjunction with leger tactics.

The second factor, which will help you decide what size of hook to use, is the size of fish you are expecting to catch. You will lose more large fish on tiny hooks than you will on big hooks, and you won't be able to hook small fish on big hooks.

Third, the hook size will also depend on how the fish are feeding. If they are taking the bait confidently, you can usually get away with a hook of a larger size than if the fish are suspicious.

The next consideration is the strength of the hook. This is determined by the thickness of the wire and the way it is made. Obviously, it pays to use the strongest hook possible. However, a hook made out of thick wire will be far heavier than one made from fine wire and thick wire might make the fish suspicious. Some hooks are forged for extra strength which involves flattening the wire. However, a forged hook has to be made from fairly thick wire. Fine-wire hooks have, through modern technology, been made very strong but make sure they are not brittle. A hook should be slightly springy.

What other points must you consider?

First, will you use spade-end or eyed hooks? Eyed hooks are good for large baits and should be used for carp fishing when a hair rig might involve attaching the hair to the eye. On the other hand, when floatfishing it is best to use spade-ends, especially for small hooks.

Modern small hooks often come with a microbarb, a tiny barb that allows perfect penetration with far less chance of losing a hooked fish through the hook pulling free. These are the hooks to go for in the smaller sizes, but use a full barb on large hooks. Always make sure that the venue you are fishing allows hooks with a barb because there are fisheries that state that barbless hooks only must be used.

Many of the more expensive, smaller hooks are treated during manufacture with a process known as chemical etching. This creates a sharper, more durable hook than standard wire models, and does not need sharpening. These hooks should never be sharpened, as this only serves to remove the outer layer and ruin the hook. Other types, however, should be sharpened periodically with a small sharpening stone, especially after landing a good fish.

Hooks come in many colours, but for general coarse fishing bronze is best. Red is favoured by bloodworm anglers – for obvious reasons – while blue is a popular colour for canals. Gold is favoured with some anglers when they are using lightly-coloured or white maggots or sweetcorn.

CHAPTER FOUR

....

Casting

The first golden rule of casting a waggler float is to always use a float that is heavy enough to do the job. A float that doesn't have the shot-carrying capacity to be cast easily to the required distance is a big handicap. The right float will be big enough to allow you to hit the right spot accurately without forcing it.

If the wind is difficult, be sure to use a float long enough to combat any downstream skim that may otherwise spoil your presentation. Just because a float worked in a particular swim on one day, it may not be right for the next visit. Conditions may have changed and a bigger shot-load may be needed.

OVERHEAD CAST

There are several ways of casting a waggler, but the overhead cast is by far the most effective and will enable you to put a float out a fair distance after only a few practice attempts. The idea is to use both hands in a push-and-pull motion. The hand at the front of the handle pushes the rod-tip forwards while the other arm pulls the end of the butt

Opposite: Start of the overhead cast. After disengaging the line-release mechanism, trap the line against the reel spool. Swing the rod back behind you to stop at about 45 degrees to the bank, directly over your head.

Left: Using the power in the tip of the rod, swing it quickly over your head, releasing the line trapped beneath your finger. At this point the float will fly out and up towards your target swim.

back towards the body. The action is one even sweep of the rod. There is no excess force required – at least, not if you have chosen the correct weight of float.

Shotting, of course, affects overall casting distance. With a waggler, most of the load is used to lock the float in place on the line, the rest being spaced as either a series of small shots or as a small bulk with two or three single shots beneath. A good guide would be to have at least two-thirds of the overall load around the float.

In order to cast a waggler well, the reel should be well forward on the rod handle. The ideal position would put the end of the butt about 3 in beyond your elbow when your hand is over the reel and your arm laid along the handle. The cast begins by winding the float to within about 3 ft of the rod-tip. Then, with the bale arm open, the index finger of the right hand traps line against the spool. Line should of course be built up on the spool to just below the lip.

Without pausing, push the rod further back, at the same time extending your arms above your head to give extra height. Both arms are nearly straight and the finger trapping line against the spool is still in position. The rod is now brought forward, the right arm pushing and the left pulling the butt back and upwards towards your armpit (and vice versa if you are left-handed). Now comes the timing, which is vital. As the rod pushes forward, line is released, so that it goes out in a high arc. If the release is too late, the arc will be low and the tackle ends up splashing down in a heap and probably in a tangle. The right timing will put everything out in a smooth arc, which gives maximum range for minimum effort. At all times keep your eye on the spot where you want the tackle to land and, if possible, the rod should remain in a true 90-degree sweeping path to the water. A tip worth remembering is that when the backward sweep of the rod is made, the tackle must have time to swing out behind you. Once you are sure this has happened, the forward motion can begin. During practice, it may pay to watch what is going on, but when fishing look forwards at all times, otherwise you'll lose accuracy.

At the point of release the rod is moving forwards at maximum speed. It should be acting like an extension to your arm as the float flies towards its target. Try to keep the tip at a point that will give maximum range and create a gentle arc rather than a high, steep flight path or one that is very low to the surface. The release point – when the finger lets line off the spool – is at around the 1.30 position on a clock face. When the tackle is in flight, keep your finger out of the way as checking the flow of line now would end in disaster.

Towards the end of the cast, when the float approaches the target spot, drop the rod towards the horizontal and feather line gently with the index finger to slow it as it flows over the spool lip. Done correctly, the tackle should straighten out nicely. Overdo the feathering and the tackle will stop suddenly, and you will end up with a big tangle. Don't feather enough, and you will end up casting way beyond the fishing area, maybe even hitting the far bank. It's all a matter of practice, but once mastered it's easy.

Once the tackle has landed safely and tangle-free, push the rod-tip beneath the surface and give the reel handle a few rapid turns. This will straighten everything out and also sink most of the line beneath the surface. If the sinking process needs to be repeated, try keeping the tip close to the surface and flicking it a few times from side to side. This will 'cut' line beneath the surface skim.

Sideways Cast

Although the overhead cast is by far the most common method used with a waggler, some swims, such as those with overhead trees, make it difficult. In such conditions a sideways action, similar to the one used for stick-float fishing, can be used.

The sideways action is a good method, too, for dropping a float very close to the far bank. Tackle cast from this position will tend to land parallel to the bank rather than stretching away from you. This method also works well when casting beneath trees hanging close to the water surface or right up against the edge of a weed-bed. It's a good method to try, too, when fish are feeding very close to the surface. Casting with a sideways action calls for concentration and some good timing. Start with the rod pointing almost along the bank and in a near-horizontal position. Sweep it out over the water, raising the tip slightly at the same time as the tackle is released by the left hand. The thing to remember is that where the rod is pointing when the tackle is released will decide where the float lands. And above all, keep your eye on where you want the float to land.

STICK-FLOAT CASTING

Casting stick float takes a bit of practice, but once you've mastered the basics it's simple enough. With the right shotting patterns and a planned approach you will soon be laying out the tackle in a nice neat line and with the minimum of fuss. Start with the underarm, or sideways, cast and once you have mastered that, try the overarm method. Even with the sideways cast, it is possible to get a float out four or five rod-lengths.

Start with the tackle wound up so that the hook is about level with the reel or just below it. Next, open the bale arm of the reel, while trapping the line against the spool with the right forefinger. With the hook in the left hand, pull slightly until the rod-tip begins to bend.

Keeping your eye on the spot at which you intend the float to land, move the rod briskly until its tip is pointing at the target area. Keep the tip low, too high and the float will travel upwards rather than outwards and the cast will fall short, probably in a tangle.

As the right hand flicks outwards, release the hook held in your left hand, at the same time letting line run off the spool. As the cast begins, the rod-tip travels in a slightly upwards direction, while also moving upstream. Take care, however, not to end up with it pointing too far upriver, otherwise the cast will also end up above your chosen swim. Throughout the cast, try to keep your eye firmly fixed on the float; and as the cast develops, control the line as it runs off the spool by feathering slightly with the index finger.

With the cast nearing completion, feather the line more firmly and at the same time lift the rod-tip high to keep as much line as possible off the water. And as the float lands, pull it back gently with the rod to make certain everything is straightened out in a neat line downstream. Get it wrong and the float lands downstream of the rest of the rig and will travel unnaturally through the first part of the swim.

Once the tackle has landed, line needs mending, or straightening out, to get everything in line from float to rod-tip. And if the wind or flow is tricky, you may have to repeat this part of the operation several times as the tackle runs through. Above all, do not let a bow form in the line downstream of the float. If that happens the bait will be pulled through faster than the flow and appear unnatural to the fish. Mending is simple enough, just lift the rod slightly and try to scribe a circle with the tip, moving it upwards and upstream in a gentle sweep. Done correctly the line will be moved into the correct upstream position without disturbing the float as it travels through the swim.

Once you have mastered the sideways cast and can lay out your tackle correctly without causing tangles, it is time to consider an attempt at overarm casting. The basic rule to remember is that the stick float must be heavy enough to cope with the extra distance required.

To cast, just open the bale arm, trapping line in the usual manner with your index finger, while holding the hook in your left hand. Flick the rod-tip upwards and just as it reaches its highest point, release the hook from your left hand and the line from the spool rim. Ideally, the tackle will land just slightly downstream of you and, with a bit of careful feathering, in a straight line. As you get the hang of it try also to turn the rod-tip in a slightly upstream direction just as it reaches its fullest height. This little movement will help lay the line upstream of the float.

A third cast – just like the overhead method used for the waggler float – can be attempted. But be warned, it is difficult and prone to tangling unless you get everything right and time it perfectly.

Above: The start of a sideways cast: with the line-release mechanism disengaged, and the line trapped against the reel, the angler prepares to flick out the tackle.

Below: For stick-float casting the rod is flicked forward and the line allowed to peel off the reel. The cast should result in float and tackle landing in a line almost parallel to the bank.

CHAPTER FIVE

Finding the Depth

Once you've chosen the right float, picked the correct rig and bought adequate tackle, it's time to start fishing. However, there is no point in casting to a certain spot in your swim and expecting to catch without first discovering the depth of the water. You may get lucky and somehow set your float tackle to the right depth, but the chances are that your hookbait will be nowhere near the contours of the river or lake bed.

It doesn't matter if you are a proficient or an inexperienced angler, you will definitely get more out of your floatfishing if you first discover the depth. Far too many anglers guess the depth and set their float with little thought. Then they complain because they haven't caught much at the end of the day. In fact, they have only themselves to blame.

You might ask why is it so important to discover the depth of your swim? Is there any point in finding out how deep it is when often the fish feed well off the bottom? Ask any top angler this question

Discovering the contours of a river swim will bring its rewards later in the session.

and the answer will be the same. Location of the bottom contours gives you a good starting point from which to fish a swim. Whether you're on still or moving water, this is a must. Even if you think you know the depth, a quick check before fishing will only take a few seconds and will confirm your estimates.

There isn't anything difficult about finding the depth of your swim. In fact it couldn't be easier. All it involves is attaching a weight – heavy enough to pull your float right under– to your hook with your float already attached higher up the line, casting out, and watching for the float to appear at the surface. Any weight will do, as long as it is non-lead, of course, but there are several different types tailor-made for the job. They are called plummets.

PLUMBING THE DEPTH

There is no doubt that the best time to plumb the depth is before you fix any shot onto the line, apart from those used to lock the float in place. It is commonsense, really, because if you put shot on the line before finding out how deep the swim is, you will probably have to move them around once you discover the true depth.

It is best to start by casting beyond the spot you intend to fish, and plumb in a line towards you. Make sure the float is considerably undershotted, so that you can easily see if it is set too deep. Once you have cast, keep a fairly tight line and watch for the float to appear at the surface. Three things can happen here. First, the float may disappear from view and not resurface; in this case your tackle is set too shallow. By moving the float up the line, you will increase the depth of the rig. Second, the float may disappear and then resurface soon afterwards. It will probably lie flat on the surface or stick up several inches above the surface. Here your tackle is set too deep and you must shallow-up by moving the float

These are three things that can happen when you try to plumb the depth.

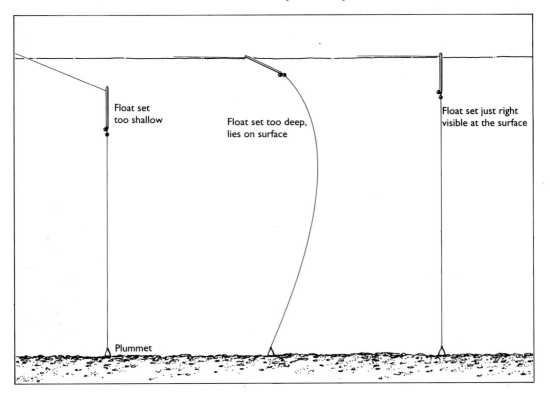

Float set too shallow

Float set too deep, lies on surface

Float set just right visible at the surface

Plummet

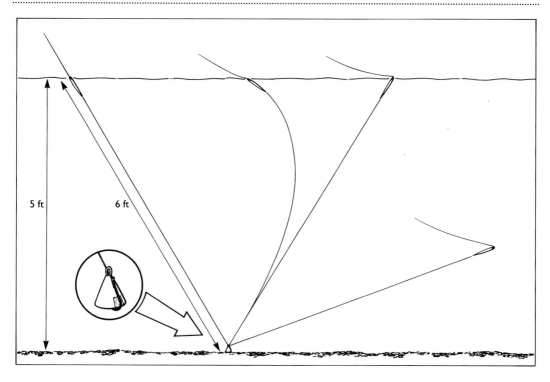

This sequence shows what happens when plumbing the depth in running water. The float moves along and eventually disappears as the plummet stays put. The answer is to keep a tight line between plummet and float.

down the line. Third, the float may disappear, resurfacing with just the very tip visible at the surface. This means the tackle is set at the right water depth, and obviously this is the situation you must aim at all the time.

Many anglers fishing running water don't bother to plumb the depth, but they could be making a big mistake. It is still a vitally important part of floatfishing, even on these type of fisheries. The reason why some anglers prefer not to spend time carrying this out is that it is quite easy to discover the depth of the swim on running water. The float simply drags under if it's set to deep, the hook catching on the bottom weed. However, it is important to discover the contours and relative depths at different distances from the bank on a river, just as on a stillwater. For example, an angler might find it comfortable to fish at three rod-lengths from the bank, but he won't catch much if most of the fish are

feeding at four rod-lengths out because there is a clear gravel run there between two weed-beds. So make an effort to plumb the depth. It is quite easy, especially when stickfloat fishing. Use your plummet carefully, again attaching it to the hook before any shot is fixed on the line.

Just as important as watching the float when plumbing the depth in running water is to feel for the moment when the plummet hits the river bottom. Once you have felt this happen, you can move the float up or down the line until you can just see its tip at the surface.

The need to keep a tight line between rod-tip and hook when plumbing the depth in flowing rivers is probably greater than in still water. This is because the angle between float and hook, with the float tip just visible at the surface, tells you whether the float is set a little deeper than the depth of the water. Once the plummet is removed and fishing begins, the end tackle will trundle nicely along the bottom of the river.

To plumb the depth effectively in this way, a fairly heavy plummet is required. Check the plummet each time, because it is a useful indicator of whether the bottom is gravelly, silty or weedy. With experience you will also get a good idea of the bottom material according to how the plummet lands. If you can lift the rod and bounce the plummet easily, the bottom is probably gravel. If the plummet moves after an initial tug, it is most probably silt. If the plummet gets stuck fast and needs a good heave to dislodge it, the bottom is probably weedy.

It is also worth spending some time plumbing the depth, not only at several distances from the bank, but also at different places along the same line. Some river swims shallow up as they progress, others get deeper. Some lake swims shelve off quite suddenly a little distance from the bank. A good angler will be aware of these potential fish-holding areas.

How do you build-up a mental picture of the swim? Start by casting your tackle and plummet to a spot a little further out than you think you will fish. Test the depth there, reeling in and moving the float up or down the line until you establish the correct length. Now cast a little shorter and find the depth again. Keep drawing the float back a little at a time, testing the depth on each occasion. You will soon discover any shallower parts or shelves. It is important to try this several times in different areas of your swim to create a mental picture of the bottom contours.

One point worth remembering is that it is easier to plumb the depth with a float attached top and bottom. Especially when you want to discover the depth in several places, working towards the bank in stages after casting to a certain spot, you will find that keeping tabs on the float attached by the top and bottom is much better. With a stick float, there are no problems, but a bottom-end-only waggler is more difficult. However, there is a simple answer. Twist the line to form a temporary loop a little way above the bottom eye of the waggler and slip this over the top of the float. This loop will be sufficient to hold the float in place at the top as well as at the base.

The starting position for the underarm plummet cast.

PLUMMETS

There are several different types of plummet available. Which you choose is largely down to personal preference, but a few points are worth remembering before making your selection.

The most traditional plummet is a weight with a cork in the bottom. The hook is threaded through the loop at the top and pushed into the cork. This plummet is good for hooks larger than a 16 and line stronger than 2 lb, but can damage small hooks and fine line. It is available in weights of $\frac{3}{8}$ to 1 oz.

There is a clip-on plummet, which originates from the continent and is designed to clip onto a hook. It can also be clipped onto a shot fixed above the hook, and is a good gauge for fishing overdepth. If you want to fish with 8 in of line on the bottom, fix a No.4 shot 8 in above the hook, clip the plummet onto this, and you will get an

Finding the correct depth: (above, left) the float is set too deep and consequently sticks too far out of the water; (above, right) the float is now at the correct depth with just the tip showing.

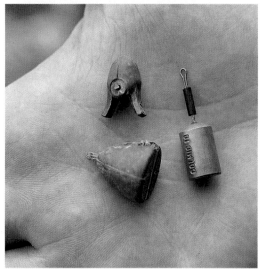

Left: Three types of plummet: clip-on, cork and silicone sleeve.

accurate reading. Like the cork plummet, this clip-on plummet can damage fine lines if its spring is too highly tensioned. Available in weights of ¼ to 1 oz, this plummet should be oiled occasionally to prevent it from rusting.

The match plummet has been introduced recently onto the fishing market and is perhaps one of the best because it cannot damage small hooks and fine lines. A wire loop at the top of the brass plummet is designed to take a hook, which is then secured by a small silicone sleeve. Available in weights of five grams, 10 grams and 15 grams, it is best to use the heaviest plummets in the deepest swims.

Some anglers prefer nothing more than a simple SSG or AAA split shot as a plummet. Quick and easy, a split shot can be fixed onto the line and removed in seconds. It is not really heavy enough for use on flowing water, however, and split shot can damage fine lines.

There are a couple of points to remember about the weight of plummet you choose. First, the heaviest plummet might be the easiest from which to obtain a true reading, and easy to cast, but a heavy plummet could also give you a false reading. If the bottom is covered with soft mud, a heavy plummet might sink several inches into it. In these circumstances, it would be better to use a lighter one. In addition to this, the plummet must be heavy enough to be cast accurately to the desired spot.

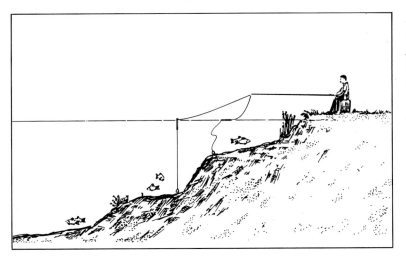

A typical canal: there are two shelves or slopes, and the good angler must discover where these are if he is going to fish effectively.

CASTING

There's no doubt that casting a heavy plummet takes time to perfect. The weight of the plummet plus the weight of the shot around the float, or even just the weight of the float itself, can result in a somersaulting effect with your tackle if you cast overarm towards the water. It's better to flick your tackle underarm. Start by holding the plummet in your left hand (assuming you're right-handed) and cast so it precedes your float towards the water.

For long distances, overarm casting can be attempted, but take care. Swing your tackle over your shoulder and wait until the plummet is out behind you before casting overarm. By feathering the line carefully, you will get no tangles, and with practice you will be able to cast accurately too.

It certainly takes time and practice to cast a plummet long distances. But it is still important, especially on stillwaters. On flowing water, you can at a push keep pulling your float up the line and trotting through as normal until your hook catches bottom and the float drags under. Then it's a case of shallowing up a few inches, or moving the bottom shot a little further away from the hook, until you achieve a perfect trot. A better alternative is to use a single SSG shot as a plummet, squeezed close to the hook. You will be able to cast this much better than a heavy plummet, although a clear reading is more difficult to obtain.

WHERE TO FISH

Once you've found the depth, how do you know where to fish? There are no hard-and-fast answers, but you look for several features on specific venues. For instance, on rivers try to find a stretch with an even bottom along which you can trot a float without it being dragged under. In a swim with uneven bottom you might be fishing parts of it with your hookbait a long way from the river bed, while in other parts it might be dragging along the bed. When it comes to lakes, look for sudden changes of depths called drop-offs or flat parts between two steep shelves. In warm weather many fish will be found on a shelf, while as the water cools, concentrate your attentions on the deeper water at the bottom of the shelf.

Shelves are even more important on canals. Plumb carefully to try to gain a mental picture of the swim in front of you. The main catching areas will be the near and far sides, and at the bottom of any shelves at edge of the centre boat-channel. Again, as the season progresses, fish will tend to move into deeper water.

Remember that plumbing the depth is one of the first jobs you should do once you arrive at the bankside. Perform the operation carefully and with a minimum of fuss, and the fish will be disturbed very little. Plumbing will definitely help you to catch more fish during the session.

CHAPTER SIX

Float Adaptors and Knots

There's nothing more annoying than watching fishing conditions alter gradually throughout the day, and finding that you need a different float to cope with the change. It could be that the wind has picked up and a straight waggler would make fishing easier than the insert float you've been using. You will lose valuable fishing time if you have to break down your rig and then tackle-up again. In the process you stop feeding, lose your catching rhythm and the day is ruined. However, changing floats should only take a second. By using a special adaptor from the outset, it's only a case of pulling the float out and substituting it with another.

TYPES OF FLOAT ADAPTOR

There are several types of float adaptor available, and your choice should be governed by which float you are using at the time. Some floats have slim-diameter pegs at the bottom, while others are fatter. Use an adaptor whose internal diameter fits accordingly.

The most popular type of adaptor is a simple nylon sleeve, around $1\frac{1}{2}$ in long, with one end melted together and a hole pushed through the two joined halves. These adaptors are available in diameters to fit onto the bottom of most floats and are soft so they damage neither line nor float, light in weight so they do not affect the float's shot-carrying capacity, and unobtrusive so they don't hinder casting potential. Several companies manufacture them in packs of three or four and they certainly represent good value for money.

Adaptors can be pushed just as easily over floats with rings as they can over floats with a simple peg at their base. Take a little care, moistening the bottom of the float before pushing on the adaptor and you'll have no problems.

Some anglers prefer an adaptor incorporating a swivel as its bottom eye. The swivel turns as the float flies through the air, ensuring a true and accurate cast with no sacrifice to distance. They tend to make the float 'fold' a little on the strike, which means that there is less resistance between rod and fish. The swivel enables the adaptor to be used to convert a conventional loaded waggler into a slider as long as the eye of the swivel is small enough.

There is a recent introduction on to the tackle market called a link adaptor. It is a clever way of using an adaptor without having to 'lock' the float onto the line with shot fixed either side of the hole. It consists of a stiff nylon peg, which pushes into a narrow piece of silicone rubber already threaded on to the line. The float is then pushed into the other end of the adaptor. Not only does this adaptor make the float want to lean upwards when held back instead of easily disappearing under the surface, it is also extremely useful for fishing with bulk shotting close to the hook. This method is much used for bottom feeding species like gudgeon and bream. No shot is wasted as locking shot to fix the float onto the line, but it can all be used where it will have the most effect – near to the hook. It's not a method for casting as there is no weight around the float, so tangles will result.

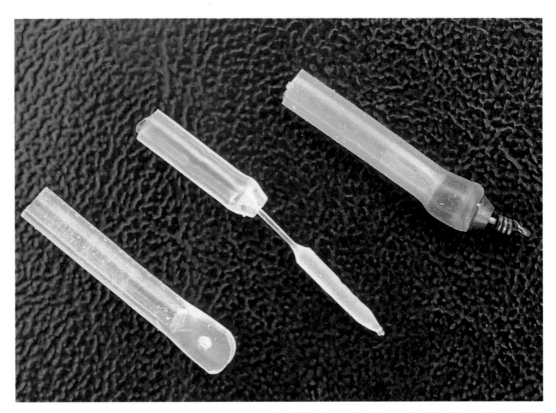

The simplest and best adaptor for conventional waggler fishing is a short length of top-quality, flexible silicone rubber with one end melted together and with a hole for your line. This is the float adaptor to use for most waggler situations, and it is available with different internal diameters, so as long as you carry a selection you will find one to suit your needs.

KNOTS

Learning how to tie a few basic knots is a vital part of the angling apprenticeship. Knots for anglers are tricky as monofilament line is one of the most slippery materials there is. Conventional knots that are perfectly adequate for string, only cause monofilament to slip, and in practice are useless. That is why, over the years, many knots have been developed especially for angling.

The knots that follow should hold you in good stead for most of your angling requirements. Before describing them in detail, here are a few tips that should make

Three types of adaptors – flexible silicone rubber, a link adaptor, and one incorporating a swivel.

knot-tying a lot easier.

You should always moisten a knot before tightening, and make sure all knots are tightened very carefully. There is also no point in 'making do' with a badly tied knot, so if you're not happy with it, discard it and start again. Don't trim the ends of a knot too close. Allow for a little leeway and you won't end up with a lost fish and a tiny 'pigtail' of line.

Another virtue is patience. Practice with any knot makes perfect. It is worth spending some time tying knots at home before using them for the first time on the bank.

Some lines have recommended knots explained on the spool. Follow this advice as some new lines are weakened considerably by certain knots.

Finally, never bite line. Whenever you have tied a knot, trim the end with a small, sharp pair of scissors. Biting weakens line and produces a messy finish.

Full bloodknot

The bloodknot is probably the single most important knot in an angler's armoury. It can be used in its various forms to join two lengths of line together, to attach line to a spool or loop, or even for tying a hook. The beauty of it is that the knot produced is streamlined, unobtrusive, and does not weaken the line excessively. The full bloodknot is really two knots in one, and the best knot for joining two lengths of line of similar breaking strain or diameter.

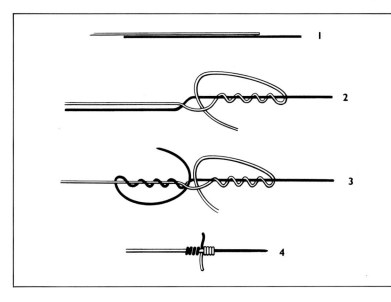

Step 1: lay both ends of line to be joined beside each other.

Step 2: twist one free end four times round the body of the other, and tuck it between the two parts.

Step 3: repeat with the other end, making sure the first turns do not unwind.

Step 4: moisten and draw the knot tight by pulling on the main part of the lines (called the standing parts), not the free ends. Trim.

Tucked half bloodknot

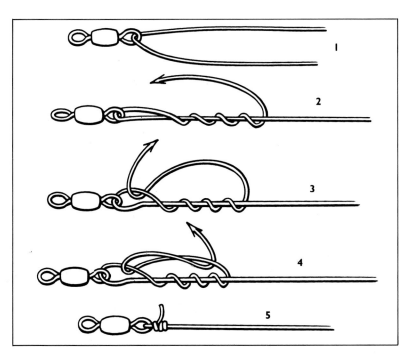

Step 1: pass the end of the line through the eye of the hook or swivel, or through the loop of line to which it is to be joined.

Step 2: twist the end round the standing part four or five times.

Step 3: pass the free end through the loop by the eye (if tightened, this is the normal half bloodknot).

Step 4: pass the free end through the larger loop now formed to produce the tucked half bloodknot.

Step 5: draw the knot together by moistening and pulling on the standing part. Trim.

Double overhand loop

Tying, a loop in monofilament line has to be done with a good deal of care. A single overhand loop knot will slip out in seconds, while other loop knots adequate for string will be sadly lacking when it comes to using them with monofilament. Here are two simple methods of tying a loop in the end of a line, and an equally easy way of joining two loops together.

Step 1: pull the end of line round against itself.

Step 2: using the loop formed, make a simple overhand loop.

Step 3: pull end of loop through again.

Step 4: tighten after moistening. The finished loop can be made as small or as large as you like, by gently moving the knot while tightening.

Grinner knot

The grinner knot can be used to attach line to a swivel or to an eyed hook. A double grinner (two knots) can be used to join two lengths of line of vastly different breaking strains, unlike the bloodknot, which is best for joining lines of similar breaking strains or diameter.

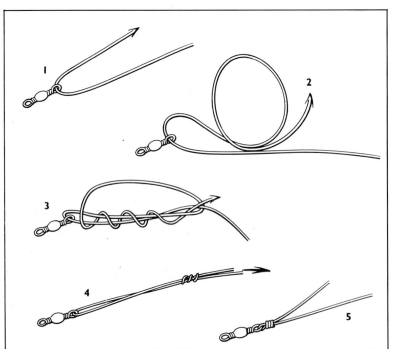

Step 1: thread the end of your line through the swivel or hook eye.

Step 2: make a large loop and place it alongside the line entering the swivel.

Step 3: take the end of the line and pass it through the loop and the other part of the line four times.

Step 4: moisten the knot and tighten by pulling on the end.

Step 5: pull the main part of the line to slide the knot towards the swivel eye. Trim close.

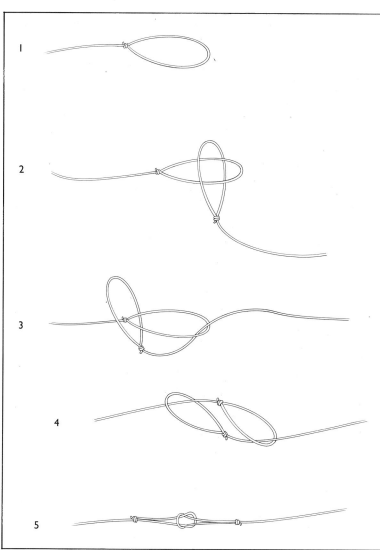

Loop-to-loop

This is a good knot to use when joining high-tech, low-diameter, pre-stretched hook-lengths to the main line.

Step 1: tie a loop in the ends of the two lines to be joined.

Step 2: push the loop at the end of the main line through the other loop.

Step 3: push the hook through the loop at the end of the main line.

Step 4: gently pull the two lines, drawing the two loops together and making sure the loop knots do not get caught up in the loops.

Step 5: continue pulling to draw the knot tight.

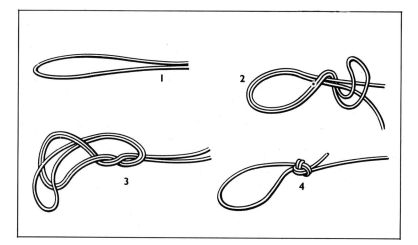

Blood bite

Step 1: pull the end of line round against itself.

Step 2: wrap the end of the loop twice around the line.

Step 3: pull the end of the loop behind and through the second loop now formed.

Step 4: moisten and tighten. It is more difficult to alter the size of this loop while tightening.

When fishing for big specimens, don't allow knots to let you down.

Four-turn waterknot

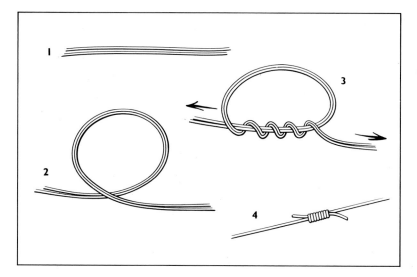

Step 1: place the two lines to be joined alongside each other, making sure there is plenty of overlap.

Step 2: with the two lines together, make a loop.

Step 3: take the end of the loop both lines) furthest from the rod and pull through the loop four times.

Step 4: moisten and tighten by pulling on the ends. Trim the unwanted parts.

Domhof knot

If you intend to fish with an eyed hook as opposed to a spade-end, then there is no better knot that the Domhof. This is a very reliable knot. Whereas the tucked half bloodknot and grinner knot are both tied to the eye, the Domhof relies on the line being secured around the shank of the hook. It definitely improves hooking a fish on the strike.

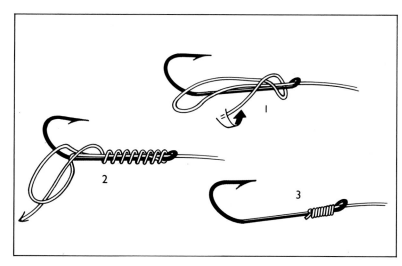

Step 1: pass the end of your line through the back of the eye and form a loop.

Step 2: holding the loop at the hook bend, take the end of the line and make eight neat coils towards the bend. Pass the eye through what is left of the loop.

Step 3: moisten and tighten by pulling on the main line while holding the other end.

Spade-end knot

There are several ways of tying spade-end hooks by hand and many anglers prefer to do it this way even though good hooktyers are now available, which can make the job easier. With a little practice, tying by hand takes only a few seconds and even the clumsiest of fingers will soon master the spade-end knot shown here. Start by tying large hooks to quite thick line and tie several before saving them for use. Then graduate on to smaller ones with finer lines.

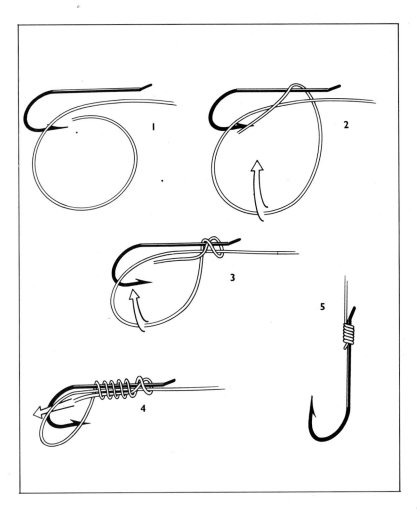

Step 1: make a loop in the end of your line and lie it along the hook.

Step 2: take the loop around the back of the hook, over the bend. Hold it in place.

Step 3: continue with another turn, trapping the line against the hookshank and making sure it comes from the front of the spade.

Step 4: carry on whipping down towards the bend until the required number of turns have been made. Modern hooks with small spades might need as many as 12.

Step 5: check the coils are neatly laid together before tightening by holding the short end and pulling on the hooklength or main line. Make sure the end of the line is passed through the loop before tightening.

POLE FISHING

Over the past 20 years the face of angling has changed beyond all recognition. Technology has heralded a new dawning in the manufacture of fishing accessories, which has benefited anglers of all disciplines. However, the area where most of the benefit has been felt – and appreciated – is in pole fishing. Poles have been transformed from the heavy, floppy, glass-fibre versions of the 1960s and 1970s to the ultra light, rigid carbon poles of today – and at an affordable price.

I was very lucky to be able to afford a top-notch pole as far back as 1981. Having just won the River Yare Championships that year, I soon converted the £525 winner's purse into a 10 m Daiwa Pro-carbon model, which set me back £400.

At that time I was one of only a handful of anglers in the Nottingham area to possess a pole made from this superb new material but I knew that to get ahead on the fiercely competitive local open-match circuit I would have to stay one step in front. Another reason was that I had endured a very unsettling experience in Ireland on a festival the previous May, when Leicester's Trev Tomlin, using a 10 m carbon pole, gave me one of the biggest next-peg thrashings of my whole career. I won't go into too much detail, but if I remember right I was about 140 lb in arrears.

In our neck of the woods the pole caught on later than in the south or the north west of England, and as a result there was little information on pole fishing techniques at grass roots level. Much of the pole angler's skills had to be obtained by trial and error. In fact, the first time I used one I tried to fish to-hand with a waggler, which was a complete disaster. However, quite clearly, there are days when the pole can be a devastating method in terms of fish-catching.

Gradually things started coming together as I progressed in the match world and discovered friends who passed on much-needed but basic tips, which I was to put to use. How I wish there had been a book like this one around at the time! One trick that helped me was always to practise with a pole if I had drawn a bad area in a match. Surprisingly enough, I caught a lot of fish, won section prizes and even got into the main list on a few occasions.

Since then, one of the many highlights of my pole fishing career was when I caught 133 lb 12 oz of roach on Lough Erne in Northern Ireland in the Brennan and Hickman Open. I only managed third because my groundbait wasn't right, but Kevin Ashurst's certainly was and he won with a staggering 207 lb.

Whether you are using a 2 m or a 12 m pole, I can promise you lots of exciting times with this delightful style of fishing. I can't guarantee breaking the 100 lb barrier, but you will have plenty of fun along the way.

Good luck and good fishing.

Jan Porter

*Elastic takes the strain as a
carp bids for freedom.*

CHAPTER SEVEN

Choosing a Pole

Buying that first pole is one of the most important decisions faced by the potential pole angler. There are so many things to be taken into consideration that it can seem an impossible task sorting the wheat from the chaff. Whereas, not so many years ago, there were only a few poles on the market to choose from, now there are hundreds from manufacturers all over the world. It is not the intention to mention too many manufacturers here. Suffice it to say that most pole-manufacturing companies have their good products, their reasonable ones and their sub-standard ones. Let's take a look at the different types available.

As with so many things in life, the angler's prime consideration has to be finance. Not everyone can go out and spend over £1,000 on a new pole, despite the advice of the angling press on what's best for this or that. You get what you pay for, and anyone with the slightest interest in polefishing will know that money buys poles. A lot of money will buy a good pole and a little money won't. It's as simple as that. So the first piece of advice has to be: save up until you can afford a pole you feel happy with. Whether this is £200 or £2,000 depends very much on the angler and his conscience. While it might be fine for the unmarried to save well-earned pennies over several months, the married mortgage-payer is often forced to have very different priorities.

Looking first at long poles – 8 m or more – you will get little change from £200, and this, in truth, will not buy you a pole you can feel totally happy with. In fact for a decent 11-m pole – the commonest length on sale – you can expect to pay £400. For this sort of money you will have a pole that you can use adequately in most conditions. Compare it to one costing twice as much and the difference will quickly become apparent. But just how much you spend is your decision. The

second-hand tackle columns in *Angling Times* can be a lifesaver. Scan these for bargains and don't be scared to make that phone call – someone else could beat you to it. It's an often-used piece of advice but worth repeating again: buy the longest pole you can afford. Buy an 8-m pole and you will probably soon want a 9-m one. Buy a 9 and you'll soon want a 10 – it's a catch-22 situation and one reason (in addition to the advent of new technology) why poles are appearing in ever-increasing lengths, and are used to great effect at amazing distances by the likes of Bob Nudd.

Assuming you have saved up enough money to buy yourself a decent pole, we now have to look at the other things you need to check before making your purchase, and the first of these is materials. The cheapest poles are made either from glass-fibre or a somewhat dubious material described as 'carbon composite'. This usually means glass-fibre with some sort of strengthening, stiffening agent added. Many companies offer poles in these materials in lengths up to 10 m and some are actually quite good. However, it is unlikely that you will be able to use this sort of pole comfortably in windy conditions, especially in the longer lengths. The pole will feel heavy, floppy and cumbersome, and sag towards the tip.

Likewise, the tip will bounce around for several seconds when the butt is moved. In practical terms this could mean lost fish, the pole's bounce pulling lightly hooked fish off the hook. It is also likely to have a wide diameter at the butt. All this makes for uncomfortable fishing, but it does provide a sound grounding for anyone trying their hand at polefishing for the first time – just don't expect to be putting in world championship performances when you take it out to the riverbank.

The newcomer to polefishing might not

notice these qualities in a 'cheap' pole, thinking all poles behave in a similar fashion. All that changes when he tries one made out of carbon fibre. As with rods, the advent of carbon brought an enormous improvement in the poles that were commercially available. Poles suddenly became usable by anglers other than those built like brick outhouses. The improvement is still going on today. The first carbon poles, although a vast improvement on their glass-fibre predecessors, were heavy, sloppy and cumbersome by today's standards. What you don't know you don't miss, however, and would-be pole anglers thought they'd struck gold. Now, all sorts of techniques and materials are employed to make further improvements in weight, diameter and rigidity. Materials such as kevlar, lithium and amorphous are used in the manufacturing process, combined with the carbon fibre in elaborate 'weaves' running the length of the pole from butt to tip. The best poles have successfully achieved a near-perfect combination of these three essential criteria – little weight, little diameter and much rigidity.

Most reasonable poles that are in the shops come at a basic length of 11 m, and this is the length the would-be pole angler should endeavour to afford. Even the most proficient of pole anglers would probably admit that they rarely use their pride and joys at lengths beyond this. It coincides with the far shelf on the majority of canals and gets them well out into rivers and lakes.

Extensions of 1 or 1½, metres are usually available to add to the butt section of these poles should a longer one be required – but again, they can cost a lot of money if the pole is to retain its good qualities. If you're worried that 11 m might not be long enough, pace it out in the back garden. You'll realize that 11 m will be perfectly adequate for most polefishing situations. An 11-m pole costing a lot of money will even feel uncomfortable at first to the angler used to wielding 13-ft float rods. It's a question of technique and the familiarity that comes with regular use. Techniques for holding a long pole in comfort are described fully later on.

JOINTS

The way in which each section of a long pole joins together might not seem very important to the beginner, but the angler who has been polefishing for some time knows that good joints can make or break a pole – literally. Pole joints come in three types – telescopic, put-in and put-over. Telescopic joints are used exclusively for short whips and highly specialized long poles, and should not be considered by the angler buying his first long pole. The two important ones are put-in and put-over. So what's the difference? Quite simply, with poles that have put-in joints, the sections nearer the pole-tip fit inside those nearer the butt. With poles that have put-over joints, the sections nearer the pole-tip fit outside (or over) those nearer the butt.

In practice, the beginner to polefishing will notice little difference between the two types. However, during recent years there has been a definite trend among good pole anglers towards poles with put-over joints. This type of pole, it is said, is better to use because put-over joints are easier to locate than put-ins. Furthermore, all pole joints wear, but when put-over joints wear, all that happens is that the section nearer the butt pushes further inside the next section, nearer the tip. When put-in joints wear, eventually the male joint on the section nearer the tip• will slide completely through the female joint on the next section nearer the butt. In addition to all this, poles with put-over joints tend to be slimmer overall than their put-in counterparts, and lighter too. Perhaps the only aspect on which put-in poles are superior is rigidity. Some of the stiffest, sturdiest poles ever made have put-in joints, and anglers who visit fish-packed countries like Ireland and Denmark often take this sort of pole with them.

No poles have put-over joints only. In fact, often the top two or top three sections are telescopic, while sometimes the top section pushes inside the next. Be careful with poles whose top three sections are telescopic. This might pose problems when a very short length of line is required between pole-tip and hook – for pushing under the branches of a far-side tree on a shallow canal, for example. With the top three sections being at least 2 m long in total, that is the shortest length of line than be used comfortably and a shorter line might be required. Poles whose top two sections are telescopic, or fully take-apart poles, are better.

SPARES

Another important point to look into when buying a new pole is the availability of spare parts. There are few pole anglers who have not at some time or other broken a section or watched one disappear under the water surface. You need to know that replacement sections are available without too long a wait, and at a fair price, too. On the subject of spares, check also whether your pole comes just as it is, or whether extra top sections are included in the price. It is certainly useful to have more than one top-three pole-tip as different elastic setups can be fitted through each one. Many pole anglers like several different rigs set up beside them while fishing. Having more than one top part certainly saves time and energy in this department. Several manufacturers sensibly provide a spare top-three section with their poles, while some tackle dealers will also provide a spare top-three for little extra cost.

TIP SECTIONS

Take a close look at the pole's tip section before buying. The chances are it will be hollow and quite long. This is the most common type of tip section and is designed to be cut back so an internal shock-absorbing set-up can be fitted. The tip sections on some poles are stiffer than those on others. The softest tip sections are usually longer and have to be cut back considerably more than the other type to allow elastic to be fitted so that the tip does not bend too much when a fish is hooked, reducing the effect of the elastic as it rubs against the inside of the tip section. A third type of tip on a long pole is known as a fiick-tip and is a length of fine, tapering and solid carbon spliced into the hollow tip. This is not designed to house

elastic – as it is solid, elastic cannot be fitted inside – but acts as a shock absorber by itself. Some accomplished pole anglers prefer this fiick-tip set-up for catching large numbers of small fish quickly, but with the lack of elastic to help with playing larger fish, it is a dangerous technique if anything at all substantial is likely to be hooked. Your chances of landing it are minimal.

ACTION

In today's technologically advanced world of polefishing, it is possible to buy poles with just about any action you want. And as the pole angler becomes more proficient, he will realize that it is not always the stiffest poles that are best. For example, anglers who concentrate most of their attentions on canals with light tackle and long poles, might place lightness at the top of their list of priorities. The fact that the lightest poles usually lose out slightly in the rigidity stakes does not bother them. However, the river angler is likely to place rigidity higher on the list than lightness. So decide what sort of action you want before making that all-important purchase.

WHIPS

Similar criteria to the above can be laid out when buying a whip, which is really a shorter pole, often all telescopic or part telescopic and part take-apart. Telescopic whips are designed for fishing with a length of line that is the same as the length of the whip. It is fishing at its simplest – the tackle is swung out to the desired fishing spot, and the fish are swung back in again! It sounds easy, but there are considerations to be borne in mind when deciding whether or not to use a whip. The action of the wind on the water, for example, can severely reduce the whip's effectiveness, blowing tackle and line all over the place. A long pole and shorter line, unshipping to catch, allows better tackle control. However, there is no doubt that a whip fished effectively can be much faster than conventional pole fishing. All-telescopic whips are available in a wide range of lengths from

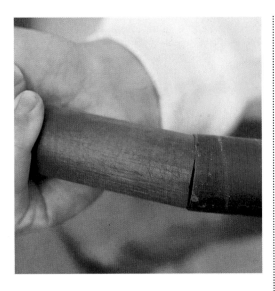

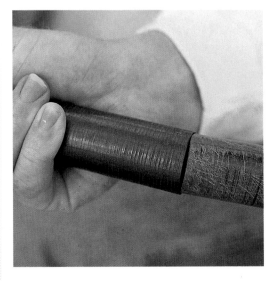

Left: Put-in joints are like this.

Below: Put-over joints are like this.

1 to 10 m although the most common lengths in use on British waters are 3, 4 and 5 m. Canal anglers will tell you that you need 2-m whips, while river anglers will always carry whips of 6 m and perhaps 7 m. However, for your first purchase, buy a whip of 4 or 5 m. On most venues between 4 and 8-ft deep, a 5-m whip will allow you to cast out far enough to find the fish.

Nine times out of ten, whips are used with fiick-tips, in order to catch large numbers of small fish quickly. An elastic set-up with a stiffish tip section would result in a lot of 'bumped' fish, so whip anglers usually prefer a fiick-tip, resorting to chance should a big fish come along to take the bait. It is quite amazing how large fish can be landed on a whip – sometimes they're in the net before they have realized they've even been hooked! The only time anglers should consider using an elastic set-up when whip fishing is for highly specialized requirements such as fishing for carp in lakes where large numbers of fish to 3 lb are taken close to the bank. These fish can be landed successfully as long as some sort of shock absorber is used to control that first run of the hooked fish.

A few years ago, it was true to say that the only whips to consider in terms of action and lightness were all-telescopic ones. Now, however, the angler is spoilt for choice and it is possible to buy one whip that can be used in several different lengths. Manufacturers

have achieved this by a combination of telescopic and take-apart sections, and there are now many excellent whips of this type available. Most have a top 3 or 4 m that are telescopic, followed by several add-on sections to extend the length. There are several advantages in this. The whip can be used simply for to-hand fishing as normal. It can be used with a short length of line corresponding just to the telescopic section, with extra sections added on to gain extra length while still retaining a good degree of tackle control in a wind. And the angler can follow the fish, adding on a section if the fish decide to move further away from the bank as the session progresses. As you can see, a part take-apart and part telescopic whip serves several purposes and is an excellent buy.

Whip action can be split into two types: those which are designed purely for catching large numbers of small-to-medium fish ($\frac{1}{2}$ oz to 6 oz), and those for larger fish. The first type are quite stiff through the fiick-tip or the second section, after which they bend. It is this tip part that acts as the shock absorber when a fish is hooked, to prevent the hook pulling from its mouth. Once hooked, however, the fish should be removed from the water as quickly as possible, and this is where the stiffer sections of the whip do their job. Shorter whips (up to 4 m) are usually of this action. However, when longer whips are used, the action is much softer. Much more of the whip bends and they often have a hollow, flexible tip section. These whips bend in a gradual curve, aiding the casting of light floats and enabling large fish to be played successfully to the net. They can be highly effective in deep-water swims, or on rivers where the flow of the water requires more line to allow the float to travel the full length of the swim. Reasonable whips can cost anything from £40 to £200. If you can afford just one, go for a part telescopic and part take-apart model of around 5 or 6m in length.

CHAPTER EIGHT

Elastics

Once you have bought a new pole, you'll be itching to get to the bank of your favourite river or lake to put it through its paces, but first there are several important things you have to do at home. In fact, half the fun of polefishing is the preparation involved – it makes that first pole-caught fish something special!

Before you even start work fitting elastic and making rigs, check the pole very carefully. It's unlikely that you will have been sold a faulty one, but a few will always slip through the net and it is worth examining every section carefully 'for cracks or splits, especially around the joints. Only when you are satisfied that your pole is in first-class condition should you start to work on it. If you feel inclined – and it's certainly a good idea – treat each joint with the special protective solution that is now available, called Jointsave. This adds strength to each joint, prolongs the life of your pole, and reduces wear, which shows in untreated poles in the form of black carbon 'dust' on the affected section. This is especially noticeable in the wet. You should also insure your pole before using it. With tackle thefts on the increase, it's a foolish angler who does not make plans for such an eventuality. As your pole is likely to be the most expensive item of kit in your collection, that should go at the top of the list.

Let us assume that the pole is fine, it's been insured, and you have taken the wise step of buying an extra top-section kit to go with the two supplied with the pole. Your next job is to fit them with elastic. The use of elastic is an alien concept to newcomers to polefishing. However, it is an extremely important fish-catching aid. When using a rod and reel, once a fish is hooked the angler simply reels in and swings the fish to hand or nets it in the usual way. If it's a big fish, he can let it run if required, either by setting the reel's clutch so that the fish pulls line from the spool, or by backwinding – turning the reel's handle backwards – to give fish line. With a pole, neither of these two things can be done there is no more line apart from that between pole-tip and hook. The answer is to incorporate a length of elastic inside the top part of the pole. It is this elastic that does one part of the job of a reel. It doesn't magically produce extra line so a fish can run and still be landed, but it extends when a fish is hooked. If the fish is small, it might only be pulled 1 to 2 in before retracting back inside the pole to

The Uni-bung (top) and Stonfo Connector: useful items for the pole angler.

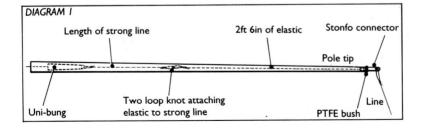

DIAGRAM 1

Length of strong line — 2ft 6in of elastic — Stonfo connector — Pole tip — Uni-bung — Two loop knot attaching elastic to strong line — PTFE bush — Line

A typical pole-tip elastic set-up. This one includes a length of strong line so exactly 2ft 6in of elastic can be used.

allow the fish to be landed. However, when the fish is big, it really does its work. The elastic is pulled out from the pole-tip, increasing in tension as it does so and eventually tiring the fish, which can then be landed in the normal way. It is an extremely effective way of landing large fish – neat, tidy and reliable as long as the elastic is checked on a regular basis.

TYPES AND STRENGTHS

There are several types of elastic designed for polefishing - all thin, circular and able to stretch a long length. It is obvious that one size of elastic will not suffice for every situation the pole angler is likely to encounter. That's why it comes in many different strengths and thicknesses, which can be used for different circumstances. Catching small fish along the far shelf of a canal, for example, should require a fine elastic, while larger fish on rivers can be handled with a thicker one. The strongest elastic, meanwhile, is designed for large species. Large fish would soon pull a length of fine elastic to its limit and the angler's chance of landing it would be minimal; using thick elastic for small fish will undoubtedly lead to a lot of 'bumped' fish, the strike being too powerful and pulling the hook through the fish's mouth. But still there are problems.

What about times when most fish will be small, but the occasional larger one can be expected? Choice of elastic is one of the skills of the pole angler, but with more than half-a-dozen sizes available, there is usually one to suit your needs. You can always change

during a session. Now you can see the importance of several top sections!

Britain's two most popular elastics are those under the brand names of Slip and Zim. Others are available that should meet your requirements equally well – check which are stocked by your local dealer. Both of these elastics are excellent, but you will notice that Slip elastic is colour-coded for easy identification That is a great advantage to the pole angler when it comes to selecting elastic before starting to fish. Pole elastics are coded according to thickness and breaking strain. Don't worry too much about breaking strain –it is merely a guide and only ever comes into play when the elastic 'bottoms out' (reaches the limit of its stretch). Your choice of strength and length of elastic should be determined by three factors: the size of fish you will be catching, the depth of the water, and the size of your float.

Consult the table as a guide but remember that the best anglers are prepared to change according to what's happening in front of them. The best way of finding the right elastic on your chosen venue is to experiment with different elastics, different lengths and different tensions. An elastic which might work on one venue may result in bumped fish on another, similar venue. Fish like skimmer bream have soft mouths, and if your elastic is not exactly right, you will lose more than you catch. In truth, all species can prove difficult to hook unless the right pole elastic and tension is used. The well-prepared angler will

A table showing elastic guidelines.

Zim	Slip	Size of fish	Size of float	Depth of water	No of sections	Diameter	Species
1	Purple	Up to 8 oz	Up to 0.7 gm	Up to 4 ft	1	0.58 mm	Roach, gudgeon
2	Red	Up to 1 lb	Up to 1 gm	Up to 8 ft	1	0.65 mm	Roach, skimmers
3	Green	Up to 2 lb	Up to 1.5 gm	Up to 8 ft	1 or 2	0.75 mm	Roach, bream
4	Orange	Up to 3 lb	Up to 2.5 gm	Up to 12 ft	1 or 2	0.85 mm	Roach, bream
5	Blue	Up to 4 lb	Up to 3 gm	Up to 12 ft	2	0.91 mm	Bream, chub
6	Yellow	Up to 5 lb	Up to 4 gm	Up to 15 ft	2	1.06 mm	Carp, barbel
7	-	Up to 6 lb	Up to 5 gm	Up to 18 ft	2	1.18 mm	Carp, eels
8	Grey	Up to 8 lb	Up to 6 gm	Up to 20 ft	2	1.37mm	Carp, eels

ensure that he has several different set-ups, then one can be changed in seconds for another. This can prove costly in the first instance, but will eventually pay dividends.

FITTING ELASTIC

Of course, if pole elastic is to do its job effectively and reliably, it has to be fitted properly – and there are specific tools for the job. It is most important that the elastic fiows smoothly from the pole-tip. An elastic that fiows in a series of awkward jerks is a recipe for disaster – lost fish at best, snapped elastic and lost tackle at worst. The main problem lies at the tip of the pole. Even a carefully cut pole-tip, smoothed with fine sandpaper, will cause abrasion and damage elastic, so something has to be fitted into the tip to provide a friction-free surface over which the elastic can glide smoothly without damage. The answer is a PTFE bush. PTFE is an almost friction-free material that is used in space rockets among other things, and it is the answer to a pole-angler's prayers. A correctly fitted PTFE bush will give years of trouble-free service, although the elastic will need changing from time to time.

PTFE bushes are small, neat and can be fitted internally or externally, depending on the diameter of the hollow pole-tip and how much is cut off. Internal bushes are generally regarded as preferable because there is no way the elastic can scrape against the rough

Internal (top) and external bushes. Internal are best.

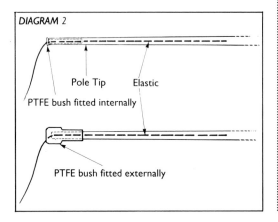

DIAGRAM 2

Pole Tip   Elastic

PTFE bush fitted internally

PTFE bush fitted externally

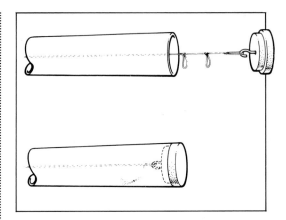

Elastic tension can be altered quickly by tying small loops at 3-in intervals.

tip of the pole. This can happen, however, with a badly fitted external bush – so take care. External bushes used to be popular because, as none of the bush is inside the pole-tip, very little had to be cut off the pole-tip, reducing the length of the pole by only a few inches. Now, tiny 'micro-tips' are available, which can still be fitted internally but without having to lose much from the pole's length.

With the PTFE bush at the very tip of the pole, what about the other end of the elastic? It will have to be secured in some way, and again there are items tailor-made for the job. Elastic securing bungs come in several shapes and sizes, and it's largely a matter of personal choice. For elastic that is to be fitted into the wider, second section, a bung which can be cut to fit neatly inside is ideal. If this bung has the facility to allow the tension of the elastic to be changed quickly and easily without breaking it and starting again, so much the better. A bung that fits inside the pole is necessary if the next section down fits inside the section with the bung, as on put-over poles. If the next section fits outside the bung section – a put-in pole – then a different kind of bung can be used, fitting neatly over the end of the joint. The put-over pole bung can be used with both types of section.

Opposite: Six easy steps to fitting pole elastic.

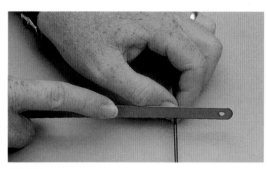

STEP I

Check whether your chosen PTFE bush – it should allow the elastic to pass through with only a tiny space all round – fits inside the pole-tip, or outside if you want to use an external bush. The chances are that it won't, so use a hacksaw blade to saw carefully through the tip of the pole a few inches from the end. Score all the way round with the blade before sawing through to prevent splinters shearing away.

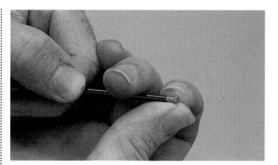

STEP 2

Try the bush for size again. If it fits tightly, push it in or over the tip. If it doesn't, cut a little more off – I in at a time is about right – until the bush fits tightly. Now remove the bush and sand the tip edge smooth with wet-and-dry paper. Fit the bush for a last time. Carefully glue it in place if you want to, but if you have cut the pole tip back correctly, you shouldn't need to do this.

STEP 3

Take your chosen bung and, assuming you want elastic through the top two sections of your pole, ensure it fits into the butt end of the second section. If you are using a Uni-bung, it should be gently scored by turning it against the bottom of the second section. Then cut and remove the unwanted part of the bung without cutting through the inner nylon tag. Sand the cut edge smooth.

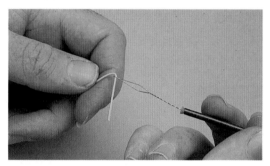

STEP 4

Attach the elastic to the special threader – all tackle shops sell them – and push threader and elastic through from the tip sections. Once it's through, attach the tip connector by using at least two overhand knots, tightening each carefully so there is no chance of the elastic slipping.

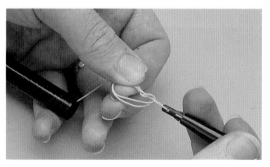

STEP 5

Once the elastic has been threaded and the tip connector tied and pulled against the bush, take the other end and, after removing the threader, pull it to the tension you require. Trim off the excess and thread the end of the elastic through the hole in the bung. Tie to the bung using a well-tightened single overhand loop. Some bungs have a hook. Here, tie a loop and hook it over.

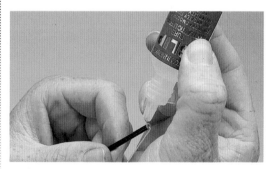

STEP 6

Test the elastic for tension, adjusting it at the bung end if necessary, and treat it with pole-elastic lubricant to ensure that it flows smoothly through the tip. You can make further adjustments on the bankside.

As well as bung and bush, you will need some means of joining the elastic to your line. An Italian device called a Stonfo Connector is great for the job, but there are other ways of doing it which are just as effective and not as bulky. The Stonfo is a simple, plastic device with a hook at one end, over which a loop in the line slides. It is secured by a plastic sleeve. The end of the elastic is tied to the other end of the connector and everything is neat, tidy and secure.

Pole-elastic lubricant is a must for the pole angler. Regular treatments with this helps the elastic to flow more smoothly through the pole-tip sections, repelling water and prolonging the life of the elastic. Use it after fitting and tightening all knots, and before every fishing session. Several drops should be poured into the tip sections.

A good tackle dealer will often fit elastic into your pole-tip sections if you ask him nicely, but it is a useful ploy to learn how to do this yourself. The things you will need are: PTFE bush, tip connector, bung, elastic, elastic threader, pole-tip section or top two sections, wet-and-dry paper, small scissors and hacksaw blade.

LENGTH OF ELASTIC

Anglers with poles whose top section is quite long often use elastic through the top section only, and in the small sizes of elastic it's unlikely that you will need any more than around 18 in of fine elastic. However, a different type of bung is required here. The best tip-section bungs are made in Italy by Stonfo and are available in 10 different diameters from 2.8 mm to 12.4 mm. Once a loop has been tied in the end of the elastic, it is attached to a plug of the correct size, which then fits on to the end of the tip section.

For many polefishing situations, elastic through one section will be enough. With a tip section of at least 12 in long, there will be enough elastic to handle fish of 2 or 3 lb as long as you are careful. This is fine for small-to-medium sized fish, but what about larger

Fitting elastic to line the Bob Nudd way.

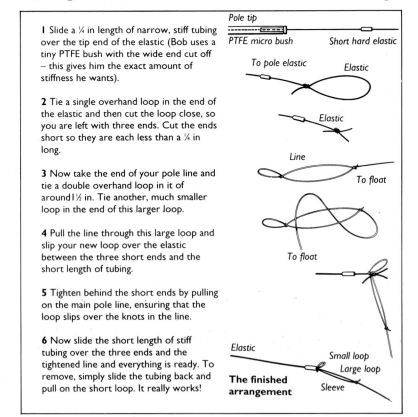

1 Slide a ¼ in length of narrow, stiff tubing over the tip end of the elastic (Bob uses a tiny PTFE bush with the wide end cut off – this gives him the exact amount of stiffness he wants).

2 Tie a single overhand loop in the end of the elastic and then cut the loop close, so you are left with three ends. Cut the ends short so they are each less than a ¼ in long.

3 Now take the end of your pole line and tie a double overhand loop in it of around 1½ in. Tie another, much smaller loop in the end of this larger loop.

4 Pull the line through this large loop and slip your new loop over the elastic between the three short ends and the short length of tubing.

5 Tighten behind the short ends by pulling on the main pole line, ensuring that the loop slips over the knots in the line.

6 Now slide the short length of stiff tubing over the three ends and the tightened line and everything is ready. To remove, simply slide the tubing back and pull on the short loop. It really works!

Pole tip

PTFE micro bush

Short hard elastic

To pole elastic

Elastic

Elastic

Line

To float

To float

Elastic

Small loop

Large loop

The finished arrangement

Sleeve

fish where stronger, thicker elastic is required? In this case a longer length of elastic is needed as there would not be enough of a shock absorber in a short length of strong elastic.

On waters where fish like chub and carp may be encountered, elastic through the top two sections is best. Some top anglers are so adamant about the length of elastic they want that they measure it out to their chosen length disregarding the length of the top two sections of their pole. The elastic is then tied using the two-loop knot to a length of strong line long enough to allow a bung to be removed from the butt of the second section.

Getting the tension right is something that comes with trial and error. The best advice is to fit the elastic so it only just slides back into the pole when pulled from the tip end. The chances are this will be too slack when it comes to fishing, but better too slack than too tight. It's easy to cut the elastic at the bung end, tie another loop and replace the bung to make everything tighter, but it's much more difficult to slacken elastic that's too tight. One way is to use a plug with a hook. Then you can tie three loops in the end of the elastic at 3-in intervals, instead of one loop, and hook over whichever loop makes the elastic work best. Another way is

to use a special sort of bung, whose diameter can be adjusted to allow it to be fitted further up or down the second section. There are also special elastic tensioners available, which can be used to tighten the elastic, or slacken it again afterwards. All these are excellent ways to get your elastic just right – it should not be hanging loose from the pole-tip, but should not be too tight either. It should do its job on all sizes of fish, pulling out when the fish is hooked, then coming into play if required as the fish is brought towards the net.

If you have just one top section, or the top two sections, for elastic, you can still change elastic on the riverbank by preparing the right length at home, with a connector tied to one end but nothing at the other. Wrap it around a pole-rig winder and store it in your tackle box. Should you want to change, you can then simply thread it through from the tip with an elastic threader, and attach a bung to the other end.

Top match angler, Bob Nudd, has come up with an innovative way of attaching elastic at the tip section, which does away with the need for a Stonfo connector. It is brilliant for fine elastic and fine tip sections, where a Stonfo connector can be an obtrusive hindrance on otherwise delicate tackle. It's simple to do.

CHAPTER NINE

Types of Pole Floats

No pole angler will get very far without floats. Not only do floats serve their purpose as indicators of a bite, they also suspend the bait at the required depth and help the angler control his end tackle. However, step into any tackle shop and you will probably be totally confused by the hundreds – sometimes thousands – of floats on display. So what makes a good pole float, or a bad one, for that matter?

Before answering that question, it is worth looking at the requirements of a float for polefishing. First is its weight-carrying capacity. Here lies the main difference between floats for polefishing and those for rod-and-reel fishing. Floats for rod-and-reel fishing need to serve several different functions but one of their most important requirements is to have the potential to carry enough weight to allow the angler to cast to the required distance without the float sinking out of sight beneath the surface once it has landed. The pole angler does not have such worries. No casting is required for

Right: Floats with wire bristles are becoming more and more popular.

Opposite: Carry duplicates of your favourite floats.

him. Put in the simplest terms, he lowers the tackle on to the water. The weight required in a waggler or stick float with running line is superfluous when polefishing – which immediately highlights one of polefishing's strongest advantages over other forms of fishing.

As pole floats don't have to be cast, they are lighter than floats for other forms of fishing. In most cases, this means that they are more delicate and more sensitive as well. A delicate float, carefully shotted, will entice more bites from a shoal of fickle fish than a heavier float, which has to take more weight in order to be cast to the right place. A pole float can be lowered on to the surface of a shallow canal with almost imperceptible disturbance, completely unnoticed by the fish beneath – imagine a heavy waggler landing in the same place.

And delicacy means sensitivity. The tiny bristle on the top of most pole floats takes only a tiny amount of effort on the part of the fish to pull beneath the surface. The fish feels no resistance and is hooked by the angler on the bank. Floats taking more weight are more likely to be felt by the fish, and the bait dropped before the strike can be made. This is especially important on stillwaters and canals, where a fish has time to inspect a bait, sucking and blowing at it and even taking it into its mouth before any indication is apparent on the float tip. On moving water it's not so important – if a fish doesn't take the bait as it drifts past its nose, it will miss out. So, pole floats are usually lighter than their rod-and-reel counterparts for fishing the same distance from the bank. They're also smaller, and this can be important in clear water like that sometimes found in canals and on many venues in winter. A small float is less likely to be noticed than a large one.

MATERIALS

Just as in floats for rod-and-reel fishing, floats for polefishing come in many shapes and sizes, and the beginner can easily become confused by the vast array available. It's a sad fact that many floats – pole floats

included – are designed to catch more anglers than fish, and despite what some pole float brochures would have you believe, you need only a few patterns to see you through most situations. Most pole floats are constructed with a bristle, a body and a stem. They are attached to the line by passing it through a tiny wire eye fixed near the top of the body and through one, two or even three short lengths of narrow rubber sleeve, which slide on to the float stem. The wire eye is a much better attachment than wide, obtrusive float rubbers like those used on stick floats but they won't stand up to the rigours of rod and reels with their continual casting and retrieving. However, for pole floats, they're perfect.

You might wonder why pole floats are attached at the top and bottom, not only at the bottom end like wagglers. In truth, of course, there are times when it pays to use bottom-end-only floats when polefishing, especially when fishing 'to-hand' with a whip, but generally speaking, top-and-bottom floats are preferable. This is because near-perfect control is possible with a pole. Bottom-end floats are used by rod-and-reel anglers because there is a need to sink the line out of the way of the wind between rod tip and float. With a much shorter amount of line between pole tip and float, the effects of the wind are much reduced, so top-and-bottom floats can be used that can be controlled much more easily and are more sensitive than bottom-end only floats. Even in windy conditions, top-and-bottom floats can be controlled when the angler fixes a small shot a few inches above the float – it's called a backshot – to sink a little of the line, which would otherwise be blown around by the wind, affecting the float and ruining the delicate presentation of the bait.

BRISTLES

The bristles on many pole floats are all part and parcel of their sensitivity, aiding the bite-detection process by all but eliminating any buoyancy at the tip of the float. A fish merely has to breathe on a bait for it to show on a properly-shotted pole-float bristle.

The most popular bristle material is nylon, probably because it's the easiest to work with. A small hole is made by the manufacturer in the top of the float body and the bristle is pushed into it. The best pole floats have between ¼ and ½ in of bristle actually in the body, and around 1 in protruding as the bite detector. Often no glue is used to attach the bristle to the float body, with the manufacturers claiming that the bristle can be changed quickly for another one of a different colour if the reflection on the water changes – when the surface goes from calm to ripples, for example. This is not the perfect solution, however, as water tends to seep inside the gap between bristle and float body and affect the setting of the float. What was a perfectly-shotted pole float at the start of a session disappears from view beneath the surface an hour later. For this reason, many anglers glue their bristles in place, changing its colour if they need to by using a quick-drying fluorescent paint (orange or yellow) or indelible felt-tip pen (black).

Nylon bristles, though not buoyant, are not heavy either and a float can be shotted quite easily so just a part of the bristle is showing. They come in various thicknesses, which is is a good thing as some of the smaller floats have ridiculously fine bristles that just cannot be seen at distances beyond say, nine metres. Many anglers substitute thicker bristles for these fine ones, or give the fine ones a coat or two of fluorescent paint as an aid to visibility. These thicker bristles are just as sensitive as thinner ones and can actually be shotted so just the very tip is visible above the surface.

Another bristle material much used in the manufacture of pole floats is cane. This material is an excellent choice when a float is required that registers bites as the bait falls through the last part of the water. Good canal anglers use cane bristles when fishing for gudgeon, weighting the pole float with its 'bulk' – most of the float's weight-carrying capacity – around 8 in from the hook and just one or two small shot between this and the hook. These shot are usually No. 8s, and as each one settles, the cane tip on the float settles a little more.

A few trial drops of the tackle soon familiarizes the angler with the behaviour of his float. Gudgeon – and other species – have a habit of coming up a few inches off the bottom as they gain in confidence. Instead of shallowing up and missing out on those fish still on the bottom, the angler has the perfect float. If a fish intercepts the bait as it is falling, once the bulk has settled, it is easily seen on the float by the failure of the cane tip to settle properly because the fish has prevented the bottom 'dropper' shot from settling. Setting a pole with a nylon bristle in this way is not so easy.

The final bristle material is one that is becoming more and more popular with top match anglers after losing popularity for many years. Floats with wire bristles used to be employed all the time by anglers on the Continent – especially in France and Belgium, where polefishing techniques were perfected long before British anglers started realizing its advantages. Now, anglers of the calibre of Bob Nudd and Dave Berrow use wire bristles for much of their polefishing. The great advantage of a wire bristle is its sensitivity – drop a wire bristle into water and it sinks like a stone. Once a float with a wire bristle has been shotted so the body is fully submerged, it takes no more effort on the part of a fish to pull the bristle under. They're impossible to beat for sensitivity. So how come anglers don't use wire-bristled pole floats to the exclusion of all others? The main reason is that the bristle cannot be shotted in order that on-the-drop bites can be spotted. Once the body is submerged, the tiniest of tiny weights will sink the float out of sight. In fact, many anglers steer clear of them, claiming they are impossible to shot correctly. There is, however, a simple answer to the problem. By smearing a little grease – Mucilin is best – over the top part of the wire bristle, you will find that the float can be shotted much more easily. You are, in effect, shotting the grease. And what could be more sensitive than a float whose only above-water buoyancy is provided by a smear of grease on the wire bristle? Wire bristles can be difficult, but the rewards are

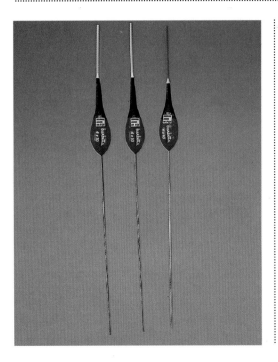

there for the taking.

Recently introduced carbon bristles have exactly the same properties. Both types are often used right the way through the body of the float, the same material forming both bristle and stem. Like other types of bristle, their visibility can be improved by a coat of white base paint followed by one of a fluorescent top coat colour.

The length of bristle depends on the size of the float. Usually the heavier floats have

Opposite: Fish like this small carp caught by Jan Porter can provide a lot of fun on pole tackle.

Left: An ideal stillwater float with body shaped roughly like a pear.

Below, left: River floats should have bodies shaped like an upside-down pear.

Below: Far side canal 'dibbers'.

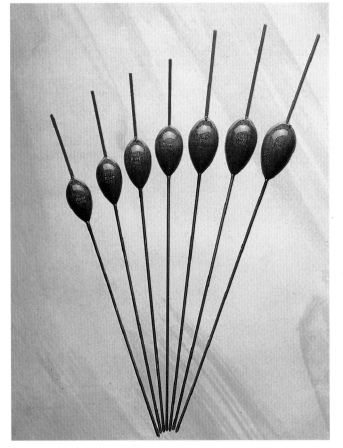

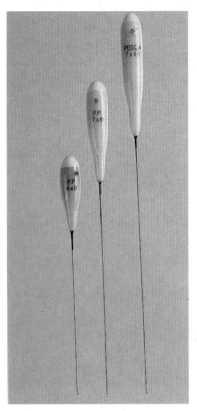

the longest bristles, but this should cause no problems as long as you follow the simple rule: shot the float so that only the bristle – or even just part of it – is showing. If any of the float's body stands proud of the surface, it will lose sensitivity, and the main advantage of polefishing would be lost.

Of course, not all pole floats have bristles. 'Dibber'-type floats, such as those used for caster fishing on canals, are usually very short lengths of balsa or peacock quill with a small piece of wire glued into the bottom. The tops of the floats are simply the tops of the bodies, painted at the very tip to make them visible by the angler on the bank. These floats hold up well at the surface, when the bait is fished with several inches of line on the bottom, and they are not susceptible to being dragged under by any tow caused by flow or by the opening of lock gates – a common occurrence on canals. They work well in choppy conditions, too. Some anglers like pole floats without bristles for river fishing, claiming that bites are easier to detect and hit with just a tiny dimple of balsa body showing at the surface. These floats resemble conventional stick floats, with a slightly thinner body top.

STEMS

Just as pole-float bristles come in several different materials, so do float stems – the long, thin length of material underneath the float body. By far the most popular material for stems is wire, which offers the desirable combination of strength, straightness and stability. The right sort of pole-float wire is much sought-after by manufacturers, and sources are often a closely guarded secret as it can make or break a pole float – literally. A long length of wire underneath a pole-float body provides much-needed stability in windy conditions, keeping the float upright despite the best efforts of the choppy upper layers of the water to tilt it this way and that. Line is attached by two or three short lengths of rubber sleeve – one directly underneath the body, one at the bottom and one half-way between. Choose a float with a wire stem for most polefishing applications,

but they work particularly well in windy conditions, when using a long pole and short line, and for fishing on or very close to the bottom as they settle upright quickly once the 'bulk' has reached its level. Check that the wire on the floats you buy returns to the straight when you bend it slightly, and that it isn't rusty.

Another popular pole-float stem material is cane. A float with a cane stem works particularly well when you are fishing with a string of small shot or styl weights for fish feeding at all levels in the water, because its lightness helps the float 'tilt' as each shot settles. A wire-stemmed float would settle in a near-upright position, quickly making bite detection difficult. With a cane stem, however, it is fairly easy to detect when a fish intercepts the bait on the way down by its failure to settle properly. Cane-stemmed floats also 'cast' better than wire-stemmed ones, and are often used by anglers fishing to hand with a whip. A word of warning, however: cane-stemmed floats are very fragile – handle them with care, especially when altering depth by moving them up and down the line.

A fairly new addition to the range of pole-float stems is carbon. This material is sometimes preferable to either wire or cane in that it gives the angler the best of both worlds – it is stronger than cane, yet lighter than wire. It can be used for on-the-drop and to-hand fishing, yet there are no problems with the float breaking.

BODY SHAPES

Pole-float bodies – that part of the float between bristle and stem – are usually made from balsa wood, but any light, buoyant material will do. One successful range of floats have bodies made from elder pith, while others are formed from man-made, dense polystyrene. Much more important than the materials from which pole-float bodies are made, is their shape, and more confusion surrounds this aspect of pole floats than any other.

Disregarding for a moment the size of the float, your choice of its body should be generally determined by two factors: flow and wind.

Many pole floats have bodies that can be broadly described as looking like a pear, either the right way up or upside down. Let's look first at those whose body is like an upside-down pear. These are the floats for flowing water – the fatter the pear, the faster the water that the float will be able to handle. The reason is simple. A float with a body like an upside-down pear can be controlled much more easily in flowing water because it will not tend to rise out from the surface when its passage through the swim is slowed down or stopped by the angler. The pressure of water on the 'shoulder' of the float will, if anything, want to push it further underneath the surface. Slightly overshotted, these floats are perfect for river fishing, easing the bait through slower than the speed of the current for shy-biting roach.

On the other hand, floats whose bodies are shaped like a pear the right way up are better for still water or water that occasionally flows very slightly in either direction. These floats offer stability thanks to their low centre of gravity, and produce very little resistance on the strike because they are streamlined. They're highly sensitive, and in the smaller versions can be used on shallow canals, drains and ponds, and on lakes and very slowly-moving rivers in their larger versions.

In between these two extremes are many more patterns of pole float. There are floats with very long bodies, whose fattest part is at the bottom for windy conditions on stillwaters; floats whose bodies are almost spherical, which work well in windy conditions on rivers; floats with long, parallel bodies and long wire stems for stability and sensitivity; and highly sensitive floats with very long, slim bodies best-suited to no-wind, no-flow conditions; there are tiny, far-side canal floats for fishing overdepth in, sometimes, only 8 in of water. The list is almost endless, and it is all too easy to become confused, but the angler who remembers the 'pear' rule won't go far wrong when it comes to selecting pole floats.

SIZE

One of the great beauties about polefishing is the fact that very light, highly sensitive floats can be used. A swim that might need a rod-and-reel float taking three BBs just to cast the distance can be polefished with a float taking a fraction of that. Three BBs weigh in the region of 1.2 gm, but the same swim could be tackled with a pole float taking, say, 0.3 gm. Even so, many anglers still insist on using a float when polefishing that is far heavier than they need. It's all a question of creating a successful marriage for the considerations of depth, flow, species and wind. For example, a float taking just a few small shot might be best in a swim where the fish are feeding close to the surface, while bottom-feeding fish in the same swim should be tackled with something a little heavier, using most of the float's weight capacity as a 'bulk' close to the hook, with perhaps just one or two small shot as 'droppers' underneath. Similarly, although a light float might work in one swim in calm conditions, a much heavier one might be required when it's windy to achieve good tackle control without the wind blowing float – and bait – around. If in doubt, start with a float a little on the light side – many anglers new to polefishing make the mistake of using floats which are too heavy.

There are occasions when a waggler float attached at the bottom end only can be used with a long pole and short line. Some anglers fishing canals, especially across towards the far side with caster hookbait, prefer a short, stubby length of peacock quill attached at the bottom end only, to one attached at both the top and the bottom. In windy conditions, sometimes the wind 'catches' the line on the surface with a top and bottom float, and while one answer is to backshot with a small weight above the float to sink the line, another way is to use a bottom-end-only float, sinking as much line as possible between float and hook.

Some pole floats give their shotting capacity as 'four x 14' and 'four x 16'. This signifies the shotting of the float in styl

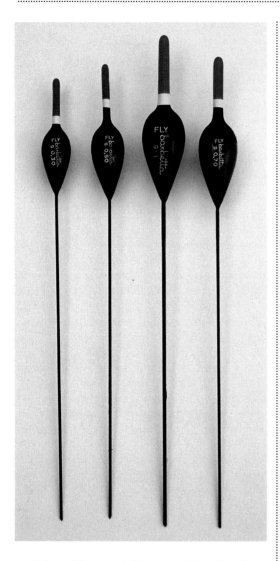

Above: The tips of these floats have been replaced with thicker bristles for better visibility.

Left: Some anglers prefer floats with no bristle especially on rivers.

weights. 'Four x 14' means that the float takes something in the region of four No.14 styls, or the equivalent, in order to shot it correctly. The problem here is that lead styl weights heavier than No.12 are, in fact, not allowed to be sold in this country because of problems associated with swan deaths in the 1980s. Here is a guide to what the floats would take if marked in this way:

No.13 styl – 0.625 gm
No.14 styl – 0.1 gm
No.16 styl – 0.125 gm
No.18 styl – 0.17 gm
No.120 styl – 0.31 gm

A float taking 'four x 14' will require a weight of approximately 0.4 gm to cock it correctly.

CHAPTER TEN

Making Winders

There are two schools of thought when it comes to tackle for polefishing. Some anglers spend hours on end at home, lovingly preparing their pole tackle, shotting floats, selecting and measuring line and wrapping the finished product around specially-made plastic pole-winders, which they then store in neat rows in their boxes. They're the envy of their friends and can be ready to fish in a matter of minutes. Others would rather do everything on the bankside, taking their time to select the float, line and hook they want from those in their box and getting everything exactly right for the session on which they are about to embark. Both

approaches have their staunch supporters and opposers. Some wouldn't even consider going fishing without a pristine collection of more than 50 winders prepared to perfection, while others don't have a single one in their box.

If the beginner to polefishing wants to do everything right, he should fall somewhere between the two. The angler with 60 winders will probably admit to using only 20 of them during the course of a season, while the angler who hasn't a single pole rig ready will at times probably regret not being able to get fishing quickly. Anyway, making up pole rigs at home is great fun and provides a sound

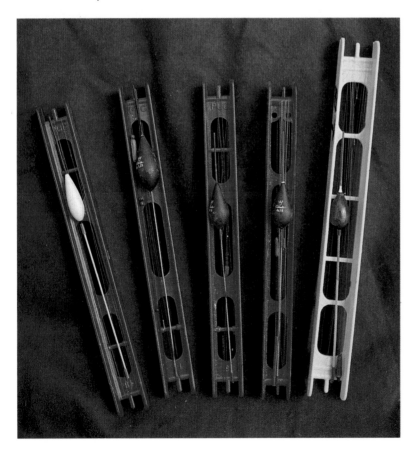

Completed pole winders make an attractive addition to angler's tackle.

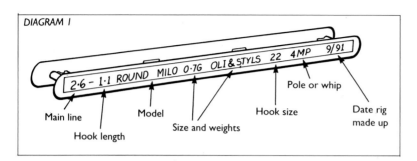

DIAGRAM I

Main line | Hook length | Model | Size and weights | Hook size | Pole or whip | Date rig made up

Some anglers like to label their winders so they know exactly what they are using.

grounding into the skills of polefishing.

There are many things to be considered when you want to make up rigs at home. These range from the float you want to use, to the line, type of shotting, and the length of the rig itself. In addition to this, you must have an easy way of discovering just what your chosen float takes in the way of shotting, without the advantage of a stretch of water in front of you into which to drop the float and shot. Fortunately, the answer to this problem is easy, thanks to special neutral-buoyancy devices. The best-known are the Dosa Piombo and the Nutroboy, and they really are easy to use. Instead of fixing weights on to the line, you simply slot your float into the top of the device, place shot, styls or olivette in the saucer around its edge, and lower the lot into a bucket of water. By adding or subtracting weights, you can shot the float perfectly. All you then have to do is fix the same float and weights on to your line and you know that the float will be shotted very accurately. You can make minor adjustments on the riverbank.

With the first problem out of the way, let's look at the other decisions you must take when making rigs at home.

LINE

Line for polefishing does not have to withstand the same pressure as line for fishing with a rod and reel. No casting power is needed, and no brute strength required to beat fish - the pressure is largely taken up by the elastic when a long pole is used. For this reason, line for polefishing should generally be lighter than that for use with rods and reels. Where a reel line of 2 lb to 2½ lb

breaking strain might be used for casting a waggler or a stick float into the river, the same swim could be tackled easily with a pole line of 1½ lb breaking strain. As long as the right knots are used, the pole angler should never be broken when using a main pole line of this strength, except in very unusual circumstances, such as when a very large fish is hooked. Even then, the elastic will do its work and the fish can still be landed by a combination of skill, experience and a little luck.

The situation has been improved – and somewhat complicated – in recent years by the influx of so-called high-tech lines into Britain. These lines are nothing like traditional monofilament. They boast extremely fine diameters for a given breaking strain, offering the angler obvious advantages: he can use the same diameter line as before, which gives him more strength in his line; or he can use the same breaking strain as before, which gives him a much thinner line. Thin lines are less likely to be seen by the fish than thick lines, so why are low diameter lines not used exclusively for every type of fishing?

The answer lies in their other properties. Most high-tech, low-diameter lines are pre-stretched. This certainly makes then thinner while retaining a good degree of strength, but it it also removes most of the line's stretch. For rod-and-reel fishing, a line must be able to stretch considerably or it will be broken easily when the angler casts or strikes – that is why pre-stretched lines should not be used on the reel. Such requirements are not so important for the pole angler, however. Line stretch is not so vital as long as some sort of shock-absorber is used in the form of elastic or flick-tip. So the pole angler has another weapon in his armoury – the potential to use line of a much thinner diameter than his rod-and-reel counterpart. As an example, a typical, conventional line of $1\frac{1}{2}$ lb breaking strain will have a diameter of 0.1 mm. A typical high-tech, low-diameter line of the same breaking strain, however, will measure just 0.08 mm. That might not seem much variance, but to a match angler fishing for hundreds of pounds, it could make the difference between winning and finishing among the also-rans.

Learn to view lines not just by breaking strain, but by diameter as well as they have been doing on the Continent for many years. It makes the whole question of lines much simpler. Don't feel obliged to use high-tech lines, however. Many people have tried high-tech lines as main line for polefishing and reverted back to conventional lines. Special knots often have to be used, the line has be extremely well looked after as it is highly abrasive, and many think it just isn't worth the trouble.

Hooklengths are different, however, and high-tech lines are perfect in this department. With diameters as little as 0.05 mm, they are hardly visible with the human eye, let alone that of the fish! The beginner is best advised to use ordinary, good-quality line for his main pole line, but high-tech, low-diameter lines are worth trying for hooklengths. Don't worry if you can't get on at all with them, however – 12 oz hooklengths of non-stretched lines are normally perfectly adequate unless matchfishing. As a guide, use $1\frac{1}{2}$ lb breaking strain line for main line and 12 oz for hooklengths.

On the subject of lines, another decision you will have to make when it comes to rigs is the actual length of line to wrap around the winder. The first point to remember, obviously, is the depth of water for which the float and shotting is designed. If you intend fishing a 6-ft deep river swim with your rig, it's pointless making the rig with just 6 ft of line – there will be no extra line between the tip of the pole and the float. If you work on the basis of at least 1 yd between poletip and float, you'll see that at least 9 ft of line will be required in this situation, although as we're

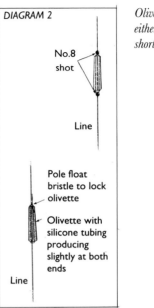

DIAGRAM 2

No.8 shot

Line

Pole float bristle to lock olivette

Olivette with silicone tubing producing slightly at both ends

Line

Olivettes are secured either by shot (top) or short piece of bristle.

talking about a river here you could even go further than that, and have even more line on your rig to allow the float to travel more of the swim without reaching its limit. Similarly, if you intend fishing a shallow canal or pond of only 3 ft deep, making a rig with 6 ft of line will be about right.

Some anglers don't like to be restricted to certain lengths, and use the same length of line – say, 15 ft – with all their rigs. They then shorten the line accordingly having decided how much they want when they reach their swim. This is a good idea, but problems can occur when they need to add line to a rig – extra line can be tied on at the top of the rig but knots are an unwelcome encumbrance on fine pole tackle. The fewer knots the better.

Although we're talking about line length in feet, in actual fact the right way to measure line for your pole rigs is against your pole – and the only way to do this, is to lay your pole out and measure the line against the number of sections you want it to equal in length. Pole lines must correspond to the end of one section and the start of another, so that a fish can be lifted safely to hand or easily netted without having to reach up or down –a recipe for disaster. The wrong length of line is an all too common mistake made even by good pole anglers.

RIGS

Making up pole rigs at home is an enjoyable occupation and can while away many otherwise boring closed-season evenings.

You'll notice no hook or hooklength has been tied to the winder. Some anglers prefer their pole rigs on winders to be stored complete with hooks, but it's better to leave hooks off them. Hooks rust with just a couple

STEP I

The things you'll need are: a bucket of water, a float, a winder that has been tested against the float to make sure the float sits neatly inside with no protruding ends, line, weights (Olivette styls and shot), styl pincers. tweezers, polefloat shotter (this is the Preston Innovations Nutroboy), scissors and pole anchor (for attaching completed rig to winder).

Take the bottom of the pole float and push it into the hole in the centre of the Nutroboy. All sizes of pole-float stem can be used with the Nutroboy, but make sure it is well-secured.

STEP 2

Start dropping weights into the Nutroboy, beginning with the largest. This float takes I gm and you want to shot it with an olivette and styl weights. So a 0.8-gm olivette goes in just (special tweezers are supplied with the Nutroboy), followed by a No.8 shot to prevent it sliding to the hook. It's a good idea to add in a No. 10 shot as well. This goes above the olivette to secure it and stop it sliding up to the float when baiting the hook.

Test the float in the bucket of water, adding or taking away styl weights until you achieve the setting you want. Undershot the float slightly to allow for the weight of the baited hook and line – polefishing is a delicate business. Final minor adjustments can be made on the bankside.

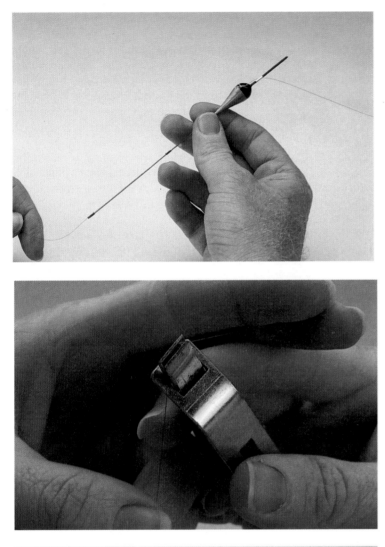

STEP 3

When you are happy with the setting of the float, remove it from the Nutroboy and keep the weights safe. Measure the line against the length of pole to which you want it to correspond, and thread the float up the line from the bottom. Use two soft but tight pieces of silicone rubber on the stem, one immediately under the body and one at the end of the stem. Really long-stemmed floats should be secured with three rubbers. With the float on the line, slide the olivette up from the bottom and secure it with the No.8 shot underneath and the No. 10 above. The fattest part of the olivette is furthest away from the float. Don't squeeze them too tightly as you will probably want to move the olivette before you start fishing. Start with it around 3 ft from the hook.

STEP 4

As many styl weights are added to the Nutroboy to make the float sit correctly. These are fixed on to the line with styl pincers. The three styls here are equally spaced between olivette and the bottom end of the line. Again, they can be moved on the riverbank. Once all the weights have been fixed on to the line, tie a loop in both ends and slip the bottom loop (the one underneath the float) over the peg at one end of the winder. Carefully wind the rig around the winder, moving the float up or down slightly so it sits neatly in the winder protected from possible damage.

STEP 5

Continue until all the line is wound on to the winder. Place the anchor end of an elasticated pole anchor through the loop and secure. Stretch and wrap the anchor around the winder, securing the other end of it around the first available peg in one end. It's worth making a note of the length of rig on the side of the winder so that it is immediately recognisable. Some anglers add other details such as line strength, float shotting capacity, type of shotting and the date.

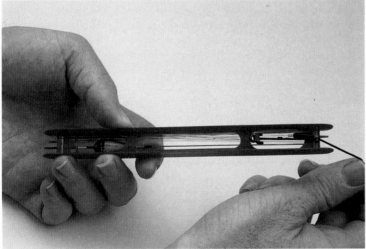

of drops of water, and fine polefishing hooklengths are easily damaged when they are stored in a box. It's better to keep your hooks and hooklengths separately, tying them at home and looking after them in small individual packets.

WINDERS

One pole winder might look very much like another, but it's worth checking on a few small but important points before making your selection. Winders come in numerous different lengths and it is imperative that you make sure they are longer than the floats they are to take. Your floats will quickly become damaged if they protrude from either end of the winder. Take care also with floats that have big, bulky bodies. With floats like these it is best to use wider winders whose centre panels are nearer to one side than the other. Make sure the float sits in the deepest side to avoid damage. Make sure as well that the winder is wide enough to allow the float to sit inside the two edges, otherwise they will cut its body. Finally, you might want to choose the colour of your winders according to the length of line wrapped around them, or the type of rig. This will make identification easier when you are faced with lots of winders in your tackle tray.

Ready-made pole rigs should be stored carefully. Not only is it important to keep them away from heat and light, which rots fine lines quickly, but you should also make sure that the winders cannot rattle about in your box – another way to damage the delicate rigs on them. It's no coincidence that Continental-type tackle boxes have become more popular in Britain since polefishing really took off. These boxes have one or more shallow trays incorporated into their lid section which are ideal for the safe storage of pole winders. They look good in them as well!

OLIVETTES, SHOT AND STYLS

Until you decide to start polefishing, you will probably never have encountered olivettes. An olivette, simply, is a streamlined weight that is often used on pole rigs instead of several weights, which might be more prone to tangling. It ensures that the bait gets down quickly to where you want it, and is probably the best bet when the intention is to fish on or very close to the bottom all day.

Most olivettes are tubular in construction with the fattest part at the bottom, and line is threaded through the middle and secured either end by small split shot, styls or with a small length of pole-float bristle. They are available in sizes from 0.1 gm to more than 10 gm in weight, and between olivette and hook, one or more small shot or styl weights, called droppers, are fixed. Both olivette and droppers can be moved up and down during the course of the session. The most popular olivettes are made from tungsten and many now come supplied with soft silicone tubing threaded through their centres. This tubing acts as a buffer at either end against abrasion. Other types include olivettes that secure the line at either end with very small pieces of silicone rubber. These olivettes are easily moved up and down the line. Only one olivette is used on a rig.

SHOT

Olivettes are fine when you will be catching fish on or very close to the bottom all day, but what about those days when the fish might feed at all levels in the water? In these conditions, olivettes can easily make you miss out on fish taking the bait 'on the drop', or as it falls through the water. The olivette simply pulls the bait down too fast. This is one of the reasons why more and more anglers are turning to shot to weight their pole floats. Shot can be used as bulk, fixed closely together to perform a similar – if slightly inferior – function to an olivette, or they can be spread out to produce a slower fall of the bait through the water. Shot are certainly the simplest way of setting a float and anglers like them for their versatility. For most polefishing situations, it's best to use shot no larger than No 8. The higher the number, the smaller the shot.

STYLS

Styls are small, cylindrical weights with a split running along their length. They become flat when fixed on to line and are much used by pole anglers when they are after the most delicate presentation possible. With care they can be moved up and down the line to make bulk and strung-out rigs, and the best styls for polefishing are those between No.12 and No.7. Unlike shot, the larger the number, the larger the styl. They are often also used when trying to catch with hempseed on the hook. Fish can easily mistake a round split shot for a grain of hempseed, taking the shot in their mouth and causing false bites – called shot bites. With styls there are no such problems. A fish mistaking a styl weight for a grain of hemp has to be very stupid indeed!

As you can see, styl weights are very tiny indeed – a No.8 split shot weighs 0.063 gm, almost exactly the same as a No.12 styl – and there are five styl weights smaller than that! It follows that for really delicate presentation of a floatfished bait, as is often required in polefishing, styl weights can prove extremely useful. With the bristle on most pole floats being extremely fine and sensitive, often a No.7 styl is all that's required to sink them from the top of the body to the top of the nylon bristle. Styls are often used as 'dropper' weights underneath the bulk of an olivette or several styls grouped closely together.

A little practice is required to fix styl weights on the line, but once you've mastered it, the process takes just a few seconds. Special, tailor-made styl pincers are a must.

1. Slide several styls from the dispenser and gently grasp one that is lying with the split downwards with the pincers.

2. Pick up the styl with the pincers, ensuring that you don't accidentally squeeze the two sides together.

3. Make sure your line is tight by pulling it under pressure, and carefully slip it into the split of the styl.

4. Now just squeeze the pincers and the styl will be lying neatly on the line. Don't squeeze it too hard or you won't be able to move it up and down the line.

A styl weight can even be removed with care, by pulling it away from the line so that the line is forced out of the split. As long as it's been fixed on properly, the line will remain undamaged.

CHAPTER ELEVEN

Pole Rigs to Use

Ask a dozen experienced pole anglers which type of rig they prefer and the chances are you will get 12 different answers. There are few hard-and-fast rules in polefishing, and a rig and shotting pattern that works well for one angler might not be as effective for another. But as you become more experienced in this branch of angling, you will soon learn that certain rigs are best used for certain conditions and certain species, and it is the angler who succeeds in working out what's best in several departments who catches the most. Only after examining several different conditions should you make your final choice from the rigs you have available, or what tackle to set up on the bank.

It is useful to look at several imaginary fishing situations and decide what's best for each one. Read each one and then adapt the suggestions to your own requirements.

RIVERS

Flow – moderate
Depth – 6 ft at 9 m Out
Wind – slight

There are several different ways in which the pole angler can tackle a swim such as this one on a river. First, you must decide on your choice of floats. As discussed in Chapter Nine, the best floats for flowing water have a slight shoulder at the top of the body which allows the angler to control them easily. By this is meant slowing down the passage of the float through the swim by slowing down the movement of the pole as it follows the float. As the line tightens between pole-tip and float, so will the float slow down or stop. Slim pole floats, or pole floats whose bodies have their fattest parts at the bottom, would soon 'ride' out a little way above the water surface, ruining their effectiveness. However, floats whose bodies have a slight shoulder will be forced downwards by the current and stay where you want them. Use a fatter-bodied float in faster water, and a slimmer one in slower flows, and for the best results add a little more shot than you would under normal circumstances if you want to hold them back hard – usually this is not necessary except in flood conditions, however.

Having selected the pattern of float you want to use, it's time to choose its weight-carrying capacity. The swim is 6 ft deep so that immediately gives you some idea – and here's where many beginners to polefishing make their first big mistake. Just because they would use a waggler taking three AAAs in 6 ft of water, they select a pole float taking the equivalent of three AAAs – and that's much too heavy. Three AAAs weigh roughly $2\frac{1}{2}$, gm, but your pole-float choice should take less than half that. Now you can begin to see why polefishing has numerous advantages – if you can catch using a three AAA float, imagine what you will catch using one taking a third as much!

For our imaginary swim you should be looking at a float taking in the region of 0.6 gm to 1 gm. Your actual final choice should be determined by the strength and direction of the wind as well as your chosen style of shotting. Let's look at wind first. If the wind is nothing more than a gentle breeze blowing in a downstream direction or from behind you, you will have few problems and can almost disregard it when it comes to float size choice. However, too light a float can pose problems in a wind blowing in an upstream direction, or into your face. In these conditions, you will probably need to use a larger float to give you the stability to move in the right direction. If the flow is slight, too light a float in either of these two wind conditions will simply not 'pick up' the flow and the chances of a good catch are reduced. In stronger flows, an upstream

Small rivers can be perfectly fished with a pole. South London angler Andy Love prepares to net a fish from Surrey's River Mole.

wind will not pose so much of a problem. The answer is to use a float that takes enough weight to combat the wind, but one where there is no excess shotting, which is wasted.

What about the style of shotting? There are several options here, ranging from the use of an olivette to styl weights – and a combination of the two – but the basic choice the angler has to make is whether to use a bulk rig or a strung-out one. Rigs that are described as bulk rigs are those which have most of the float's shotting capacity bulked together at or below mid-depth, while strung-

out rigs have several smaller weights fixed at equal distances from each other, either all the way from float to hook, or in the bottom part of the rig.

Many pole anglers would opt for a bulk rig in our imaginary swim, choosing an olivette to be fixed around $2\frac{1}{2}$ ft from the hook, followed by several small styl weights between the olivette and the hook. In this instance, four styl weights of sizes 10, 9, 8 and 7, with the No.7 nearest the hook, would be about right.

This is the simplest way of tackling this swim and it would undoubtedly catch you fish. Choosing a float taking about 0.8 gm would be right. The olivette would pull your hookbait quickly through the water until it reached its settling point, after which the styls would produce a slower, more natural fall

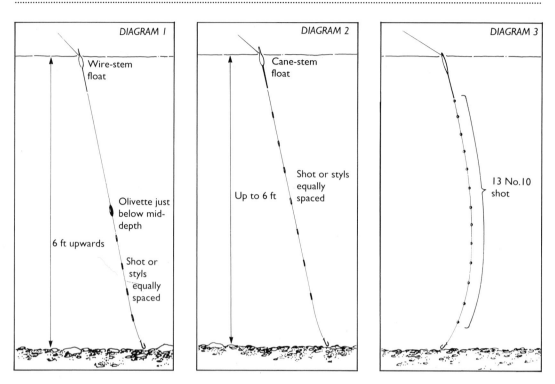

Three ways for rivers. Pole-float shotting patterns.

through the bottom section of water. The rig would allow fish to intercept the bait from around mid-depth right to the bottom, and the olivette can be moved closer to the hook if the fish are feeding close to the riverbed. However, the big disadvantage of an olivette is that it cannot be separated out, and this is why lots of good pole anglers now rarely use them, except for deep water or fishing for bream or eels. Instead of the olivette, they would much prefer the versatility offered by split shot, which can be bulked together or strung out as required. They're not as neat as an olivette, but they certainly offer the angler more versatility. It's all about experimentation – an olivette rig might work on one day, but on the next day the same swim might respond best to a strung-out rig.

The third point for the angler to consider is line length. With a moderate flow, a depth of 6 ft and little wind, you would do well to use a rig length corresponding to the top five sections of your pole. Most top five sections will equal around 15 ft long, so taking away the 6 ft between float and hook, you are left with 9 ft of line between float and pole tip. This is much too much for stillwaters, but on a flowing river that extra 9 ft will mean that you can use most of your swim, following the float at it goes. In windy conditions, that 9 ft might have to be shortened, as it would if the river was moving very slowly and most fish were being caught at the upstream end of it. In that case, the extra line would simply get in the way. Don't just sit there, if the line length needs altering, do it! It only takes a minute or so to remove the line from the top of the pole, cut through it and remove or add about 3 ft. Remember that we are talking about a swim that's 6 ft deep – you'll need more line still if it's deeper, or less if it's shallower.

LAKES

Depth – 8 ft at 11 m out
Wind – strong

Let us assume that this imaginary lake is full of bream, roach and tench that live close to the bank. They are great fun to catch on pole tackle, but only if you present your

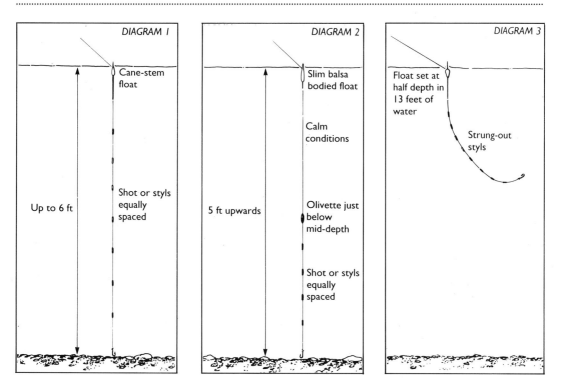

Three typical lake pole-float shotting patterns.

tackle to them in the right way. Choice of float is just as important as it is on a river, but on a lake there's little flow to worry about. Lakes do flow in one sense, of course, when the lower part of the water moves in the opposite direction to the wind, which is pushing the top part towards one bank. When this top part of the water has nowhere else to go, having hit the bank, it turns under and moves in the opposite direction. It is something to be aware of, but rarely will the undertow be so strong that you need to use a float with a shoulder like those you should use on rivers.

In fact, a typical stillwater float has a body that is an upside-down copy of the river float – instead of being fattest at the top, it's fattest at the bottom. This fattest part of the body provides the float with stability, and the lower down the float it is, the greater the stability that is offered. It's absolutely no use trying to polefish a windy lake with a float that is being blown around all over the place. A long wire or carbon stem also helps the float's stability, serving the same purpose as those floats with long, tapered bodies that were popular a few years ago. For our windy lake, in 8 ft of water,

a float taking between 1 and 1½ gm would be about right. As conditions worsen, use a bigger float.

Fishing for mainly bottom feeders like bream and tench demands a bait fished on or very close to the bottom, and a strung-out rig is therefore no use. The angler's first choice might be an olivette fixed towards the bottom end of the line, with one or more droppers underneath in the form of small shot or styl weights. It's unlikely you will need the delicacy of half a dozen strategically placed styl weights – just one or two should suffice. If you are fishing with 6 in of line on the bottom – an excellent way of catching good-quality fish in lakes – it might pay to rest a No.8 or No.10 shot just on the bottom. Bites will often be slight lifts of the float here.

Other species – and even tench – will sometimes come up in lakes to feed close to the surface, and for this a different type of rig is required. First, you'll need a much lighter float. Second, there's no need for an olivette. Just use a float taking 0.5 gm at most and shot

Above: Worsbrough Reservoir near Barnsley, S.Yorks. A superb lake for the poles.

Left: A string of shot is often better than an olivette.

Opposite: At 11m wide this is a typical canal venue and ideal for the pole.

it with round split shot or styl weights, strung out between float and hook. A cane-stemmed float is ideal for this sort of fishing, because it will tilt slowly in the water as each small weight settles and registers. Bites will be seen either as the float failing to settle, or shooting away out of sight – and then the fun starts!

When casting this type of rig, make sure the tackle is laid out on the water in a straight line. Roach, skimmer bream and carp are typical species that will come up to feed close to the surface, especially on a hot summer day. Keep them happy with generous helpings of maggot loosefeed, dropping your hookbait among them.

Length of line on stillwaters should be determined mainly by two factors – wind and water clarity. In ideal conditions, the best advice is to use roughly 3 ft of line between float and pole-tip. This will give you enough line to allow for a little pole-tip movement, when feeding, for example, without upsetting

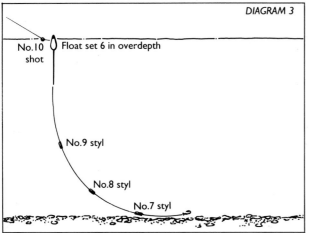

DIAGRAM 3

No.10 shot

Float set 6 in overdepth

No.9 styl

No.8 styl

No.7 styl

The best way of tackling the far shelf of a canal.

the float. The exceptions to the 3-ft rule are when it's windy – more line will probably be required to prevent the wind blowing the pole-tip around, pulling the float around as well; and when the water is clear. Shy fish are easily spooked by a length of unnatural material waving around over their heads. It is amazing what can be seen from the bottom of an 8 ft deep swim.

CANALS AND DRAINS

There are several different ways of fishing canals and drains with a pole, all of which require slightly different rigs made up either in advance or on the bank. It would be useful here to talk about species and baits rather than conditions, as the basic rigs will stay roughly the same regardless of wind strength, although the float shape and size should be altered following the same general guidelines as those already suggested for rivers and lakes.

The first point to remember is that you should always use the smallest float that will give you adequate control – in fact, this is a good policy to adopt for 90 per cent of polefishing, whatever the venue. However, there is an exception – small, bottom-feeding fish like gudgeon on canals can sometimes be caught at great speed by anglers using floats taking a surprisingly large amount of weight. It's nothing to see them with floats of 1 gm, or even more, fishing whips 3 m from the bank. These floats are of the stillwater type,

with bodies whose fattest parts are at the bottom, and they're shotted with an olivette only a few inches from the hook and one, or at most two, droppers in the form of No.8 or No.10 shot below. The tackle is dropped into the water right under the end of the whip, and seconds later another gudgeon or ruffe is in the net. Many 'towpath' anglers who specialise in this sort of fishing like to use floats with cane bristles as opposed to nylon or wire ones. These cane bristles are slightly more buoyant, and if a fish intercepts the bait after the olivette has settled but before the droppers have, the bite will be easy to see by the failure of the cane tip to settle.

What about fishing for roach on canals and other small waters? With small baits like squatts and pinkies, the best type of rig to use is one composed of shot or styl weights – and here styl weights definitely have the edge in terms of delicacy of presentation and effectiveness. A favoured float type has a simple, rugbyball-shaped body and wire stem and takes in the region of four No.12 or four No.14 styls – that's roughly 0.25 gm and 0.4 gm respectively. Don't fall into the trap of believing that just because a float suggests it takes four No.12 styls, that's exactly what you should fix on the line. It's far better to split these styls further to allow more, but smaller weights to shot the float. In a 3 to 4 ft deep swim, try fixing a No.7, No.8 and No.9 styl weight at 3, 6 and 9 in from the hook, followed at just below mid-depth by a string of No.10 styls fixed so they are just touching

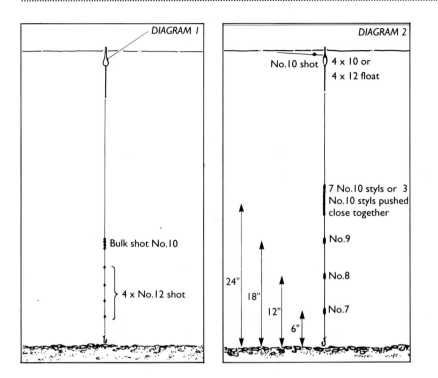

Two shotting patterns for canals and drains.

each other to weight the float right to the tip. This rig gives you the best of both worlds – it allows a slow drop of the bait in the bottom half of the water to catch roach from mid-depth onwards, and the small bulk of styl weights can be separated if required to provide a slow fall throughout the whole depth.

That's a popular rig for catching roach, but what about the swim you've chosen that has a lovely looking bush opposite, which you think might be home to some big roach, and even a chub or carp as well? Here, there's no bait to beat casters, and canal anglers have developed a highly successful rig for fishing with them. These big fish will usually want a bait presented right on the bottom, but the problem with conventional, bristle-tipped pole floats is that if there's any wind or tow caused by the opening and closing of locks, the bristle will be constantly pulled under and bites will be impossible to spot.

The answer is to use a different type of float, with no bristle but a thicker, more buoyant tip made from material such as peacock quill or balsa. Not only are these floats buoyant and ideal for combating wind

and tow when fished overdepth, they are also easy to see when shotted correctly so that only the barest tip is visible at the surface. These floats are usually tiny, short, stubby affairs, ideal for the sometimes very shallow water they will be used in. And they take only a few shot or styls. Plumb the depth carefully, and then move the float so that at least 6 in of line is on the bottom. At least one tiny weight should be allowed to lie on the bottom as well, but be prepared to go deeper, with more weight on the bottom if the wind or tow increases. The trick is to reach the ideal combination of perfect tackle control and successful bite-to-fish ratio – big canal roach have a habit of giving seemingly perfect bites but avoiding being caught – usually because the angler is fishing with too much line on the bottom. A typical shotting pattern for this type of fishing would be a No.9, No.8 and No.7 styl (or the equivalent in round split shot) weight equally spaced between float and hook (smallest nearest the hook and on the bottom). Scant caster loosefeed and caster on the hook should then do the damage.

What line length should you use for these types of waters? Two to three feet is ideal, but use more in windy conditions so that the movement of the pole-tip won't drag the float off line, and when the water is clear. Shallow-canal fish are very easily scared.

Lancastrian Dave Roper used casters to take this fine bream catch on the pole from the Lancaster Canal.

CHAPTER TWELVE

Starting Off

You've now done the hardest part. You've bought your pole and floats and have made your decisions over the rigs you intend to use. Perhaps you have them neatly lined up on pole-winders in your box, or maybe you've just a dozen or so floats, which you can make into rigs on the riverbank. Now it's down to the important part – fishing! Even so, the job will be much easier if you have a few specially made polefishing accessories.

First, beginners to polefishing usually like to use a pole rest, and there's nothing at all wrong with that. A pole rest consists of two supports, which attach to one side of your box – if you are right-handed, they attach on the right side. One of the U-shaped supports hooks around the top of the pole very close to the butt, while the other supports it from underneath, 1 ft or so further along. The best ones are adjustable so that the pole can be slipped in, leaving it in exactly the right position – with the tip just above the water. They really are a boon for the beginner to polefishing when it comes to feeding, as you can place the pole in the rest, leaving both hands free. However, as you will see later, there are other methods of feeding while still holding your pole. Make sure the rest has wide supports with no sharp metal edges and you won't go far wrong. Don't place your fully extended pole in its rest and then stand up – all that will happen is that your pole-tip will smack on to the water, perhaps taking your box with it!

Another useful piece of equipment for the pole angler is a roller. This looks like a painter and decorator's paint roller – only for painting round corners, as it is really two rollers at right angles fixed to the top of a bankstick. Many of the country's best pole anglers swear by a roller, especially when the bank behind them is awkward. So what does a roller do? It makes catching a fish much easier, and losing a fish much more difficult. Hook a good-sized fish using a long pole, or any fish for that matter, and it can easily be lost during the unshipping process as you push the pole back behind you. The butt hits the ground, the resulting bounce shakes the tip of the pole, and the fish falls off. The properly used pole roller prevents this happening, as the butt of the pole is laid in the V of the rest and then pushed back. The rest takes any bounce out of the unshipping process. Sounds easy, and it is. However,

The presence of cables is often signposted but check nevertheless.

make sure the rest is positioned properly, so that after you have unshipped the pole and pulled the sections apart to lift or net your catch, the butt part doesn't lift up into the air out of reach when it's time to push the pole out again. This happens when the part of the pole behind the rest weighs more than the part in front of it, so you might need to make a few adjustments before you're happy. There is, however, a way to stop the butt sections lifting away out of reach, and that's by strategically placing your keepnet so that the front end of the unshipped part can be wedged just under the top ring with the rest placed far enough back to avoid too much pole behind it. Practise this technique and you will eventually reach a happy medium.

Apart from the simple V-type pole rest, others are available that are used with two banksticks and give the angler more space on which to rest his pole. These have two vertical end pieces to stop the pole falling off, with a horizontal roller in between them. Do not, however, assume that you should always use a pole roller when unshipping. Flat, even banks can be handled perfectly well without one while your rod holdall can also often do the job for you. In fact there are some anglers who never use one at all – it's all down to personal preference.

CABLES

There is no greater danger to the pole angler than electricity cables. Carbon fibre, for all its excellent qualities, is also a good conductor of electricity. Touch an overhead cable with a carbon pole and at best you'll be badly burned, at worst you'll be dead. It's a tragic fact that every season the angling press has tales of anglers killed or injured in these circumstances.

HOLDING A POLE

A short pole or whip can be easily held with one hand. However, when it comes to wielding 11 m of carbon fibre, it's a different ball-game altogether – and it has to be said that this very basic aspect of polefishing puts many anglers off taking it up in the first

place. There is really nothing to it, however, and a little practice will soon see you holding the pole like a world champion.

As in many aspects of the sport, there is never one answer to a problem – several different ways can be employed to hold a long pole. The first way, and the one most easily mastered by beginners, is to grasp the pole right at the butt with one hand (right hand for right-handed anglers) reaching behind, while holding it with the other hand (left hand for right-handed anglers) resting on one knee. The upper leg is used as a rest for the pole.

Perfect, comfortable control can be achieved by holding a pole in this way, but as you become more proficient, you will probably want to hold the pole with both bands close together. Again, the butt section rests on the upper right leg. This method of holding a long pole is favoured in calm weather conditions and works well with lighter poles. It is also conducive to making a clean strike when a bite occurs.

Another way of holding a long pole is to wedge it under and between your legs, leaning out from your box and supporting the butt section with both hands. This is good in a wind, but a little cumbersome, especially after a fish is hooked as you have to move the pole around in front of your body before you can begin to unship it.

Finally, highly proficient pole anglers and those with expensive, lightweight poles sometimes fish with just one hand holding the pole, grasping the butt section, while supporting it on the upper leg. Again this is something for the expert.

Standing up to use a long pole is not something for the beginner, although as you become more proficient in polefishing the techniques required will gradually become second nature. Even so, it is only really advisable to stand to polefish when fishing with long rigs and highly specialised whips or long poles, such as 'to-hand' fishing on the fish-packed lakes and rivers of Ireland and Denmark.

As you can see, holding a long pole is one of the first disciplines for the would-be pole angler to master. It is best done not only

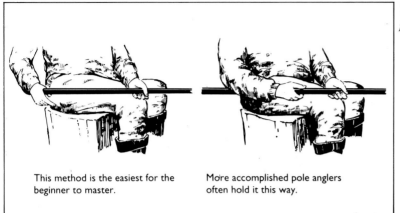

Two ways of holding a long pole.

This method is the easiest for the beginner to master.

More accomplished pole anglers often hold it this way.

seated, but seated on the level. This is where platforms and box legs come in handy. Although the purchase of a platform might seem a little excessive to the pleasure pole angler, there really is no excuse for not investing in a set of box legs. It takes just a few minutes to attach these to a box, drilling holes in the box according to the manufacturer's instructions and attaching the legs. They might add a little weight to the box, but their advantages far outweigh this small matter. Once on the bankside, all you have to do is spend a couple minutes adjusting each leg so that you end up sitting comfortably, not having to worry about balancing on the edge of the box or perched in such a way that holding the pole is the last thing on your mind.

If you do decide on a platform, you will soon wonder how you ever got by without one. Not only can you use it to place your box on in the shallow margins of a river, drain or canal; even if you don't need it for your box, you can set it up alongside you as a platform for your tackle sundries. It goes without saying that care should be taken when erecting a platform in the margins. It's best to make this your first job when you reach the bankside, setting it up and then leaving it for a good 15 minutes before sitting on it on your box – you will probably find that you can tighten the four legs still more. Extra-wide feet for the legs will help prevent them sinking into soft mud or silt.

CHAPTER THIRTEEN

Your First Bite

Everything is ready. You've found an attractive swim and you've decided to fish with all but one section of your 11-m pole. The swim itself is 4 ft deep and hardly moving, so you plump for a rig whose length corresponds to the top four sections of your

Above: Pushing the pole back before unshipping.

Opposite: Kent tackle dealer Charlie Lovell starts to push his tackle out to the water.

pole. How do you get your tackle into the water? Although this might seem hardly worth mentioning to accomplished pole anglers, the simple act of 'casting' with a pole can be a daunting prospect for the beginner.

Step 1

With the length of your pole corresponding to the length of the rig in your right hand, and holding your line just above the baited hook in your left, pull the line a little to check that the elastic is flowing freely. If it is not, it's tangled and needs looking at. If it pulls out but in a series of jerks, it needs treating with some elastic lubricant. If everything is fine, flick the tackle overarm into the margins, making sure that it doesn't land on any weed and that your hook doesn't end up fouling your keep-net.

Step 2

Assemble the rest of your pole except for the butt section, ideally going away behind you with the front end of the fifth section wedged into the top ring of your keepnet or simply lying on the ground if the bank is flat. Take this front end and push it into the rear end of the fourth section.

Step 3

Now comes the process known as 'shipping'. This involves carefully pushing the pole and tackle out into the water between both arms until the whole of the pole you intend to use is out in the swim and you're holding on to the butt section.

Step 4

During the shipping process, make sure that the pole-tip doesn't become tangled with the line, and try to keep the float and rig in the water, ensuring that the pole-tip doesn't bounce, which usually has the result of wrapping the rig around the pole-tip. Once you have reached the required distance, lift the pole sharply to pull the rig from the water and move it so the tip makes a rough half circle, resulting in the tackle flicking over and landing in a straight line in the water. This action is important and practise it. Not only does it avoid tangles, it makes sure that the bait falls through the water well away from the pole tip and in a natural fashion. Laying out your tackle in a straight line can also be done underarm in favourable wind conditions, but it requires more practice to achieve the correct technique.

STRIKING AND UNSHIPPING

When you're using a long pole, every tiny movement of your hands is magnified considerably 10 m away at the pole-tip. For this reason, the strike must be a controlled exercise, totally different from the one you would make if you were fishing at the same distance with rod-and-reel tackle. Watch for every movement of the pole float. If you've shotted it correctly and just the very tip is showing, it should simply disappear from view under the surface of the water. Perhaps if you're fishing for roach feeding at all levels

in the water, the float tip might hold up slightly when a fish intercepts your slowly sinking bait as it falls through the water. It might even start to move slowly against or a little faster than any current. Whatever happens, if you think you've got a bite, you must strike. The best strike to employ when polefishing is slightly to the diagonal, making sure you don't 'hit' the float by striking too much to the side. Similarly, if you strike directly upwards, you might then have to lower the poletip again to allow you to push the pole back behind you without the butt hitting the ground.

Step 1

This is the real test of a pole angler's preparation. If you have done everything correctly, the strike is met by a few inches of elastic being pulled from the poletip as the impact of the hook penetrating the fish is absorbed even if it's a small fish. In shallow water, this strike should be a diagonal movement of the pole-tip through a relatively short distance until the resistance of the fish is felt. If the water is deeper, you will probably need to increase the movement. Once you have hooked the fish successfully, you must try to assess its size as quickly as possible before starting to bring it to the bank.

Step 2

Having assessed the size of your fish, you can begin the process known as 'unshipping'. Let's assume it is a small fish. Look behind you and pass the pole through your hands, resting the butt on a smooth surface or in the V of a pole roller, until you reach the 'joint that leaves the pole length equal to the length of line you are using.

Step 3

Once you have reached the right joint, pull the pole apart. Rest the section of the pole that is behind you so that it won't swing round or up (one way is to wedge the front end of the fifth section in to the mouth of your keepnet - we're using a four-section rig, remember). You must make sure it doesn't slide into the water, something which can be a problem on sloping banks.

Step 4

Check that the fish is still hooked – if you've done everything right, it should be – by watching the elastic from the pole-tip. Take your right hand (now redundant) and swop it with your left so that it now holds your pole, and swing in the fish or net it as required.

Although this sounds a difficult process, with just a little practice you will find it becomes second nature and is one of the most enjoyable of all aspects of polefishing. You can make the job easier still by using hooks that have a small barb, rather than barbless ones. Even if a little slack line is created during the unshipping process, the barb will help prevent the fish from slipping the hook.

PLAYING LARGER FISH

What happens if the fish you have hooked is much larger than you bargained for? You'll

soon know, because the elastic shoots out from the pole-tip as it makes its bid for freedom and heads for the far side. Here is another test of your preparation. Any weak links in hook, knots, line or elastic will be revealed and the fish will be quickly lost. It is a common scenario on canals where the angler is happily catching roach using casters, and suddenly the swim goes quiet for a few minutes before a carp is hooked.

The first thing is not to panic. With skill and a little luck there is no reason why the fish should not be landed. Pole elastic is an amazing material and although you have no extra line to give a running fish, elastic can stretch a long way. And as it stretches, its tension increases. This is your major ally when it comes to landing fish. Another good tip is to have the next section of your pole – if there is one – strategically placed behind you so that if you do hook something substantial and it starts to charge away, you can add this section to catch up with the fish. Don't rush things. Hold the pole as still as you can, letting the elastic do the work it's designed for, and be in no rush to start the unshipping process. It's better to let the fish run in open water than give it the chance to dive under the near bank by unshipping too early. Soon the fish should start to tire and you can start unshipping. Usually it is just a case of pushing

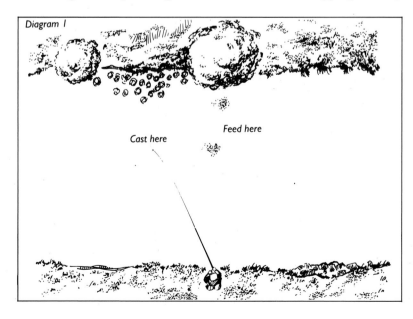

Diagram I

Feed here

Cast here

Two swims on a canal will allow fish to be caught all day. Make sure you drop your tackle a little downwind of your feed.

the pole behind you and pulling it apart at the relevant section. You can still do this with a big fish, but be prepared to push the pole back out again before unshipping if the fish makes a sudden run. Another way with big fish is to unship one section at a time, resting each of the unshipped sections behind you as you go. If you've done everything right, eventually the fish will be beaten on the surface and you can unship fully before netting it.

NETTING

With small fish, lifting them from the water simply means unshipping the pole at the right section and swinging them to hand. When it's a case of netting them, however, sometimes you might need to unship at a different section. This all depends on the behaviour of the fish once it reaches the

Above: Some pole anglers like to feed by leaning over to trap the pole.

Opposite: Large fish can be landed on pole tackle with a little care.

surface. Take chub, for example. They tend to stay still at the surface once they have a mouthful of air, and you can then use the pole and elastic to pull them to the waiting net. The process is made easier if you unship one section fewer than normal so that more elastic is pulled from the pole tip and the fish can be netted. The elastic stretches to put the fish under pressure, but as long as it remains relatively quiet on the surface no losses should occur. The same process can be employed with bream. For carp and roach, however, you would do better to unship to your usual section with

less elastic out from the poletip. These fish tend to thrash around on the surface more, and they can easily be lost if the elastic is stretched to put them under considerable pressure.

FEEDING

Beginners to polefishing often like to feed by placing the pole in a pole rest attached to the side of their box. By doing this, they have both hands free to throw or catapult groundbait or loose feed to the desired area. However, when it's a case of feeding regularly, it is time-consuming to place the pole in a rest every time, and can waste a lot of time over the course of a session. The answer is to learn how to feed while still holding the pole.

There are several ways in which you can feed without having to place the pole in a rest, and the method you choose should depend on personal preference, the distance to be achieved, wind conditions and whether you are using groundbait or loosefeed. The golden rule before feeding anything is this: always make sure your feed is at pole level. You do not want to be reaching down to the ground every time you want to feed. Trays at roughly the same height as the top of the box will make the job much easier. Let us assume that you want to introduce regular helpings of loose feed to your swim, which is 11 m out into a lake. Three methods can be employed with a catapult – throwing loose feed is out of the question at such distances.

Perhaps the best way for the beginner to feed is by wedging the pole butt between his legs. By doing this and crossing his legs, a sort of temporary pole rest is formed and both hands are free to feed.

The second method, affectionately known as the 'beer-gut' method, involves leaning over and feeding by wedging the pole between your foreleg and the bottom of your ribcage or, better still, your stomach. Drinking anglers enjoy a considerable advantage here!

The third method is one practised by the majority of accomplished pole anglers and involves controlling the pole by wedging the butt section between your upper leg and forearm. With the bait at box-lid level to your left and your catapult pouch hanging from your bait-tray, loose feed is dropped into the pouch. The left hand then takes the catapult frame and passes it in front of the body so that the right fingers can grasp the pouch while it still maintains its hold on the pole. Bait is then fired into the swim by pulling the frame away from the pouch with the left hand and releasing the pouch. The bait will be propelled along the pole and with practise it will become easy.

This last method, although the best one to use in most conditions as it requires very little movement of the pole, can be difficult when it's windy as the pole is not held as tightly as it might be with the others.

With all three feeding methods, it's important that you are not sitting too high on your box. Some Continental boxes see the angler almost dangling his legs because there are so many trays incorporated into the lid. If you're to feed easily and correctly with a catapult, one or more of these trays will need to be removed and placed to one side before you start to fish.

It is also a good idea, when feeding with a catapult, to use a small one, with a triangular as opposed to a mesh pouch, and short elastic of only 6 in or so. Bait can be dropped inside this type of pouch easily, whereas with a mesh pouch maggots would quickly fall off. And the short elastic minimizes tangles.

If you're in any doubt about these feeding techniques, the simple answer is: don't try them. It doesn't really take very long to unship your pole to feed, or to feed before casting. Especially when you are feeding only occasionally – caster fishing on a canal, for example – there is no point in running the risk of spraying bait all over the river. For regular feeding of maggots, pinkies and squatts, however, it is probably worth the trouble of practising until you get it right.

Groundbaiting can also be carried out while you are holding the pole, by placing the bowl of mixed groundbait at hand height to the right of your box and squeezing and throwing the ball of groundbait with your right hand while wedging the pole butt into your groin and supporting it a little way up the butt section in your left hand. Some anglers prefer to stand while they feed but the process remains the same.

While on the subject of feeding, it is worth pointing out that great care must be taken to ensure that it lands in the desired place. Many's the time a pole angler has missed out on a good catch because he was fishing nowhere near his feed. There were plenty of fish in front of him, but he was fishing in the wrong place. On a flowing river, it is imperative to feed a little upstream of where you are fishing, and you must make sure that you let the tackle travel far enough down your swim to make the most of that feed – again, you can see the need for a longer line between pole-tip and float on flowing water than you often need on still water. The deeper the water and the faster the flow, the higher up your swim you will need to feed and the further down your swim you will need to let your float travel.

There is another way of allowing your tackle to 'cover' as much of your swim as possible, useful in windy conditions when too much line between pole-tip and float is hindering good bait presentation. That method is to use pole one section longer than you need, but start the trot through the swim by holding the pole so that the extra section is behind you. As the float nears its downstream limit and the line between it and the pole-tip starts to straighten, pass this extra section between your hands to give you extra length in front of your body and the float will be able to travel further.

*A bream safely in the
net brings a smile to
Dick Clegg's face.*

SECTION THREE

LEGERING

There have been hundreds of books published about fishing generally, about catching big fish of all species, about floatfishing and about pole fishing. However, I can't think of one that has been exclusively about legering, and this is an astonishing omission when you consider that more big fish are caught on leger tackle in this country than by all other methods put together.

There are many anglers who won't leger because they dare not try something different, while others simply like watching a float. And, inevitably, there are some who have tried legering but not had much success because they weren't doing it properly. I have been in the tackle trade for much of my working life – first as a tackle dealer and now as a tackle wholesaler – and my heart bleeds for all those anglers who do their best but who don't get results, because I know how much effort some of them put in. Yet all of us, when we tackle something new, need help, whether it's in the form of advice from friends, magazines or books, that's how I learned. So I welcome this book in particular, as it is filling a huge gap in the market. And if it introduces just a few anglers to the basics of legering I will be a very happy man.

In 1993, I competed in the World Championships in Ireland – an event in which legering is banned. And I can safely say without any fear of contradiction that if legering had been allowed in this match the anglers would have caught many times more fish than they eventually did. That's how good legering is when conditions are difficult.

Having said that, I must point out that I am not, in fact, in favour of allowing legering in this particular event, because it would greatly reduce the spectator-appeal. And many Continental countries ban legering in their matches, so it would be grossly unfair on many teams.

As a specimen hunter before I became a matchman – and later manager of the England team – I know just how many advantages legering (and I include swimfeedering) can give anglers of all abilities, from the rank novice to the very experienced, on both still and running water. It's a method no-one should be ignoring, for it will catch you fish – and lots of them – when floatfishing is out of the question because of either the conditions or the sheer casting distance involved. Yet it is also a winner at times in conditions that are perfect for floatfishing. And because of this I urge you not to fall into the trap of becoming addicted to legering just because it's easy – for it will ruin your enjoyment of fishing. The leger man who ignores other methods will miss out on as much pleasure as the float angler who ignores legering. Treat it as just another weapon in your armoury, to be used only when it is definitely the best method at your disposal.

Frankly, I wish a book like this had been available when I started fishing. It would have saved me many hours of heartbreak and unsuccessful experiments. My advice is to read it and adapt the ideas for your own waters. Some will work; others might not. However it can't fail to start you on the right road if you have never legered, or to give you plenty of ideas if you're already experienced at it.

Good luck, and tight lines!

Dick Clegg
Manager of England World
Championship Team.

CHAPTER FOURTEEN

The Quivertip

Seeing a bite is probably the novice's biggest worry when legering. In fact, it's no more difficult than seeing a bite on a float. And many people consider it easier because the rod is much closer than a float would be. Some anglers with failing eyesight leger for that very reason. The quivertip is certainly the most popular bite indicator now. And for the beginner it's probably the best choice. Not only is a quivertip slightly easier to cast than a swingtip, but it also tends to adjust itself more easily to the current or drift than a swingtip. It is, in fact, just a sensitive extension of the rod tip.

BUILT-IN OR SCREW-IN?

You have two choices. Either you get a rod with a special, slim, sensitive, tip already built in as part of the rod, or you can buy a leger rod with a special threaded tip into which you can screw a quivertip of your choice. The screw-in type are on sale in most tackle shops and will range from very thin, and hence very sensitive, to much thicker, and less sensitive. Broadly speaking, you should use the thin ones on windless days on stillwaters, and thicker ones on windy days on stillwaters or in running water, when a current would pull a thin tip right round.

Most experienced leger anglers have at least one favourite rod with its own quivertip built in. However, there's a type of rod that is becoming more and more popular – a leger rod with three or even four different top joints, each with a built-in quivertip. This will give a range of quivertips from very sensitive to very strong, and which between them will suit almost every occasion, except perhaps very fast rivers like the Severn when you will need a special, extra-strong swimfeeder rod.

Screw-in tips, however, can give the angler a huge range of tip strengths, colours and tapers, and in addition can be used with the same rod as a swingtip so you need only one leger rod. One disadvantage is that when a screw-in tip is screwed into the tip ring it's a matter of luck whether the rings on the tip line up with those on the rod. The answer is to slip a piece of stiff tubing over the quivertip thread – a piece of a ballpoint inner tube is ideal – which will allow you to align the rings easily and still get a good, solid fit.

For the beginner a rod with a threaded tip, allowing you to use a variety of tips at very little extra cost, is a good compromise. Later you will probably get at least one special quivertip rod suited to the waters you fish most.

TYPES OF QUIVERTIP

This is largely a matter of personal choice, but on a stillwater the best sensitive tips tend to be long and tapered, and after a while you will be able to use such a tip in a great variety of conditions. On a perfectly still day such a tip will be straight out, and you will watch the very end for bites; on a windier day the end will bend round as the line is moved by the wind, and you will watch a point 1–2 in from the end to spot your bites. In both circumstances, you can see a bite developing very well and begin to visualise what the fish is doing with your bait, and when to strike. This is not as difficult as it sounds, particularly if you are able to sit in the open, without an umbrella up. You will be able to feel the gusts of wind as they blow round you, and get a better idea of the effect of the wind on the tip.

However, where you have a very sensitive, tapered tip you may find that when you are playing a fish the top few inches of the quivertip – perhaps most of it – doesn't come into play. This is no great problem so long as you realise what is happening, and don't slacken off when the tip starts to bend right round as a fish swims away.

Straight tips – those that have no taper at all – tend to be used on running waters, and help iron out the little bumps and quivers made by the current or by wisps of weed flowing down the river. In other words you get fewer false alarms. With a straight tip you are likely to be exerting pressure on the fish right from the top ring of the quivertip, which can be a help in giving you a little buffer if your rod is a bit stiff.

The material the tip is made from (it's nearly always fibreglass or carbon) is not particularly important. It's much more important that you can see it well and can 'read' it as a bite develops.

LONG OR SHORT?

Long tips are normally used on deep, still waters as they take longer to straighten after you've cast, or tightened up, and make it easier to see bites 'on the drop' – that is, as the bait is sinking within, say 30, seconds of casting. You will find, when you start quivertipping, that a lot of your bites come just after you've cast in, or adjusted the tension on your line, or after you've moved the weight along the bottom. And a long tip gives you a much longer time to spot these bites – the process is more fully described in the chapter 'Tightening and Twitching'. With a short tip you may have to turn the reel every couple of seconds to tighten the line because the tip will spring back immediately. However, a short tip is very useful on medium-to-fast running water, on very windy days when a long tip would be blown all over the place, and on very shallow water, say up to no more than 3 ft deep. In these shallow

stillwater swims a short tip can get you in touch with the tackle more quickly after you've cast than will a long tip.

POSITION OF THE ROD

Most important of all is to get approximately a right-angle between your rod and the line. This will give the maximum amount of movement of the tip for the least effort on the part of the fish. And nine times out of ten you will have your rod placed approximately parallel with the bank, but with the rod tip over the water, clear of bankside vegetation. If you're fishing directly in front of you, you will get away with the rod at anything up to 45° to the bank, but if it's more than that you're going to struggle to see bites unless they're real sail-aways.

On running water, unless the flow is very slight indeed, it's generally better to sit facing downstream. Then, when you make a strike, you are tending to strike with the current.

On a stillwater, it's usually better to sit with your back to the wind. Not only is this more comfortable, especially if it starts to rain, but you are helping to shield the butt end of your rod from the wind. And although you may not realise it, the effect of the wind on your rod butt is probably at least as important as that on the line and rod tip – every little movement of the butt makes the tip dance horribly. If the rod is set perfectly solidly, you'll be able to see proper bites much more easily. Check that next time you're fishing in a wind.

In a strong wind one way of minimising false bites is to tighten the line so it holds the tip under pressure. This is against all the rules, which say it's not necessary to tighten

The angle between line and quivertip needs to be around 90°. If you're fishing in front of you the rod will need to be roughly parallel with the bank, as shown.

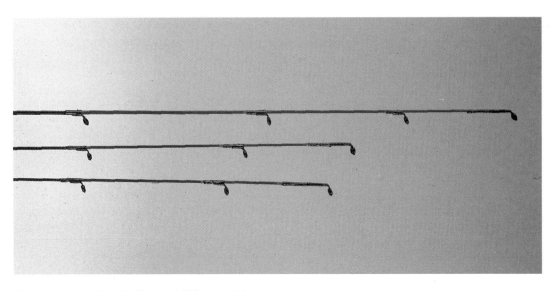

Some rods come equipped with several different top joints, each with its own built-in quivertip.

line completely, but it may be your best compromise in very difficult circumstances.

The colour of the tip is optional, though most commercially made, screw-in quivertips seem to have 2 or 3 in of red on the end. Certainly the vast majority of anglers like a bright colour here. White is also a good colour, and many anglers carry a bottle of typist's correction fluid to colour the tip quickly.

A METHOD OF SPOTTING DIFFICULT BITES

Most anglers will be looking for the quivertip to bend obviously when they get a bite, and indeed the quivertip is capable of showing minute movements. However, there is a useful method of seeing the tiniest of bites. If you sit directly behind the rod so it looks straight, or as straight as you can make it, you can move your head so that the side of the tip ring just peeks out from the side of the rod. Settle in that position, and when the tip ring is pulled round by even the tiniest fraction of an inch, you will see it. It's a method for those days in winter when small fish are hanging on to the bait without giving any obvious indication – the silver of the tip ring will make it very easy to see.

TARGET BOARDS

Target boards are extremely popular with leger anglers and most useful with a quivertip. They are usually black and rectangular and screw into a bank stick. They have lines or a grid marked on them, and are placed beyond the end of the rod, so the angler can line up his tip ring with one of the lines. Once the tip is set into position it is easy to see it move even a fraction of an inch.

In addition, when there is floating weed about, the board can be set so it diverts the weed round the tip so that it does not catch on the line, provided you are sitting with the board upstream of the rod tip. And it can also keep wind off the tip. If you are caught out without a target board, a bank stick pushed into the bottom just beyond the rod tip is a useful substitute.

POSITION OF THE ROD TIP

You will find, nine times out of ten, that the best position for your tip ring on a stillwater is just above the surface – perhaps no more than a $\frac{1}{4}$ in – with the rest of the line beneath the water. This position stops the wind buffeting the line. It also helps you spot some of the tiny bites you might otherwise miss, as your eye will quickly become accustomed to judging the gap between water surface and tip ring. If the gap is a $\frac{1}{4}$ in, then a movement

Left: The line should make approximately a right-angle with the rod. In windy weather drop the tip to the surface so the wind doesn't blow the line about.

Below: It's usual to sit with your back to the wind when legering. A target board like this helps you spot bites.

of your tip of only a ¼ in will reduce the gap by anything up to 50 per cent (given that the line is at an angle) – and the human brain is incredibly adept at spotting this. However, if there is marginal weed you may have to lift the rod high, and perhaps even have it set pointing towards the sky. Then you can do nothing about the effect of the wind on the line – like all types of fishing, legering is always a compromise between what you would like to do and what the elements and circumstances allow. If you can get that rod point low, then do so.

TYPES OF BITE

Experience will enable you to decide what is a bite and what isn't and – just as important – when it's worth striking at a bite. Most often, the sort of bite that pulls the tip round by about 1 in and then immediately lets it flick back to its original position is unhittable. And after a few outings you will start to learn that this sort of indication is simply not worth striking at.

Often this is a line bite, caused by a small fish flicking the line somewhere between your rod tip and the leger weight. If it's not that, it's likely to be a very small fish that has nipped the end of your maggot and given it a quick tweak. Line bites caused by bigger fish tend to pull round fast, but usually pull round further and hold the position for perhaps half a second before flicking back into place. Unfortunately, these bites often give you sufficient time to make an instinctive strike before you realise it's a false alarm.

If you are missing bites, and suspect line bites, the best thing is to sit on your hands – literally – so you can't make a premature strike, for continual striking and re-casting into a shoal of fish that hasn't settled down to feed can eventually unsettle them so much that they move away. Better to allow too long than to strike too quickly. In other words, it's better to let a fish get away with your bait than to risk either pricking it in the lip and losing it or scaring it by striking when the line is lying across, or perhaps round or underneath, its body.

A proper bite, contrary to what many anglers may imagine, is often no more than a tiny, slow, nudge – the sort you will never see unless you are concentrating really hard. This is frequently from a fish that is slowly cruising around the bottom and picks up your bait confidently, never imagining there might a hook in it. It has no reason to bolt away; it just carries on cruising around, perhaps moving only 1–2 in at a time. When you get a series of these tiny, little nudges you almost always connect with every one, as opposed to the real sail-aways, when the quivertip may hurtle round and keep on going, half of which you miss!

STRIKING ON A HUNCH

Don't worry to begin with about whether you're able to spot all your bites – you most certainly won't. Once you're comfortable with your tackle don't be afraid to strike on a 'hunch'. All experienced quivertip anglers suddenly find themselves striking without being really sure whether they've had a bite or not. It's almost as if the human brain can programme itself to recognise a strange movement of the tip and give the orders to strike before you realise it is happening.

The more relaxed you are, provided you're really concentrating on the tip, the more likely you are to get the feeling – no more than that – that there's a fish at the bait. Sometimes the tip doesn't bend round – it just 'quivers', hence the name quivertip.

CHAPTER FIFTEEN

The Swingtip

A swingtip, as its name implies, swings about on the end of the rod, and lifts when you get a bite. It's most useful on deep stillwaters, but can be used effectively on all waters, including rivers where the water is moving. However, it's usual on really fast rivers to discard the swingtip in favour of either a strong quivertip, or a special swimfeeder rod, when you watch the rod tip for bites.

As with a quivertip, it's possible to buy a rod with a swingtip already whipped on to the end. For most anglers there is little point in buying one of these, because there is a huge range of swingtips, which will all screw into the same threaded end ring as any quivertip.

On quivertips the ring spacings at the rod tip are not particularly important. However, there is one point you should watch when buying, or making up, a swingtip. You must have a ring near the threaded end. If you don't (and many swingtips are sold with no ring here) you will find that the line can flick over the tip of your rod, causing a break when you strike.

The swingtip can be left hanging vertically downwards after you have cast, but, at least to begin with, you will probably feel more confident allowing it to hang at a slight angle, under very light tension. You should be certain of seeing an indication when a fish takes the bait.

WEIGHT AND LENGTH

There's no taper to worry about with swingtips, like there is with a quivertip – all swingtips are straight. Your choice will be concerned with weight and length. Obviously a heavier one will tend to swing about less in a wind and will not be pulled up so far by a heavy drift or in running water. This means that it will be easier to see bites, as the tip will have a greater distance to travel before it's pulled out perfectly straight. That's a broad generalisation, but to begin with you should aim at using a light swingtip on stillwaters when there's not too much wind, and heavier swingtips on moving water or in really bad conditions on stillwaters. As for the length, a short one will swing around less in a wind, while there may be some circumstances in which it is essential to get your rod as close as possible to the water – bankside or wind conditions may dictate this. In that case a short swingtip will be needed.

However, in reasonable conditions on slow

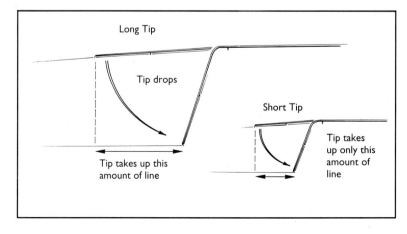

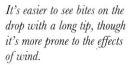

It's easier to see bites on the drop with a long tip, though it's more prone to the effects of wind.

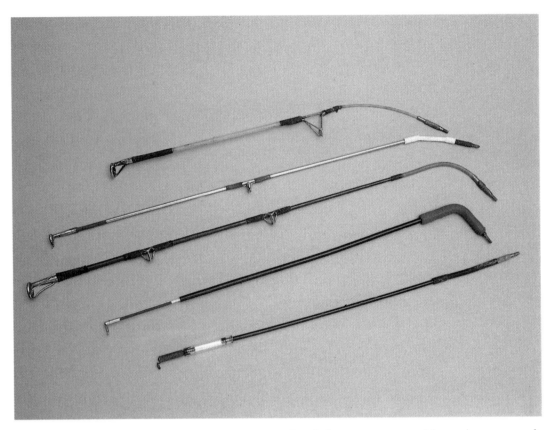

Swingtips come in different models and sizes. (From the top): the Clayton one-piece nylon swingtip; extra-heavy metal; heavy cane with three rings; stiff link for strong wind; fluorescent-tipped for night fishing.

or still waters the average-length swingtip – about 10 in – will be a good choice. This gives you enough time to spot bites 'on the drop' combined with a reasonable amount of stability in a wind.

Some anglers fish with swingtips almost 2 ft long. Each time they are tightened, they take up more slack line than a shorter one, and this is an advantage when bites occur as the bait falls ('on the drop'), or soon after the bait has settled. Also, the longer the swingtip, the easier it is to see bites – a 1-in pull on a short tip may be hardly noticeable, but on a very long tip it's more obvious because there is more swingtip moving! However, you are better off using a normal-length swingtip until you have completely mastered the basics. Taking up slack line in such a way that

it helps you see bites is a much misunderstood part of legering, and the swingtip offers the best way of doing this.

THE CLAYTON TYPE

If there is an 'all-round' swingtip it must be the original Clayton-type marketed by the late Jack Clayton, a Boston, Lincs, tackle dealer who popularised the swingtip in the 1950s. This is a one-piece swingtip made of extruded nylon. The link is pliable, but with enough stiffness to hold the tip under just a little pressure against the wind. It's a light tip, and not easy to find nowadays. If you can find any, especially the medium-to-long ones from 10–18 in in length, buy some. They'll come in handy in the future.

PLASTIC TYPES

In any typical tackle shop there will be many modern swingtips, probably made from some sort of plastic. Look for weight, length and

Left: The take-apart model has weights which are inserted down the hollow swingtip, so you can adjust its weight. The swingtip pushes into the rubber link.

Below: Waiting for a bite! Note the special long rod rest near the tip.

the type of link. It's advisable to have a reasonable selection to begin with, though later you will probably end up with just two or three favourites. Perhaps the most important thing about the 'average' commercial swingtip is the link. On a stillwater it really is useful to have a link that has a little stiffness in it, enabling you to increase its resistance to the wind by turning the rod slightly.

HEAVY CANE

There are also heavy cane types, most useful on medium-moving water. They'll probably have a simple pliable rubber link, which makes them liable to be blown all over the place in wind. That doesn't matter so much on moving water, when the current puts the line and the swingtip under tension, tightening the line and reducing the effect of the wind.

TAKE-APART

The take-apart swingtip is an extremely handy and greatly underrated item of tackle. It consists of a standard, threaded end, onto which is pushed a piece of rubber tubing. Into the tubing is pushed a hollow swingtip, and it comes with a set of metal weights that are slipped down inside the swingtip. This enables you to adjust the weight more quickly than with any other method, and is faster than using lead wire.

POSITION OF THE ROD

The swingtip is much more versatile than the quivertip when it comes to positioning your rod. Whereas with a quivertip you aim to get approximately a right-angle between the rod and the line, with a swingtip this angle is of no real importance. This is because the link will allow the swingtip to be pulled upwards in any direction. So you can place the rod anywhere in the 180° arc in front of you: pointing to the left, parallel with the bank, or straight out, or round to the right, or at any spot in between. However, for the sake of comfort the average angler will instinctively sit with his back to the wind, and this helps shield the rod from the wind. The swingtip can also be shielded by tucking the rod into the bankside vegetation. The only proviso is that the rod will need to be approximately parallel with the surface of the water.

In moving water most anglers will tend to try to sit with the rod facing downstream. Then when they strike they are doing so across the flow rather than against it, assuming they are fishing a spot somewhere out in front of them. There are times when the wind and the water are coming from opposite directions, of course, and that's when only you can decide on your priorities. The position, though, makes a big difference to the way you see your bites. With the rod straight out in front of you, you are watching the tip move directly away from you, and it can be difficult to spot bites in wind. However, if the rod is parallel to the bank, you are watching the swingtip move across your line of sight when you get a bite, and most anglers find these sorts of bites very much easier to spot. There's also a difference with the striking. With the rod resting to the side, a strike pulls the line roughly along its

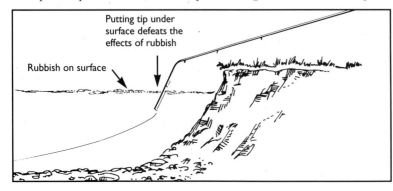

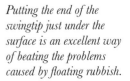

Putting the end of the swingtip just under the surface is an excellent way of beating the problems caused by floating rubbish.

own length, or through its own 'tube' as it was once described, and this means the line meets very little resistance. With the rod put straight out in front of you, however, a strike is, in effect, pulling the line upwards through the water.

In theory, the sideways strike means that you are striking directly to the fish, while the upwards strike means that the line is meeting lots of resistance and the strike is not direct. However, some of the top bream anglers prefer pointing the rod straight out in front of them if conditions allow, so the final choice is up to you. Where bream are concerned, most anglers strike too early anyway, so it can be worth trying the straight-out approach if you are missing bites, as this may slow your strike fractionally.

On most occasions you will want to position the rod so that the very end of the swingtip just touches, or is just above, the surface. On a really calm day when there's just a tiny drift on a stillwater you can, with a little patience, allow the drift to take the line up so that the tip is just held down by the surface tension of the water. That's the perfect scenario – the tiniest of bites will flick the tip above the surface in a way you can't possibly miss.

On a windy day it can actually pay to allow $1/2$ in of the swingtip to remain in the water as this has a steadying effect. It helps if the bottom inch or so is brightly coloured, in which case you watch the top edge of the coloured band for bites, and not the very tip. The colour is a matter of personal preference. Some of the modern glowing colours have been known to cause migraines. A black swingtip with a white tip or white bands can be effective. My preference in good light is for a black swingtip with a single white band about 1 in from the end. When I sink the tip I drop this band to surface level and watch it for bites.

When you have gained experience in legering you may find that you can see bites in a good light no matter what the colour of the indicator you are using. However, undoubtedly there are times, during poor light conditions, when you will be glad of a bright colour on the end of your swingtip. As with floatfishing, a pair of polaroid spectacles can help reduce eyestrain when you're looking at a tip for hours on end.

BITES

A swingtip is, generally, more affected by wind than is a quivertip. A swingtip is fatter, while a quivertip is very thin; and even under some tension a swingtip is liable to be blown in almost any direction, while a quivertip's movement is much more restricted. This is the price you pay for being able to use a swingtip in almost any position. However, to begin with you may find a swingtip harder to read.

The ideal bite is a slow lift, with the swingtip ending straight out, almost parallel with the water. You should rarely miss a bite like this. The difficult bite is the one that lifts the indicator perhaps $1/2$ in and then allows it to drop back, and this can happen before you realise you have a bite, especially in a wind. On a quivertip this would register as quite a good pull, and you would probably strike. In fact, it rarely hurts to leave a bite like this and wait for a better indication, and you are more likely to find yourself doing this if you use a swingtip. The end result is that most swingtippers tend to hit a greater proportion of bites they strike at than quivertippers.

If you get that tiny lift and nothing else, it's worth striking the next time you get one, even if the tip has fallen right back. And you are likely to hit a higher proportion of bites by striking late using a swingtip than when using a quivertip. I can't work out why this is. It may be something to do with the fact that the tension on a quivertip increases noticeably as it bends, while the power needed to pull a swingtip up varies very little during the lift, and the fish feels more confident, and keeps the bait in its mouth. Also, the amount of line that can be pulled by the fish is greater with a swingtip than with a quivertip. A 12-in swingtip hanging vertically won't be out straight until more than 12 in of line have been pulled, while a 12-in pull on a quivertip will probably pull the rod off the rest

There are times, though, when little fish do seem put off by the weight of the

The ideal setting for a swingtip – just touching the surface.

swingtip, and keep jerking it without ever making off with the bait. A change to a quivertip, which is lighter, is then probably the answer.

Line bites, caused by fish hitting the line between bait and rod tip, are likely to be more easily recognised on a swingtip than on any other method. The tip will, without warning, shoot out and immediately fall back, probably leaving some extra slack line – this slack line can be the result of the fish moving the leger weight. And you are less likely to hit a bite like this instinctively on a swingtip than with a quivertip, which is a point in favour of the swingtip, especially when fishing for bream.

CHAPTER SIXTEEN

End Rigs

The simplest leger rig consists of a drilled bullet running on the line, stopped by a split shot or a leger stop at a point above the bait. The distance between bait and bullet depends on whether you particularly want the bait to sink slowly during the latter part of its descent, and would normally be between 1–3 ft. This rig is not, in fact, particularly suited to presenting a slowly falling bait, and would normally be used on moving water, when the bullet's round shape rolls nicely along the bottom, allowing the angler to present a moving bait. However, it can be used on stillwaters, and has the advantage of allowing a 'straight through' rig to be used; that is, with the hook tied direct to the reel line. This does away with all knots, except the one joining line to hook, and gives

the strongest possible rig.

A variation is to put an Arlesey bomb on the line, also stopped above the bait with a shot. This is popular with carp anglers, and when the bomb is a big one it forms the basis of the 'bolt' rig – the fish runs for a few inches and then another shot, positioned above the weight, comes up against the weight and the fish hooks itself. This particular rig is used almost exclusively by carp anglers, and is not suitable for other species, which tend to feed much more timidly. The weight in this case needs to be quite heavy, to ensure that the fish hooks itself.

The basic rig, with just the lower shot or stop, is a perfectly workable rig on stillwaters. For the average angler, though, it is unsophisticated as the line can become

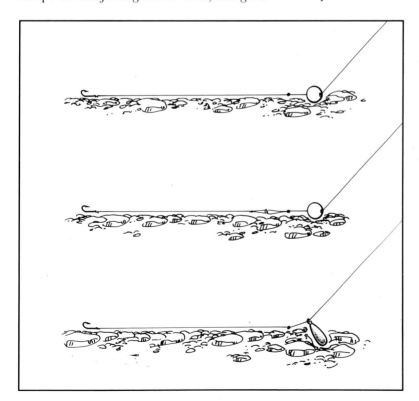

Three very basic rigs: (top) the simplest drilled bullet rig with the hook whipped direct to the reel line, and a shot on the line; (middle) a similar rig, but with a hook length looped to the end of the reel line; (bottom) an Arlesey bomb is favoured on stillwaters as it is more streamlined for casting.

twisted above the eye of the weight, in which case it would be acting as a dead weight and the fish would feel it as soon as it tried to swim off with the bait. On fast-running water it is a rig worth considering, however, as the shape of the Arlesey bomb gives it a tendency to lie still. Yet when the line is tightened, provided the bomb is the correct weight, it will roll round a little. This allows you to search the swim. The rig's simplicity and the fact that you can fish it 'straight through', as with the drilled bullet, makes it popular with specimen hunters. The biggest problem with a 'straight-through' rig is always the tendency of the heavy weight to knock a split shot down the line to the hook, so a leger stop is the usual, preferred method, as this holds the line quite tightly.

PATERNOSTERS

By far the most-used rigs are those based on the paternoster principle, in which the weight is tied to the end of the line and the hook is on a length of nylon attached somewhere above the weight. The hook length can be short, leaving the hook above the weight or, more usually, longer, putting the bait beyond the weight. The point at which they join can be tied, or the weight can be on a short piece of nylon tied to a swivel running along the main line and stopped, as with the drilled bullet or Arlesey bomb, above the bait. To make this rig, the main line is threaded through a swivel, and then through the collar of a leger stop, and the hook whipped to the end of the line. Three feet above the hook the wedge of the leger stop is inserted into the collar, and this holds tight on the line; then 9

in of nylon are tied to the swivel, and the leger weight is tied to the other end of the nylon. As with the drilled-bullet rig a split shot can be used instead of the leger stop, but it can be difficult to get this to hold really tight on the line, although the new non-toxic shot are harder than the old-style lead shot and do, in fact, hold quite well.

Whether the join is tied or sliding is largely a question of personal preference. However, on stillwaters there seems no point in adding a swivel and perhaps a split shot if you are trying to get the bait to sink as slowly as possible – all that extra ironwork simply takes the rig down more quickly. And there is also the possibility, particularly on stillwaters, that the line will snag the swivel as it sinks, so it will not run smoothly. However, if you especially want to fish a paternoster rig with the hook tied direct, with no knots in the line, then the sliding paternoster is your best option.

The weight can also be attached to a piece of Power Gum, which stretches when put under pressure and is popular with river anglers using a big weight to hold bottom. It absorbs some of the pressure of the strike, so the angler does not have to move the weight before he hits the fish. Power Gum has the advantage over elastic that it will stretch only a short way and that once stretched it retracts only slowly, without the typical springing-back you would get with elastic. For this reason it is also popular with fly anglers, who use it between fly line and leader to absorb the sudden smash strikes from big trout.

Instead of the swivel you can use one of the many little adaptor beads now on sale in tackle shops. A ready-made Power Gum link, complete with swivel on one end and a clip

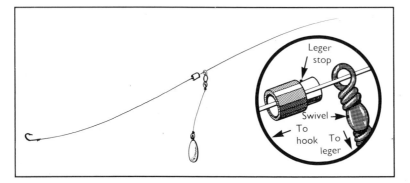

A sliding rig like this has the advantage that by moving the leger stop below the swivel the effective length of the hook snood can be altered in seconds. Inset, close-up of the set-up.

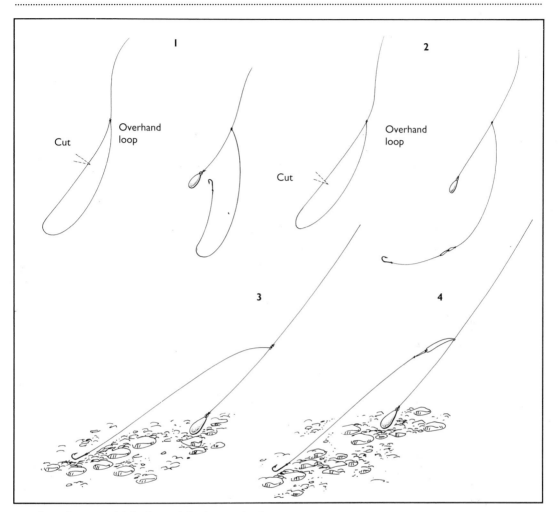

Four simple leger paternoster rigs:
1: A loop is tied in the end of the reel line, cut, and the hook tied to one end and the leger weight to the other.
2: The same procedure is followed but a lighter hook length can be looped on.
3: A hook length is tied to the reel line with a water knot.
4: A loop is tied in the reel line above the weight and a hook length looped to this.

on the other to which the weight is attached, is also available. It was designed for use with swimfeeders, but can be used just as effectively with a leger weight.

There are several ways in which a fixed paternoster can be tied:

• By tying a large loop in the end of the reel line, using a simple double overhand knot, cutting this loop 9 in from the knot, and using the shorter end for the weight and the longer end for the hook (in this case, both hook length and reel line are the same strength).

• By using the above system but tying a small loop in the end of the longer hook length to which a ready-tied hook, on thinner nylon, can be attached.

• By using a water knot, leaving 9 in of reel line and 3 ft or more of the thinner hook length.

• By tying the bomb to the end of the reel line and then tying a small loop 9 in above the bomb, to which a hook-to-nylon is attached.

There are other methods published from time to time in the angling press, but most are based on the above. It is worth

Above: There are several types of leger weights. This one is flattened to hold bottom better in a flow.

Left: Power Gum links have a snap swivel on the bottom, allowing you to change your leger weight or swimfeeder in seconds.

experimenting until you find one you are happy with, though. Of the four, the last method is probably the easiest to tie, but slightly less neat. The third is the least easy to tie, since it involves learning the water knot. However, it is the neatest, and favoured by experienced leger anglers.

Tying the line instead of using a sliding system has advantages in moving water when there is weed or rubbish floating along, as it presents a much smaller spot where the weed can lodge when compared with a swivel and split shot, which picks up a lot of weed on occasions. This can not only cause the rig to stop sliding, but reduces its sensitivity and gives false bites in a current. For weedy swims on both still and running water there is no doubt that the tied paternoster rigs are to be preferred to the ones containing a swivel and stop.

There is one big advantage in using a sliding paternoster rig. By moving the position of the shot you can increase or decrease the hook length at will. And on occasions, when you are having trouble finding the best length it can be a real boon. At all times you should keep the swivel or sliding bead, and the leger stop, as small as possible.

With both fixed and running paternosters, the weight is normally on a piece of nylon around 4–6 in long. There is no real advantage to be gained in lengthening this as it only increases your chance of the hook length tangling in it.

HOOK LENGTHS

The length of the piece of nylon you use for the hook length is very important on the day, and probably the biggest single consideration once you have cast. Overall it's probably even more important than the bait you use, for it determines how the bait behaves, and how (and sometimes even whether) you will see your bites.

On running water in particular, and especially when using a swimfeeder, it can pay to go down to just a few inches, while on stillwaters a hook length of up to 6 ft might not be too much if you're aiming to present a slowly falling bait.

CHAPTER SEVENTEEN

Tightening and Twitching

These are the two most important and perhaps most misunderstood and neglected aspects of legering. The way you tighten the line and move the bait is just as important to the leger angler as control of the tackle is to an angler using a stick float, and especially so if you're fishing a slowly-sinking bait. The line doesn't have to be tight to the weight for you to see a bite, but most anglers prefer it this way; while twitching the bait can have the same effect on a fish as a cornered mouse has on a cat – one movement and the cat pounces. It really can bring a lot more bites on occasions than leaving the bait static.

SINKING THE LINE

The first thing to look at is the process of sinking the line after casting. And this is made

Moving the leger weight will cause the bait to move, which may prove attractive to fish. This is known as twitching the bait.

much easier if it does not float. It helps to treat the line with washing-up liquid – by running it through a sponge filled with the liquid when you retrieve. A line that does not readily sink below the surface causes enormous problems, especially in windy weather, when a bow is inevitably formed when you cast. If the line sinks it can be tightened slowly without the leger weight being moved; but if it floats, you will not only take a lot of time tightening it, but will also be likely to move the leger weight while doing so. That in itself may not matter, but you may not be fishing in the place you think you are. The line is sunk either by twitching it by pulling and flicking the rod tip, or by

Most baits have a slow natural rate of fall which you should try to imitate. Bread flake is particularly buoyant, and a fish may watch it sink for some time (left). If you tighten the line (right) it will pull the bread quickly downwards and this may make fish, particularly bream, suspicious.

plunging the rod tip well below the surface and reeling in with a series of short, sharp turns of the reel handle. Often you can see the line being pulled beneath the surface. You must be sure to get it properly sunk, otherwise the action of the waves will start giving you false bites.

In strong side winds you should always 'feather' the line (use your finger to control the speed with which it leaves the spool) while you cast, and stop the line coming off the spool as soon as the weight has hit the surface. This reduces the size of the bow that forms. If you can then push the rod under the surface as soon as you have cast, and before the weight hits the bottom, the line will sink

much more quickly. You can keep a tight line as the weight sinks, which will ensure that the line, or at least most of it, will be below the surface by the time it has hit bottom, though the rig will inevitably kite towards you as it sinks. Then sink any remaining line by twitching or reeling in. So if you use this method overcast. The deeper the water, the more the rig will move forwards as it sinks.

Alternatively you can keep the rod tip below the surface but keep the bale arm open so the weight sinks vertically. Then you will have more line to sink by twitching and reeling in. Experienced anglers tend to prefer this latter method, but for the novice the first method is probably easier.

Leaving the line slack after you have cast (left) will allow the bait to sink naturally. It may take 30-40 seconds, but still allow the line to lie slack (centre). Any fish which has watched it fall should now not be wary, and may take the bait. Be aware that tightening the line will cause the bait to move, even if you do not move the weight!

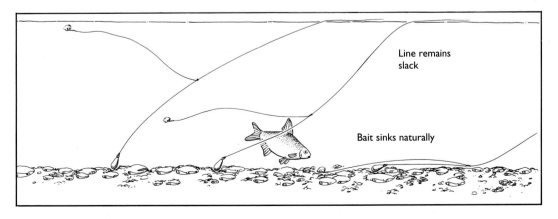

Below: The violin pluck – just tightening the line upwards in slack water can cause the bait to move.

Above: When you pull the line, it's easiest to grip it between the reel and the first ring.

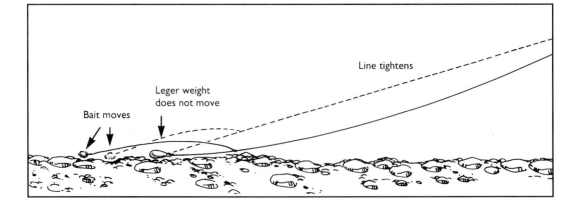

Line tightens

Leger weight
does not move

Bait moves

TIGHTENING WITH A QUIVERTIP

The process of tightening should normally be done slowly. The reasons for this can be most easily explained by an imaginary situation on a lake. Let us assume you have a piece of bread flake on the hook and are after bream, using a quivertip rod, on a reasonably windy day. You've cast out using a 4-ft tail to give a slow sink. Immediately the bait has hit the water, push the rod tip under the surface to sink the line between the rod and the point of entry. Watch the quivertip bend round as the weight sinks then flick back when the weight has hit the bottom. Now put the rod on the rest so that it's parallel to the water, but don't reel in yet! Let the line lie slack – it's against what most books will tell you, but the following is what happens.

As soon as you reel in, even a few inches, you will be pulling the line towards you, and on the end of that line is the bait. It will be falling reasonably naturally through the last 4 ft of water, and suddenly it will twitch and move quite unnaturally because it is being pulled towards you and down. Not only is this making the bait behave oddly, but it's reducing the amount of sinking time, which is short enough anyway.

There's another reason for tightening slowly that applies if there are bream in the swim. Some of the country's top bream anglers are sure a bream will watch a bait sink and then eye it on the bottom before making up its mind to eat it. An unnatural movement at that stage might put the fish off. Of course every bream angler knows that twitching a bait along the bottom can bring a response, but there will be plenty of time for that when the bait has been in the water a couple of minutes. You'll never go far wrong if you try to get the bait to sink as slowly as possible.

Once the bait has been out for about a minute or two, it is time to start tightening the line. If you get a bite in the meantime – as the bait is sinking – you will still see it as the line doesn't have to be tight to the quivertip. Even with a bow, it will bend round when a fish takes the bait.

Now tighten quite slowly, and each time you turn the reel the bait will twitch, even though the weight is not being moved, so you should be prepared for a bite even at this stage. Wind in until the quivertip is well bent, then stop, and watch the quivertip slowly straighten as it takes up the slack line. Wait 15 seconds and repeat this. Keep repeating this operation until the quivertip won't straighten any more, and then wind backwards to give a little slack line until it straightens. A bite can come at any time, and is liable to be good, and unmissable – probably either a very slow bending of the quivertip after it has straightened, or a quick jerk or two as you reel in. You will probably strike instinctively at this latter bite, almost without realising you have done it.

Now – with the bait on the bottom and the line tight to the leger weight – the time to start pulling the bait towards you. This is not only creates the right movement, but also makes little puffs of mud spurt up from the weight as it is moved. However, a piece of bread flake can easily be pulled off, so the twitching trick should be kept until you've a worm or a maggot on. If you have a heavy bait on the hook, like a worm, you can begin to tighten after, perhaps, 30 seconds. Even then, however, it's often a good idea to leave it as long as you dare.

With a really big bow in the line after casting you will have to tighten more quickly – not because you won't see the bites, but because you won't be able to hit the fish on the strike. On water which is moving, the line will tighten itself, of course, and the faster the current, the more quickly you will see the quivertip bend. Then you tighten the line by winding in and waiting until the quivertip has resumed its normal bend before repeating the excercise. Inevitably on moving water there will be a bow, and provided it's not a huge one it should make little difference to your ability both to see bites and hook the fish. In fact, leaving a big bow will help a light weight hold bottom more easily.

THE TWITCH – QUIVERTIP

Let's assume you have a single maggot on, in the lake swim, and have tightened as described – nice and slowly over a period of a couple of minutes. The length of time you wait before starting to move the bait is optional, and some bream anglers will leave it 10 or 15 minutes. I've never been that patient!

There are several ways of twitching. The one I favour is to reel in about a turn, until the quivertip is bent right round. Then take the line between reel and butt ring and pull it towards you until the tip springs back straight. Let go of the line in your hand, and reel in until just a small amount of slack is left. Usually the drift on the water will inch this line through the rod rings and put just a slight bend in the quivertip. An alternative method is to reel in and watch the quivertip bend right round and then spring back. Then reel in until the tip is almost straight. A third option is to lift the rod and pull the weight along the bottom, and then replace the rod on the rest and tighten.

Bites will frequently come as you tighten, and you will suddenly realise that there is resistance. This makes it difficult to know exactly when to strike, of course. The best bites are those which occur just after the tip has been allowed to straighten, and drift is tightening the line. Then the line will suddenly be seen to tighten more quickly, and the tip will just bend round in an almost-unmissable bite.

THE VIOLIN PLUCK

This was a term coined by Cambridge matchman, Percy Anderson, and is a surprisingly effective little dodge. It involves no more than pulling the line tight, so the quivertip pulls round, and then letting it go, without the leger weight actually moving. The drift will take up the slack line and tension the tip again. The tiny movement of the line seems to impart a tremble to the bait, and will frequently bring a bite. On narrow waterways, or where the fish seem to be concentrated in a small area, this is a useful trick, as it doesn't pull the bait out of the swim. Experienced anglers will allow a little more slack line out each time they pull, which gradually takes longer to tighten. Then they will reel in so the excess slack line is taken up (you get a lot of bites at this point), and start the sequence again.

TIGHTENING WITH A SWINGTIP

Sinking the line when using a swingtip is done in the same way as with every other method – by plunging the rod tip beneath the waves and reeling in. The swingtip then gives the advantage of allowing better bite indication as the bait is sinking than the quivertip does. You'll see bites on both, but the swingtip has a potentially greater distance to move, so it's easier to see the bite develop.

After the line has been sunk, the rod is placed on the rest and the reel turned until the swingtip is out straight (or at least as straight as it will go). Then it is allowed to fall back until it's vertical to the water; and this process is repeated until the tip stays at an angle to the surface, when some slack line is let out until it's vertical or almost so. Most swingtip anglers like it to rest at a slight angle from the vertical as this readily shows drop-back bites. The swingtip will tend to take up the slack line more slowly than a quivertip, and you will get many bites as it is sinking back. These range from a rocket-like lift to a little tremble. However, because the swingtip is larger than the quivertip most anglers find it easier to watch. The longer the swingtip, the more line it will take up on each drop, and the fewer number of times you will have to reel in. This decreases the chance of getting a bite as you are reeling in – the most difficult bites to spot and hit.

THE TWITCH – SWINGTIP

The options are the same as with the quivertip: reel in until the tip is straight, then pull the line above the reel until the tip drops down, finally reeling in to take up the slack. Or keep winding until the tip straightens and drops back. Or lift the rod and pull until you feel the leger weight move. In all cases, you

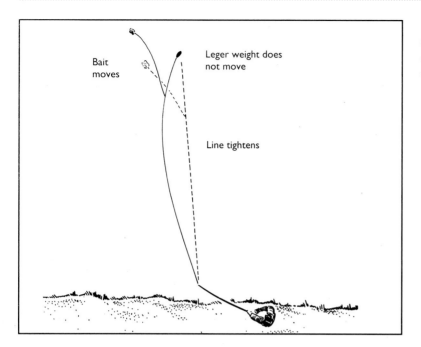

Bait
moves

Leger weight does
not move

Line tightens

The violin pluck in moving water – tightening the line against the current will also cause the bait to move.

judge the tension of the line by the angle the swingtip makes with the surface, always remembering that not all swingtips will naturally hang straight down, of course.

OTHER INDICATORS

Whatever indicator you use the method of tightening the line will be the same, although the twitching may vary slightly. With a butt indicator you will find that slack line may not be so easily taken up by drift or flow because of the increased friction between line and rod rings. With slack lining the opposite happens, and you may find that the drift takes the line quite straight, and you can't see bites so well. In that case you will either have to change to a quivertip or a swingtip, or you can fix a butt indicator, weighted if necessary to take up the slack line.

SIZE OF THE LEGER WEIGHT

The lighter the weight, the easier you will find it to move. However, in a wind a lighter weight will be less accurate to cast, and will be moved more easily as you tighten if there is a bow. It won't take you long to work out whether you are moving the weight as you

tighten up, so you should take a range of weights, say $^1\!/_8$ oz, $^1\!/_4$ oz, $^3\!/_8$ oz (a very useful size), $^1\!/_2$ oz, and $^3\!/_4$ oz. Be prepared to change them if necessary so that you get the best compromise between accuracy of casting and ease of twitching. If you have a link into which you can clip the weight you will be more likely to change it if necessary. Aim to get the lightest weight that will hold still as you tighten up. The one exception to this is when you're fishing in a swim holding a lot of bottom weed. In that case, when you have found a clear patch and are sure you can cast right on to it, you may be advised to increase the weight of the leger to ensure you don't drag the bait out of position as you tighten. The same advice applies in running water.

STRIKING

A word of warning: bites resulting from twitching the bait are liable to be be fierce, and you should try to restrain yourself from reacting in the same way. Every season, anglers twitching a bait, with their hand already on the rod, see their quivertip hurtle round. They strike hard, either breaking their hook length, pricking the fish, or taking the bait out of its lips. Few fish are lost by the angler striking too softly – lots are lost by striking too fast or hard. So take your time.

The correct way to approach any strike, particularly when a big fish like a bream or a tench is the quarry, is to 'lean into the fish'. It can be misleading to watch a Fenland bream angler give a huge strike over his head, for he may simply be taking up slack line and then reducing the power when he feels the fish. At the same time, he will be trying to get the fish moving immediately to separate it from the shoal. It's a complicated combination of actions he is performing, all in what appears to be just one sweep.

For your first efforts, don't try to emulate the experienced bream angler. He may have 20 years of experience, doing it weekend after weekend. Just try to lean into the fish to begin with, no matter what its size, and then keep a tight line. The rest will come naturally.

It's essential to set the clutch of a fixed-spool reel so it gives line if you hit something big. Not only does this prevent the line from breaking on the strike, but it tells you immediately that there is extra pressure on the clutch. This is especially useful in windy weather, when it can sometimes be difficult to judge the size of a fish you are playing.

PLAYING A FISH

Most fish caught in this country can be played without giving line from the reel. So the favourite method of striking is to click on the anti-reverse and rely on the clutch giving if you hook an extra-big fish. Then you simply click off the anti-reverse, and give line by back-winding if this proves necessary. However, if you are fishing for carp, big tench or barbel, you may find the first run of these immensely powerful fish is so fast that either you can't click the anti-reverse off in time, or if you do the reel spins backwards so fast that you can't control it. Either way, there is great danger of the line breaking. In these cases, it is essential to play the fish on the clutch, or with a combination of the clutch and some backwinding. You should set the clutch a little lighter than you would normally do, and hold the spool with you finger when you strike. Many anglers use reels with the drag adjuster on the back of the reel, as these can be altered in a split second while the fish is still running, just by turning the knob. Reels with the drag on the spool are much more difficult to adjust during a fight, although they are still popular with matchmen, as the spool can be tightened right down.

CHAPTER EIGHTEEN

The Open-Ended Swimfeeder

The swimfeeder has made an enormous impact on angling in Britain in the past 30 years, and deservedly so, as it helps the angler get his bait out to the spot where he is fishing without fail. It was introduced to a sceptical angling fraternity by Londoners, who had been using it for many years, and has been refined to such a degree that there is now not only a whole range of swimfeeders, but also a range of groundbaits for them. The two main types available are block-end, which has plastic caps on both ends, and the open-end, also known as a groundbait feeder, on which the ends are open. There is also the very versatile frame feeder and variations on this.

Swimfeeders (from the top): large and small block-ends; large and small open-ended feeders; a new-style cage feeder.

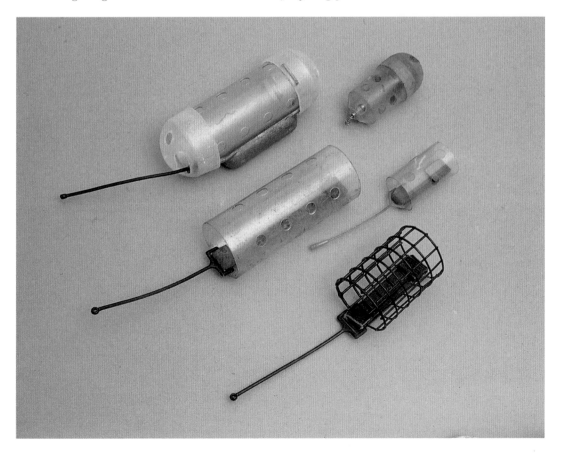

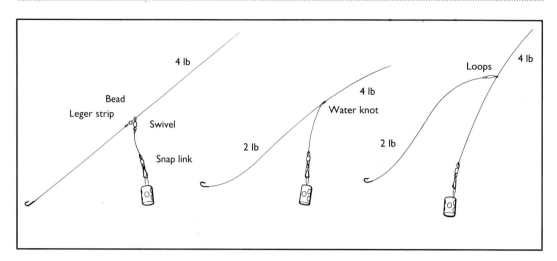

All types of swimfeeder can be used with all the indicators already mentioned, though in medium-to-fast running water a purpose-built feeder rod will usually have to be used. With this you will see the bites on the rod tip, which acts in the same way as a quivertip.

As for choosing which feeder to use, an open-ended feeder must have its ends plugged with groundbait, which slowly disintegrates and allows the contents to form a little heap on the bottom, so this is the usual choice for stillwater; and a block-end is usually filled just with maggots which crawl through the holes in the side and in the ends, and is the usual choice for running water. Block-ends are, however, frequently used for stillwater fishing and are marginally the more versatile of the two types, especially ones that have two easily removeable end caps, allowing them to be converted to open-end feeders in seconds.

Frame feeders are a new introduction. Groundbait is squeezed around the cage-like feeder and disintegrates quickly once it hits the water. These are used almost exclusively by stillwater anglers. There is also the cage feeder – a type of open-ended feeder made of wire instead of plastic.

RIGS

Rigs for swimfeeders are basically the same as for the straight leger, with the option of using fixed or sliding paternosters, and with the block-end feeder the option of running

Typical swimfeeder paternoster rigs:
Left: The very strong 'straight-through' rig, which has no knots in it. The bead is optional.
Centre: The neat water knot rig.
Right: The easily-tied double-loop set-up. The snap link allows quick changes of swimfeeder to be made.

the line straight through the middle – the equivalent of the simple drilled bullet rig. As with the straight leger, anglers use a paternoster nine times out of ten. On stillwaters or slow rivers the fixed paternoster is most popular, while on fast waters the sliding rig has some advantages. At all times, the advice to keep it simple is of paramount importance, always remembering that a swimfeeder exerts more pressure on rod and line, and a hooked fish, than a straight leger rig, so tackle tends to be slightly stronger than that which would be used by an angler legering in the same conditions.

Probably of more importance for the inexperienced leger angler than the exact rig used is when, and how, to use a swimfeeder, and which sort to choose.

OPEN-END FEEDERS

Shop-sold models are usually made from clear plastic, and have no ends. The various makes have all sorts of different fittings to attach them to the line. For the beginner it makes little difference which fitting you choose, so long as you are confident you are seeing bites. However, once you are familiar with using feeders of any kind you should pay some attention to this point, particularly if you have experienced any tangling of the hook length round the link connecting the feeder to the line. They all have holes along the side, though these are not, in fact, strictly necessary, and some top anglers use home-made feeders without holes because they plane towards the surface when you retrieve them, bringing them over any snags and also over the heads of any feeding fish.

Any feeder can be tied to the line paternoster-style or allowed to run on the main line. For the beginner, a running swivel will allow you to experiment with the length of the hook drop, which is important on both still and moving waters. To alter the effective hook length you just push the swivel stop (the purpose-made leger stop is probably best) up the line.

For a fixed paternoster you would use a water knot, using a lighter line for the hook length than the reel line. Most authorities say you should use a four-turn water knot, but I usually manage only two turns and it's never let me down yet! As with a straight leger, it is as well to begin with a good hook length – 3–4 ft – as it is easy to shorten it if necessary, but not so easy to lengthen it.

The open-end feeder tends to be reserved for stillwaters or slowly moving rivers. In fast water the groundbait is quickly dispersed, and here a block-end would be the usual choice. The best use for an open-ended feeder in fast water is probably to get sweetcorn or cubes of luncheon meat out to the swim, using a very big feeder plugged at each end with stiff groundbait. On one fast Trent backwater I always set up a big feeder rod with a big open-ended feeder just for this purpose, and don't always even put a hook on it. Four or five quick casts is all I need to get a fair load of luncheon meat out into the swim.

However, it's on stillwaters, where there are roach and bream, where the groundbait feeder comes into its own. You can either fill it with a mix of cereal groundbait and maggots or casters, or you can plug it firmly with groundbait at one end, pour your bait

Bream are big fish, and there's a greater chance of a big swimfeeder hitting one on its side, and scaring it, than a leger weight, which is much smaller.

Use fingers and thumb to fill an open-ended feeder.

into the middle, and plug the other end. This latter takes longer, but is particularly good for getting worms into the swim. Most anglers mix squats or casters with the cereal and fill the feeder with the mixture, pinching the groundbait firmly between finger and thumb when it's in the feeder so it doesn't fall out during the cast.

LAKE FISHING

To illustrate the way you use a groundbait feeder, let us look at an imaginary situation on a lake:

Depth – 15 ft at 30 yd out
Wind – strong from the side, but warm
Season – late summer

Locals have told you that the bream will probably be 30 yd out. And since you can't loose-feed you must get your casters and

squatts out some other way – either in balls of groundbait put out with a catapult, or thrown out, or in a feeder. The wind makes throwing out of the question, so you have a choice between catapult or feeder. On any big water when a strong wind is blowing, accuracy with a catapult may be affected, and in 15 ft of water the groundbait must be pretty hard to get to the bottom without starting to disperse, because there will also be quite a strong drift, which will take any loose groundbait and casters or squatts to one side, out of the swim. The drift will, in fact, probably be the opposite way to the wind because on big waters a strong undertow can develop. You can't be sure of this, however, so there will be a lot of guesswork involved. If you are confident that you can mix your groundbait so it won't break up until it nears the bottom, and think you can put it accurately into place

Adding crushed hemp sets a stream of particles rising to the surface, and then falling, attracting fish.

with a catapult, then you can fish over it with a straight leger. But if you are not sure of your abilities, then a groundbait feeder is the perfect answer. It will always take your groundbait to the spot you are casting to.

First job, even before you put your tackle together, is to mix some groundbait. The proprietary brands produced especially for swimfeeders are excellent.

MIXING GROUNDBAIT

Each day requires a slightly different approach to mixing groundbait, and in these conditions you need a fairly dry mix that will hold together well when squeezed once, tightly, in your hand. It will be slightly wetter than that used by, say, pole anglers who are only throwing it out a few feet from the side and expect it to break up as soon as it hits the surface. The mix for the feeder must stay intact until the tackle gets to the bottom. Experience will tell you when you have the mixture right – better still, check with an experienced angler, who will know instinctively when the consistency is right. For this swim it is better to err on the side of getting it too hard, so it gets right down, rather than too soft so it comes out when the feeder hits the water. White breadcrumbs need to be added to the main ingredients, as these tend to stiffen the mix, (brown breadcrumbs make it softer).

Many books tell you to sieve the groundbait as well, but for bream this is rarely necessary, although it does help get all the lumps out. However, the extra-large crumbs give them something to eat, and won't fill them up, so don't worry about them. When you are more experienced you may be happier using a sieve, as this does make the groundbait more consistent in its texture.

As always, add water in tiny amounts and mix thoroughly each time. When you think you have the consistency right, try it in a feeder. Pinch the ends to see if the groundbait holds in well, even when you drop the feeder back into the bowl from a height. If it does, leave it and tackle up. You will be amazed at how much the groundbait is going to dry out in the next 15 minutes, so be prepared to add a little more water when you start fishing, especially as you are going to add squatts and casters, and the groundbait will need to bind together even better to hold these in. Don't add any maggots to the groundbait yet.

This may seem time-consuming, but it is probably the biggest single factor that separates the competent but unsuccessful angler from the successful ones, whether you're floatfishing, leger fishing or using a pole. It really is that important.

TACKLE

As the wind is so strong, in the sample situation, we will choose a medium-sized feeder with $1/4 - 1/2$ oz of lead in a strip down the side. When groundbait is added it will weigh more, of course, and should carry the 30 yd to the swim fairly easily. And because bream are finicky feeders, tie 4 ft of 2-lb hook length to the 3-lb main line, using the water knot. In the wind this can be a bit tricky, so it helps to practise at home. Four ft of line not only gives a long, natural fall but also ensures that later, if you move the tackle along the bottom, the bait will be at least 3 ft from the feeder. This can be an important factor when bream fishing, although less so with most other species.

The choice of bite indicator can be difficult. Conditions are nearly perfect for slack-lining, but there will certainly be some undertow as the wind has been blowing hard for some hours, so unless you are experienced, you will be better off using a swingtip or quivertip. And, all round, the quivertip is the more versatile of the two, provided you can get a good angle between the tip and the line. So a quivertip it is – quite a light, sensitive one – and three rod rests go in to hold the rod steady. Sit with your back to the wind, as this is most comfortable, and no-one fishes well if they are uncomfortable.

The hook is a size 20 – a good all-round size that will take small roach and will also be capable of landing bream. The main requirement is that it should be forged, as hitting a bream at 30 yd in a strong wind will easily straighten a fine-wire hook unless you are very experienced in using this sort of tackle in these conditions. It should be a spade end whipped direct to the end. This is something else you can practise at home, and is essential for the leger angler to learn. If you buy only ready-whipped hooks you are stuck with the length and strength of nylon you are given. Whipping your own is not only quicker, but also cheaper and, most importantly, gives you complete freedom of choice of hook and line.

If you want to use a bigger bait like a worm, you will have to move up to a size 18 or a 16, or perhaps even a size 14. The 2-lb line will be quite sufficient to take these sizes, and is a good reason for starting off with a 2-lb hook length. If you start with, say, 1 lb, you are approaching danger level if you try to pull a size 16 into a fish at 30 yd, and using a size 14 to 1 lb line can easily result in a break. If you use a 2-lb hook length, you will be more likely to swop hook sizes when you need to.

In short, unless you are one of the small

minority of anglers who will take the trouble to change your tackle as soon as it is necessary, you will need to take the middle road all though your fishing career. Using the 3-lb main line is a great compromise, as it will cover almost all the situations you are likely to come across in an ordinary day's fishing. The only alternative is to have two or three leger rods set up, all with different main lines and hook lengths.

USING THE GROUNDBAIT FEEDER

When you are ready to start fishing, you should check the groundbait again. Almost certainly you will need to add a little more water and give it another good mix. You will have to add water at intervals during the day to keep it at the right consistency. Conversely, you should also make sure that if it rains your

Groundbait exploding from a feeder attracts fish. If your hook length is 3 ft longer than the link to your swimfeeder (top), then pulling the rig (centre) will pull the bait nearer to the cloud. If you get it dead right and pull it exactly 3 ft (bottom), your bait should be lying with the other free offerings. After you've had several casts the fish should, of course, be hunting over a wider area, because you can't get every cast into the same spot. Note, that as the feeder moves it may also kick up little clouds of mud.

3 ft

Above: Some top anglers camouflage their feeders.

Opposite: Small bream like this just love groundbait.

groundbait is covered, as too much water is worse than not enough! A mist spray such as those sold at garden centres is absolutely invaluable for adding a tiny amount of water, spread all over the bowl. If you work quickly you can get away with tipping some in, but this tends to wet the groundbait in one particular spot; a mist spray is much better. They are cheap as well, and probably as good value for money as any other accessory the leger angler will ever buy, because mixing groundbait to the wrong consistency is the worst mistake he can make (apart from smashing off when he strikes).

The next job is to bait the hook. You must always do this before filling the feeder, whatever type it is. If you don't, you will have to lay the feeder down for several seconds, during which time the maggots may start to break up the groundbait, especially if you have added a few pinkies, which are a very active maggot. Laying the tackle down also increases your chances of tangling the line in undergrowth. Use just a single hook maggot as bait, as this will take any size of fish which swims, and should at least bring a bite or two, which always gives the angler confidence.

Now is the time to fill the feeder, and you have a choice of adding either a load of

squatts and casters to the bowl of groundbait, or just a few in one spot, mixing them in and filling the feeder from part of the bowl. This latter is the way all the books and experts tell you is best, but it is not easy. So put in the squatts, give a mix round, and add a few casters in one spot, just mixing them in with your finger. Using just one hand (usually your left if you are right-handed), push the feeder lengthways through the groundbait for 1–2 in and shovel the feed in with your thumb at one and and your fingers at the other, packing it in fairly hard. Finally, pinch both ends together to make sure it is firm.

If you are clever, you will now try a little experiment. Drop the feeder into the water close to the bank where you can see it. Drop it from a fair height, and see what the groundbait does. Odd little pieces may float out as it sinks, but the main bulk should stay in the feeder for several seconds at least, before it starts floating out. After 30 seconds jerk the feeder to see whether this leaves most of the feed on the bottom. If it does, the consistency is about right. If you have used one of the special feeder groundbaits, you may see a sort of 'explosion' as the feed inside absorbs more water and forces its way out through the holes, making a little cloud. If this happens congratulate yourself – you have got it dead right. You can try this experiment at home to check your mixing procedure. Indeed you should do so. Twenty minutes spent experimenting like this is worth a whole season of trial and error on the bankside.

TACTICS

Bait the hook, re-fill the feeder and cast the rig out. Two to three feet of line between rod tip and swimfeeder is about right as you cast. Keep it nice and smooth, and stand if you find it easier. When the feeder hits the water feather the line with your forefinger to stop a big arc of line being blown out to one side by the wind, but don't click the bale arm shut. Put the rod tip down to surface level and watch as the tip is bent round by the sinking feeder. Then you will see the tip jerk back a little, and that is the time to shut the bale arm. As a very rough guide, an average leger

weight or swimfeeder takes about one second to sink about 2 ft, according to how tight the line is. The stronger the wind blows, the tighter the line tends to be.

Now is the time to take up the slack line and watch for a bite. However, you cannot do this properly until all the line has been sunk between rod tip and swimfeeder. Any line still lying on the surface will give all sorts of false indications as it is buffeted by the wind and waves. So plunge the rod under the surface as far as you can and reel in two or three turns very quickly. If you can see your line on the surface you will be able to see it cut through the water as you tighten up. Experience will tell you when you have sunk all the line, and then you can begin to watch for any indications of fish. Tighten as described earlier, so there is a tiny bit of slack line at the end of the quivertip, which will be straight. The drift will take up the slack line and the tip will probably end up with the tiniest bit of a curve in it.

If, as is common, nothing happens in the first five minutes or so, it is time to start moving the bait in the hope of getting a take. And as a general rule you should start by giving just tiny twitches. The reason for this is that the feeder is a large object, and could possibly frighten finicky fish at this stage if it suddenly jumps a long way, so the less movement you can give it the better for the moment, and a twitch of only $\frac{1}{2}$ in on the bait could be enough to induce a bite if a fish has its eye on it.

COUNTING THE RETRIEVE

If you catch a fish it is essential that you know the direction and distance at which you caught it. So you should always make a habit of counting the number of turns of the reel handle when you retrieve, and especially when you hook a fish. Then you will know whether you are getting back into the same spot each time. And after a little experience you will be able to make a fair guess at how far you are casting. The technically minded among you can, in fact, work out the approximate distance at which you are fishing by checking the retrieve rate of the reel and working out a simple equation. The equation gives you the circumference of a circle: 2 x pi x r, when r is the radius of the spool. Most modern match spools are about 2 in across, so the radius is 1 in. One squared is 1; and 2 x pi = 6.284, so one circle of the spool will retrieve about six inches. If the retrieve ratio is 4:1, you are retrieving about 2 ft of line per turn. The faster reels are nearer 5:1, which gives 2½ ft per turn. So 30 turns will, on average, work out at around 20–25 yd.

Counting is essential on lakes and wide rivers such as the Welland, Huntspill, Thames, Witham or the Great Ouse Relief Channel. On these waters an error in re-casting of two to three turns (about 6 ft) is usually acceptable, provided you have the direction right. Use some sort of marker on the opposite bank to achieve this. However, it is also useful on narrower waters, when an error of no more than about 3 ft may be needed to get you bait plum into the right spot. Then, one turn too many or too little may be sufficient to warn you that you do not have the distance quite right.

If you are fishing in a match on a lake it's definitely worth checking, early on, how many turns your competitors are taking to retrieve. Even if you can't see their hands you can always tell each time they make a turn by the way the rod tip bobs up and down! And if they have a good fish on, make every effort to check the turns if you can. It is also useful to count the number of turns you make when playing a good fish, so you get some idea of how far away it is at any one time.

FINDING THE FISH

There's an excellent chance, given that the conditions of a warm, strong wind are good for feeding fish, that you will get a bite or two as you search around the swim with the straight leger rig. If they are just small roach you may need only to remember the spot for exploring later and, having now given your groundbaited place a short rest, cast back into this swim with your leger tackle. If you don't get a bite it's worth considering whether you have the groundbait in the right place. Local knowledge, or advice from other anglers,

should be what you rely on most. And if you decide to groundbait another area you should make a mental note of how many turns it takes to retrieve your tackle from the original baited swim, for it's likely you will want to go back to it at intervals during the day.

A good tip is to slip a rubber band on to the spool when you think you have gone just a yard or two past the right spot. Then when you cast you can pull line off until the band is reached and reel in, say, five turns. If the line is then tight, you have it dead right. The books tell you to put the band on when you have it dead right, but I doubt whether the authors have ever actually done this – you need a few turns extra to allow for error. Alternatively you can slip the line under the little clip that is provided on some models for holding the line when you pack up. Or a dab of typist's correction fluid on the line can mark the required spot.

Bites in these warm, windy conditions are likely to be good, with fish putting a real bend in the quivertip. And you should be certain to set the clutch so it gives, and clicks, when you hit a fish, as in a strong wind it can sometimes be difficult to be sure whether you have a fish on, especially when using a swimfeeder. Watch the rod tip carefully so you can tell how much pressure you are putting on and where the fish is running. If you get good fish, stick with the groundbait feeder if everything works out all right, and if you want to introduce more feed do so using a bigger feeder. Remember that it will now weigh more, so you should consider changing to a 4-lb line. The 3-lb line is, however, a good all-round strength for this sort of fishing, and will comfortably cast up to ¾ oz or more provided the cast is smooth. There's no reason why you shouldn't introduce balls of groundbait by hand at any time, but only if you are certain you can get them into exactly the right position. At 30-yd range you can do a lot of damage by spreading the groundbait around, so you may put out six balls and get only one dead on target. Generally a feeder is the best bet at this range unless you have experience of adding groundbait balls. At worst, if you miscast a swimfeeder you put some feed outside your swim; at best it feeds your swim at the same rate at which you are getting bites – more bites, more feed; fewer bites, less feed.

The groundbait feeder is quite versatile, and if you want to put worms into the swim plug one end with groundbait, put the chopped worms in the middle, and plug the other end. Be sure to press firmly; don't risk the lot blowing apart as you cast. You may need to add just a little extra water for this job; it doesn't matter how the groundbait behaves, so long as it eventually discharges its contents. The main aim is to get the worms into your swim. In fact, without doubt this is the best method of all of getting worms into any swim. Even if you have been feeding groundbait by hand, it's worth putting on a groundbait feeder for that specific purpose, as they tend to break groundbait up.

Later in the day you may want to use a block-end feeder, which will allow you to put in maggots without groundbait. On the whole, in the conditions we have described there will be no advantage in doing this, as small roach, gudgeon and bream of all sizes love groundbait, and it's mainly in cold, difficult conditions that maggots on their own may bring more bites.

If you do get into a shoal of bream there's a very good argument for swopping the groundbait feeder for a straight leger, as a feeder dragged through the swim can disturb the bream. Worse, if you hook a fish the feeder is hanging from the line and is more likely to whack a fish than is a straight leger, because it's many times larger. In Ireland, where the bream shoals tend to be bigger than in England, and where they get less attention from the angler, this is not a consideration. In England, especially on waters that are match-fished, the fish almost always become finicky after a time, and it may mean the difference between getting four or five fish and going on to land a dozen or more.

With carp or roach, swopping to a leger weight will probably not be necessary, as the fish in the shoal soon recover from any fright. In fact, with carp in particular you may find that you play the fish for so long that while you are doing so the rest mop up all the groundbait you've put out. So a change to a larger feeder may be called for simply to get plenty of feed into the swim again.

FRAME FEEDERS

Though different from other feeders, the frame feeder is most closely aligned with the open-ended feeder. You can't put bait inside it, so you squeeze groundbait around the feeder. This means that it has to be just a little bit more 'sticky' than that used in most groundbait feeders, both to hold together while being cast, and to avoid it breaking up too soon when it hits the water, if this is what you require. A little extra water added to the mixture will help achieve this, as will looking round for a proprietary groundbait that has a good binding property. A frame feeder tends to be just a little quicker to use than filling a normal feeder, but you have to be doubly careful that the contents don't break up when you cast – so squatts and casters are much better than pinkies and hook maggots. You can also use sweetcorn in the groundbait.

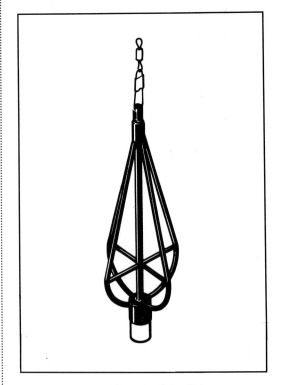

The strange-looking Thamesley frame feeder – groundbait is squeezed around it, but it works well.

CHAPTER NINETEEN

Block-End Feeders

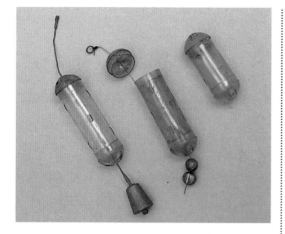

The Feederlink is a versatile feeder. Use it with the link provided (left); or on a nylon link with shot (centre); or you can cut it in half, replace the cap, and use it when you need only a few maggots inside (right).

For fast water, block-end feeders may need extra weight added. Special weights are sold for this purpose. In fast water you may have to glue a big ski weight on. This one (right) has also been wired on for extra security.

These are rather more versatile swimfeeders than the open-ended type, as they can be used easily on all types of water, from those that are completely still, like canals, to fast-moving rivers like the Severn or the Upper Trent.

Both ends have a cap, one of which must be capable of being removed so the feeder can be filled with maggots and replaced. It is important to make sure that this cap is attached to the line in some way so that it cannot be lost if it happens to work loose. Baits other than maggots can, theoretically, be used inside, but on a stillwater maggots are the obvious choice, as they will wriggle out through the holes along the sides and in the caps. On a faster water the current may be sufficient to force the bait out, and casters and hemp are often used either with, or instead of, maggots.

Several different models are on the market, and there is no real alternative to trying them to see which suits you best. The

Drennan Feederlink is particularly useful, because it can be easily cut down, and used with about a dozen maggots on winter days when the fish are finicky. This is a small, light feeder and would be used only on still or very slow-moving waters. On fast rivers the choice is very important, because the feeder must be strong enough to withstand constant casting and – even more important – constant filling. Unfortunately the action of repeatedly taking off the cap and replacing it, perhaps once a minute for five hours, always finds the weak spot if there is one. So until you settle on a particular model you will have to resign yourself to carrying several spares if you are going to fish one of these fast rivers that requires constant feeding. Feeders with screw-on caps are the strongest all-round, but it's easy to spend several seconds getting the cap screwed on properly, which is frustrating when the fish are feeding well. All may, at some time, need extra weight attached to them, because the secret of fast-water fishing with a swimfeeder is to get the weight absolutely right.

You will find that when several ounces of lead have been added, as may be necessary in really fast swims, the feeder itself is liable to disintegrate because of the extra strain it undergoes during casting, hitting the water and trundling along the bottom. Special ski-leads, which look like a couple of parallel skis, are sold for swimfeeders that need large amounts of weight added. The intended method of attachment is with short lengths of lead sold specially for the purpose, or with short spikes incorporated in the main weight, which go through the holes in the side of the swimfeeder. However, these tend to tear the feeder apart after a time. I have never found a better method of attaching ski leads, or similar large weights, than glueing them to the side with Araldite. This is a tip given to me by matchman Tom Bedder.

RIGS

The same type of paternoster as that used with a straight leger is probably the most popular set-up. And for stillwater fishing, or on slowly moving rivers, this is usually fine, allowing the bait to be fished 'on the drop' with a tail of up to 5 ft. However, for fishing fast water there are several points to be looked at, and two main methods of attachment, – paternoster-style, or with the line running through the feeder in exactly the same way as through a drilled bullet – both of which will work very well at different times.

On fast water the length of drop rarely needs to be longer than 2 ft or so, and often it is much shorter. The main problems are technical ones: making sure that the tackle is adequate, that the line doesn't twist round the link joining the feeder to the main line, and developing a routine so that as little time as possible is lost when the fish are feeding. It's useful to cover the two different types of water on which a block-end feeder is used, by fishing two imaginary swims. Wherever you use a block-end feeder, you are likely to need to adapt one of these techniques.

STILLWATER FISHING

Venue – very slowly moving river
Depth – 5 ft
Current – left to right
Wind – none
Sun – bright
Season – winter

These are conditions in which fish are likely to be very finicky, so a very cautious approach is called for – not only in the way you physically move up to the water, but also in the way you tackle the fish. The first point to make is a very important one that applies to almost all situations in which you will use a swimfeeder. You should use the minimum amount of weight that will allow you to cast to your chosen spot, provided this will also allow the feeder to just hold bottom. Although there is a slight movement here, the basic tactics will apply equally to a stillwater in winter, when the amount of wind and the distance you are casting will govern the amount of weight you use.

THE FEEDERLINK

With little or no movement on the water and no wind to inhibit casting it's likely that you will be able to use a tiny amount of weight – perhaps just a couple of swan shot. This is where the Feederlink comes into its own. It's a block-end feeder, but small and light with a nylon link running through the centre, and a weight attached to the end of the link. If this weight is too large, take out the link, thread your reel line through the centre of the caps so the line runs down the centre of the feeder when it is assembled, and pinch two swan shot on the end to hold the feeder on to the end of the line. This will provide all the weight you need for casting, and gives the extra advantage that if the feeder happens to become snagged when you have a fish on, constant pressure will pull the shots off the line, leaving the feeder behind, but at least

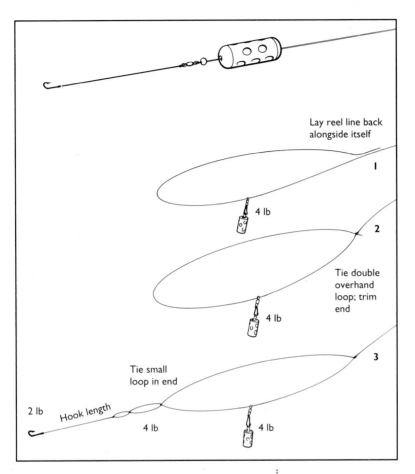

Lay reel line back alongside itself

I

4 lb

2

Tie double overhand loop; trim end

4 lb

3

Tie small loop in end

2 lb

Hook length

4 lb

4 lb

Two easy block-end feeder rigs.

Top: the line runs through the feeder, stopped by a bead.
Bottom, 1: The line goes through the swivel and a loop is formed.
2: The loop is tied in a double overhand knot.
3: A small loop is tied in the end of the large loop. This is used to attach a hook length using the Two-loop method.

you will still get the fish. It's also extremely easy to add or to subtract weight using this method, and you will be much more inclined to do so than if you were using a feeder with an integral weight – so your catches should increase.

There is no point in using a sliding swivel set-up with a light feeder such as this – everything must be kept as delicate as possible. So with the Feederlink tied to the end of the reel line the hook length can be attached using the same water knot as that used on a straight leger rig, or by tying a loop about 6 in above the Feederlink and looping the hook length to this. The water is cold and the sun bright, which both point to fish feeding not very actively (if at all) and only on the bottom. So there is no need today to set up a 'long tail'. The Feederlink is, though, a good tool to use if you want to present a slow-sinking bait, as it is light and will itself sink

fairly slowly. In summer when fishing at short range you can do worse than to use no weight at all on a Feederlink, just filling it with maggots to give it weight for casting and allowing the bait to sink slowly among the falling maggots. Today, choose an 18-in tail, which can be shortened if necessary, while the Feederlink is on a 6-in link. This set-up ensures that when the bait is in the water it is within 12 in or so of the feeder, and with fish perhaps unwilling to move many inches to pick up a bait it should pay dividends when they arrive in the swim. Two swan shot added to the feeder as described will be sufficient weight for casting, allowing the feeder to hold bottom but to be easily moved when necessary.

With no wind the choice of rod is not particularly important unless bankside vegetation dictates that you use a short one. However, it does mean you can use a very

light quivertip to see the most delicate of bites. If there is no movement at all, slacklining would also work.

Feederlinks are small, which is fine for the conditions in this swim, when not much feed will be needed. Should you ever need to put out a larger amount of bait you can always adapt another feeder by attaching it in the same way. However, you will find good anglers reluctant to use large block-end feeders on stillwaters. If the fish are feeding

A simple set-up, with the feeder running on a length of nylon between two swivels.

well enough to warrant using a lot of feed the open-ended feeder is the usual choice, as this gets rid of the groundbait and maggots more quickly than a block-end. You should always try to ensure that your feeder is empty by the time you retrieve, otherwise you will be spreading the bait over a much greater area than you may think. So the medium-sized or large block-end is usually used only where there is a definite current to push the maggots through the holes.

Put simply, if you fill a medium-sized feeder with maggots it could take them five to ten minutes, or even more, to all crawl through the holes on a stillwater. And if you're waiting that long for a bite you probably don't need as much bait as that anyway. As with all groundbaiting you can add more later, but you can't take it out once it's in the swim.

ROD POSITION

The river here is narrow – about as wide as the average canal – and because the sun is bright, and the fish will be easily spooked, you want to fish from as far away as possible. Start by casting downstream, to the right, about 15 yd away, and into the deepest water right in the middle of the river, which is only about 10 yd from your bank. While the general rule is that the rod is placed parallel to the bank when you are quivertipping, the conditions today suggest that you will be better off putting your rod straight out in front of you with the line streaming away to the right, but still forming a rough right-angle with the rod tip. You will find it easier to fish like this, as there is virtually no sideways pressure on the line from any current or wind. It would be perfectly all right to use a swingtip, but for most anglers it's easier to spot the tiny little nudges and quivers, that you are likely to get in these cool, bright conditions, on a quivertip.

CASTING DOWNSTREAM

You should almost always cast downstream if the water is moving slowly, as the current drifts the maggots in the feeder down and away from you. This ensures that the fish in a feeding shoal are working their way towards you, and they see your bait before they come across the feeder or see the line (fish almost always feed by keeping their heads into the current and working their way upstream). If you were to cast upstream to your left, you would encourage the fish to travel under your rod, past your reel line, and up to the feeder to find the source of food, with the result that you will almost certainly scare them in these clear, bright conditions when you strike, if they have not already been frightened by seeing the line.

Try to guess where the depressions are – on the outside of bends, wherever the flow is fastest, and opposite tributaries or culverts are obvious choices. Alternatively you can plumb the depth with a float, but you must take care to do it as quietly as possible on a cool day like this when fish may be timid. If you do this, then often a pole is the perfect answer – you can drop the plummet in, and lift it out, with very little disturbance. A good tip is to use a big plummet, as it is easy to tell when it has hit the bottom.

LINE TWIST

A single maggot on the hook is the obvious choice, and a pinkie is a good one to start with. A single maggot, of whatever type, helps prevent line twist, which can happen when you are using two maggots, and which is the bane of the leger angler's life. The line is less likely to twist if you retrieve slowly; or you can put the hook through the whole length of one maggot and nick a second one just on the point. After many years wrestling with the problem of line twist, which is especially bad if you use a hook length of less than 1 lb, I have plumped for using just one maggot on the hook as my usual solution.

If your hook length does twist, you must change it, because it has been weakened, and will only twist again and again, even doing so as the bait sinks, not just on the retrieve. It's a real bind in cold weather, so try to avoid it at all costs. I have found that ½-lb line is much less liable to twist than the lower strengths, but on a day like today you must aim simply to get a bite or two to give you confidence, and that will mean starting with a size 24 to a 12-oz bottom and a single pinkie. If that does not bring bites, change to a single squatt, which is even smaller.

Just one point about a size 24 on 12-oz

nylon. You would be well advised to buy such hooks ready tied unless you have a hook tier and are extremely confident that you can whip the hook on without kinking the light nylon. I have whipped hooks on by hand, on the bank, for 35 years. However, I would not attempt to do so with 12-oz nylon as it is so delicate, and I leave a kink of some sort on two occasions out of three, which means I have to re-whip it – a time-consuming business even when the hands are warm, and next-to-impossible in cold weather.

A TYPICAL DAY

Let's start fishing. Bait the hook with a single pinkie, then fill the feeder, ensuring that the cap is firmly replaced. Cast immediately, otherwise the maggots in the feeder may start falling out. If the holes are too large you will know immediately, as you will see pinkies falling out as you cast. In that case some strips of electrician's tape wound round the feeder in a spiral will make the holes smaller. You make the first cast 15 yd downstream, and after five minutes and three or four little twitches, you haven't had a bite. Repeat this routine, but casting 1 ft closer each time.

Thirty minutes go by, and you've made six casts and haven't had a bite. It's worth trying a couple of yards further out; cast, tighten the line just a little (in this shallow water there's not a lot of slack line anyway), and put the rod on the rest, allowing the very light flow to take up the remaining slack. Suddenly there's the tiniest of nudges on the tip – hardly enough to strike at. Retrieve and examine the pinkie. At first sight it looks untouched; but if you look very closely you can see it has been mouthed, as the skin is slightly scratched – there's no other way to describe it. It looks rough when compared with a pinkie from the bait box. It's important to look very hard at the bait after every single cast on a day like this, otherwise you can easily miss these markings. And to re-use that maggot will be a waste of time as you will probably never get a bite on it. You can tell by the fact that the skin is scratched well up the maggot that the fish has had it in its mouth, which is a good sign, showing that they are willing to feed

properly, although they may have to be enticed.

The other main damage you'll often find on a maggot is that the tail has been sucked. You can clearly see when a fish has just marked the very tip. This indicates either a very small fish having a go, or that the fish are very finicky indeed and is, on the whole, a bad sign, suggesting that you may struggle to catch anything. If there are bream in the water the pinkie may just look limp. It's not easy for an inexperienced angler to spot this, but the maggot looks soft and stretched, although it may recover within a few seconds. Don't worry too much about checking this today, as the cold water can also make the maggot stretch and go lifeless.

This is the time to put a squatt on the hook, though for the moment keep filling the feeder with pinkies, as it's better to get them feeding on the larger-sized maggots if you can. The squatt is only half as big as the pinkie, and the size 24 hook is about right for it, anything much larger will look conspicuous. Re-cast and start concentrating – just one bite can set the adrenalin flowing. At least you know that there's something out there. And it's worth laying your hand very lightly on the rod handle ready to strike, being careful not to move the rod or you may get false indications. Even your heart thumping can transmit itself to a sensitive quivertip on a calm day like this.

After only 10 seconds there's a definite movement of about $\frac{1}{2}$ in on the quivertip and you've struck instinctively. It's not a big fish, but remember that you've only a 12-oz hook length, so take it easy. It's a roach of about 2 oz, which you can just about lift out. Anything larger will need the landing net as the hook length is so fragile. Better to net all small fish than have one wriggle, as you swing it in, and break the very delicate nylon.

The 10-second delay between casting and getting a bite shows that the fish probably took the bait before it hit the bottom. The hook is only a fine-wire model, and very small, so with the maggot on it sinks slowly. If you should move up to a size 20 forged hook it will sink very much faster. You should bear this sink-rate in mind when fishing with small baits like a single squatt or a single pinkie. Anyway, if you get two or three bites quickly it will be worth lengthening the drop from 18 in to 3 ft, in case the fish come up in the water.

Out the line goes again, and again you've got a roach. There must be something in this spot that's holding the shoal, so try to pinpoint it. In this case it's right on the point of the reflection of a bush growing on the far bank, and in a direct line between you and a church spire in the distance. Pole anglers don't have this problem because their pole and fixed-length line ensure that they get the bait into the same spot each time.

It's worth putting a pinkie on again, to see whether the fish will take a bait this big, especially as you have kept using pinkies in the feeder. So out the tackle goes again, and you wait for a bite. Sure enough the tip moves just that $\frac{1}{2}$ in and again you've got a fish on. This is a small bream of about 3 oz, which fights quite well on this delicate tackle and should certainly be netted.

BITES

As with all legering, you will often find that the small, definite movements of the quivertip or swingtip produce a much higher percentage of successful strikes than the days when fish take the tip right round. This probably happens because when the fish are feeding well, they are taking the bait casually, and, feeling quite secure they stay where they are, looking for more feed. So the movement at the tip is minimal. On the days when the tip really cracks round, this could be due to the fish being nervous about feeding, but suddenly making up their minds to take the bait, and going screaming off with it as if they are half-expecting a problem. It's noticeable on heavily fished carp waters that lots of bites nearly take the rod out of your hand. Whatever the reason, today has produced three fish from four bites, so far, and all have been slight, but confident.

CHANGING CONDITIONS ON STILLWATERS

It's now about 10 o'clock in the morning, and a slight breeze is springing up. This happens on perhaps three out of four calm days, and is almost always a good sign, provided the wind is not too cold. On waters up to 5–6 ft deep, you can now expect the fish to feed with much more confidence, as the ripple on the water makes movement on the bank less obvious. And even on deeper waters – up to 15–20 ft deep – that ripple definitely makes a difference. Also, cloud is now covering the sun, which is an excellent sign as nine times out of ten sport is better on an overcast day than in bright sunlight.

The next cast has produced another small bream – a good sign, as bream tend not to roam about quite as much as roach, though they are both shoal fish. And now, with the ripple and cloud cover, the next fish is about 6 oz. As things look like hotting up a bit, it would be wise to change the hook length for something stronger. If you are experienced you could try a size 22 hook to 1 lb; if you do not feel confident about playing reasonable fish on this tackle, you could use a size 20 to $1\frac{1}{2}$ lb nylon.

A change to the 20 hook means re-tackling completely by cutting the reel line above the water knot, tying the hook length on via a water knot, 9 in above the feeder, and then re-tying the Feederlink to the end of the reel line. It would be wise to allow a 3-ft hook length to give a longer drop. Then the spade end hook is whipped direct to the hook length. The beauty of this system is that you can use any combination of nylon and hook size. And if you can't whip the hook on by hand on the bank, buy a hook-whipping machine. They cost only £1–£2 and are worth their weight in gold, saving you their cost many times over if you are used to buying ready-whipped hooks. The disadvantage of this water knot system lies in the time it takes to re-tie it – probably only a couple of minutes, but it can seem like a lifetime when the fish are feeding.

With a 3-ft drop on the bait you now have

a chance of picking up more fish. However, if things should get hard and you think you are getting bites you can't see reduce it back to 18 in. If that doesn't work, go back to the size 24 hook on a 12-oz bottom. However, the cautious start has paid dividends, and on a winter's day like this you can expect fish to feed on and off until about 2 pm or slightly later. When you suddenly feel the temperature drop, that's the time to be prepared to go home, for the fish are likely to stop feeding altogether.

MOVING WATER

Venue – fast-moving river
Depth – 6 ft
Current – left to right
Wind – strong downstream
Sun – bright
Season – summer

The first objective in this swim is to get a fairly constant stream of bait out to at least the centre of the river some 20 yd away. Loose-fed maggots will probably be swept away in seconds, before they have had time to sink; and an open-ended feeder could have its contents washed out very quickly before even it hits the bottom. Heavy cereal groundbait might work, but you will have to make it very stiff indeed, which is not easy, and groundbaiting like that gives you no chance to search the river. You would have to put several very big balls into one spot and take a chance on that spot holding fish. The answer is a block-end feeder, which will be baiting the swim with 40 to 50 maggots every time you cast out. In addition you can use a heavy feeder, with at least 2 oz on it, so it gets to the bottom immediately and stays there, releasing its contents slowly. Use hook maggots, as they are heavier than pinkies or squatts, and will not be swept away quite so quickly. In any case you need to use a fair-sized hook because you are after chub and barbel from 6 oz up to 4 lb or even more.

TACKLE

With a feeder weighing 2 oz you must use a proper feeder rod. An ordinary light quivertip will not have enough power to cast a heavy weight, nor to retrieve it, nor to play a big fish in this type of water. The exact make is not important, but you should be prepared to pay a fair amount for a powerful rod to do the job properly. If you don't have a feeder rod, a carp rod will do quite well.

The line will need to be around 5 lb or more, to cope with the strain of continual casting and retrieving as well as the bumps it will receive as it rolls down the swim and possibly into snags.

The reel should be strong, though you'll get away with your normal match reel with a bit of luck. If you are going to fish a water like this consistently, you should get a big, strong reel – the sort used by specimen hunters, as the continual hard use will eventually ruin a delicate match reel. It should not be automatic – the weight of the big feeder on the line will certainly affect the automatic spring system. If you have to use an automatic, be sure to open the bale arm by flicking the arm and hold the line with your finger when you cast.

The rod rest is very important. The line is so strong and thick that the current has a far greater effect on it than on the thin lines used for stillwater angling. To reduce this pull, it's usual to hold the rod high so as little line as possible is in the water. Unfortunately these fast rivers almost invariably have rocky bottoms into which it is difficult to push a rod rest. Some anglers use a sea angling tripod, which is absolutely perfect as it can be positioned anywhere in a second or two. The best alternative is the commercially produced rest, which has to be pushed into the bottom but which has a swivelling arm to hold the end of the butt at elbow level. This means that the rod tip is very high indeed. If you haven't got this, you'll have to use two normal rests – one high and one low.

On waters which hold big chub and barbel the hook must be forged. You can still go down to a size 20 if you wish, but a fine-wire hook is asking for trouble. You'll stand a better chance of hooking a fish on a forged size 20 than on a fine-wire 14, which will almost certainly straighten when you hook a decent fish.

THE FEEDER

For simplicity, use a Mal Storey Feeder, which has a large strip of lead down the side, with the ends bent round the edges of the body. The cap on the bottom is stapled to the body, while the cap at the top is removable. This has a long slit in it, through which a loop of line will go if you want to use it paternoster-style. This loop is then fixed to the main reel line via a sliding swivel. The other end of the loop is attached to the feeder by looping it under the strip of lead.

The alternative method of fixing the feeder is rather easier, and becoming quite popular among anglers who regularly fish these fast rivers for chub and barbel. The line goes through the centre of the feeder, and is prevented from hitting the bait by a bead. This, in turn, is stopped either by the knot joining the hook length, or by a swivel. Easiest of all is to carry the feeder already threaded on to an 18-in length of nylon with a tiny swivel at either end, and a small bead at the bottom so the swivel does not jam into the feeder. Just tie the top swivel to your reel line, and tie the hook length to the bottom swivel. Then you are ready to start fishing. You will find, when you first fish fast water like this, that simplicity is the key to catching fish, and if the feeder happens to become damaged it takes only seconds to tie on another. This system also does away almost completely with tangles.

The paternoster method involves having about 4 in of line from the feeder to a swivel, through which the reel line runs, also stopped by a bead. To prevent tangles you can cover this link with rubber tubing. The great advantage of this method is that should the feeder become jammed in rocks or a snag the fish can still be played. The line runs through the swivel, and there's an excellent chance of the fish pulling the feeder free. A Power Gum link is also available. This cushions the strike, and you should certainly carry some. Apart

from being ready to use, they work very well, allowing you to hit the fish, when you strike, before you move the feeder. And they could considerably increase your hooking rate.

As to the make of feeder, this is a matter of personal preference, and it largely depends on the type of river you fish. The solid green feeders are very strong indeed and are deservedly popular, while there are also flat feeders, which theoretically hold bottom better. These are nice in snaggy water where you need to cast to a spot and hold the feeder there. The round ones, particularly those that have a groove down the side to take a strip of lead, are good if you want to search a water by rolling the feeder along the swim in the flow. You must realise that lead attached to the outside of the feeder will always inhibit the rolling effect. Some feeders have a compartment inside in which you can insert extra weight. These are a delight to use, although just a little bit fiddly. On most feeders there is a weak spot somewhere that will cause them to break after prolonged, hard use. Sometimes this is the body, or it could be the point of attachment. You must be prepared, therefore, with some spare feeders in your box. And you must also have some small, add-on weights. These come in two or three shapes. The most popular are the simple $\frac{1}{4}$ oz strips, each end of which is inserted through a hole and bent round inside to hold it. These small weights are the key to success with this type of fishing.

Today you can use the simple set-up with the line running direct through the feeder, which holds 2 oz of weight, and a forged size 14 to 2 ft of 3-lb line tied to the bottom swivel.

FILLING THE FEEDER

As with the Feederlink, it's important to bait the hook first and then fill the feeder and cast straight away. The size of the holes can be very important on this fast-running water. If the feeder seems to be releasing the bait too fast, the strip of electrician's tape partly blocking the holes will work; but if, as can happen when the fish are feeding well, you are getting a bite before the feeder is completely empty, the holes should be enlarged. The pliable plastic type can be easily cut with a pair of scissors. It's important not to be playing a fish with maggots still pouring from the feeder, as this disperses your bait instead of concentrating it in one spot.

An apron is essential on this type of water, as it's often necessary to stand in the margins. A pint or two of maggots is put in the front of the apron, and it saves an enormous amount of time. Just pull the feeder over the apron pocket and as you scoop maggots in it doesn't matter if they fall out – they just end back in the apron. Start with three hook maggots from the same pocket, as bait.

It's difficult to know where to start fishing if you have no local knowledge. However, the fish tend to stay within 1 to 2 ft of features on the bottom, and these will often be given away by swirls on the surface. The snag itself will be above the spot where the swirls start, and perhaps a few feet upstream. If there are no obvious features, start by casting just upstream. This way the maggots will not end up too far downstream. If you were to cast well downstream, the maggots could finish up 40 yd below you, and you would have no hope of trundling the feeder down to the shoal. This goes against the advice given for fishing a slowly moving water, but in a fast water the fish are likely to be much more active, ignoring the line in their eagerness to get at the bait. And getting the shoal feeding is your first priority.

Bait the size 14 forged hook with three maggots, fill the feeder, replace the cap, and cast out just upstream, to your left. The cast is more of a swing than a whiplash cast such as you might give a light leger lead, and now you can see why you need a proper swimfeeder rod. Two ounces doesn't sound much to cast, but in fact it's a very heavy weight. Don't tighten the line – leave the bow – the current will tighten this up in just a few seconds.

THE BOW

The secret to fast-water swimfeeder fishing is the bow in the line, which should be quite big. And the bigger the bow, the lighter feeder you will be able to use to hold bottom. If you have the weight of the feeder correct, a fish taking the bait will dislodge the feeder, which will hurtle downstream, pulled by the bow. This will pull the hook into the mouth of the fish. And that's all there is to it! You would not believe the number of anglers who make things difficult for themselves by ignoring this simple procedure. Of course, there are days when it doesn't work out quite right, or the fish are feeding too cautiously. But you must get the basics right before you

1: In fast running water you should allow a bow to form in the line.
2: A fish will normally approach the bait from downstream.
3: It will continue upstream until the line to the swimfeeder is tight and it starts to move.
4: If you have the weight exactly correct, the moment the fish dislodges the swimfeeder it will be swept downstream and will hook the fish itself. This registers on the rod as a slack-line bite.

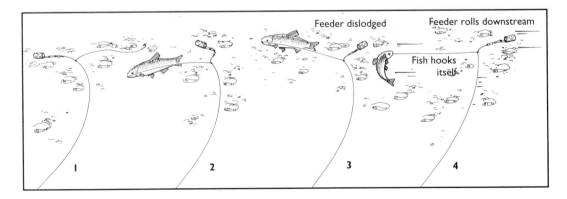

Feeder dislodged   Feeder rolls downstream

Fish hooks itself

1   2   3   4

start adapting them. It's exactly the same principle as beach anglers use; and it's probably the biggest single fault most of them make – they don't get the bow big enough.

In a match, it's against the rules to cast upstream, of course. Even so, many clubs will allow you to pinch the odd yard in this fast water, and since everybody is fishing the same way there's no problem. It definitely helps improve catches. Today you are not in a match, so it's upstream, and the feeder is swept by the current downstream, to rest a few feet to your right. Leave the bow in the line where it is, put the rod on the rest and watch the rod tip.

The first priority on a water like this is to get plenty of maggots into the swim. After about 45 seconds retrieve the tackle and repeat the exercise, checking that no maggots are left in the feeder. When you first wind the feeder back against a fast current you'll probably think you've got a fish on – everybody does. However, after a few casts you get to know how much resistance the current puts up. When you get a fish on, you'll be left in no possible doubt!

Ten casts later, without a bite, and it's time to leave this one a bit longer. Three minutes go by and there's still no response. Now pick the rod up and ease it upwards slowly, watching the line tighten. Suddenly, as the feeder starts rolling downstream, the line will slacken. Now just put the rod back on the rest. Did you see that? As you put the rod down the tip started jerking violently back and forth. The movement of the bait obviously tempted a fish to take it, and it dislodged the feeder again. The bite is not that described in text books ('...suddenly the rod tip slammed down'), but a real dance. Pick the rod up. There, you have a fish on. Hooked by itself. And it's really bending the rod over. You have 5-lb line on, with a 3-lb bottom, so you can afford to give the fish some wellie. It takes a few fish to get used to the tackle, and you'll be amazed at how the current magnifies the power of the fish.

Now the fish goes across the current, and you're keeping the rod high, which is good. Lowering it only gives the current more line to push against, helping the fish and increasing your arm strain. Try to get the fish into the side, where the water is slacker. It's been on two or three minutes and it's in the side, about 15 yd downstream. You'll need a bit of patience now, bringing it up against the moderate flow. It's a chub, and when it opens its mouth the current almost sweeps it downstream again. Bring the fish in close – it is a slow process. You'll find that you need to bring it well over the net. You can't lean forward to push the net that extra foot out because as you do so the current takes the fish downstream and out of range. So bring it well upstream, and don't lift the net until the fish is completely over the rim, remembering that as soon as you release pressure, even slightly, the fish will sweep downstream again.

Now you can examine your prize. The fish you thought was at least 3 lb turns out to be about 12 oz! You have to experience this type of fishing before you can truly believe it. Incidentally, if the feeder runs directly along the reel line you have a small advantage when you land fish; the feeder appears above the surface of the water earlier than it would if it were on a paternoster link, and this reduces the current pressure. It's a small point, but a good reason for choosing this method for your first trip or two.

HOLDING THE ROD

It's impossible to beat holding the rod all day. You can feel weed catching the line, the feeder bumping over stones, and even fish mouthing the bait – something you can't see on the rod tip. This creates a sort of rasping feeling, as if someone was sawing through the line. You also get to distinguish gudgeon bites from 'proper' bites given by better fish. Best of all, you can move the feeder just the smallest amount and be prepared for a bite a few seconds later. Many times you will find yourself playing fish without remembering how you struck – it's an instinctive reaction. On a snaggy water, if you are holding the rod, you also have that second of extra time to hold the fish away from its safe haven, for a big barbel will often be almost in a snag when it takes the bait. It's not unusual for even the best anglers to have days when almost every

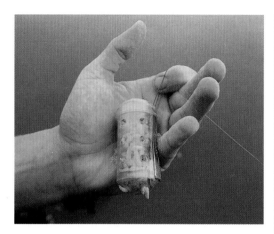

Always bait your hook before filling the feeder, as maggots will soon crawl out of the holes.

fish seems to get snagged. Whether they come out is in the lap of the gods. All you can do is to keep a tight line for as long as you think you have a chance of getting the fish, or give it slack line when you're desperate.

Tactics

As a general rule, fish will feed in quite a small area of the river – perhaps in a depression, or near a bed of weed or a rock. And as long as you keep catching fish you should continue to cast to the same spot, and fish the same way. At some time, though, bites will dry up, and then it's time to alter tactics. When the fish are feeding, a drop down to a smaller feeder, which is quicker to fill and easier to cast can pay dividends. You can go back to the big feeder, containing more maggots, if the fish go off the feed. Alternatively, they may have moved to another spot, and you should start searching the whole length of your swim, rolling the feeder down as far as you can. Often the fish will have holed up in a spot downstream and be waiting for the next lot of maggots to float by. If that doesn't work, try casting close to the far bank, or close to your own bank.

Look for obstructions in fast water, as these tend to hold chub and barbel.

A 12-oz chub will put up a good fight in stream water.

There are plenty of times, however, when you get the feeling that the fish are still there but not taking the bait properly. Perhaps you are getting half-hearted bites, and still hooking the odd fish. Then you should consider changing down to a size 20 hook with a single maggot; the hook must be forged, though. You might also want to drop the hook length down to 2 lb, or perhaps even 1½ lb if you are really desperate. Before you do that, however, you should consider changing the weight on the feeder. Try increasing the weight first (it's easier that way) by adding the small strips of lead available from many tackle shops, or by inserting weight in the little compartment provided on some models. An increase in weight help you to fish more accurately, although it will mean it's not so easy to twitch the bait.

More likely is that you should lighten the weight, and put a bigger bow in the line to hold it on the bottom. At least 50 per cent of the times when I have had fish go off in this fast water, lightening the feeder has put me in touch with the fish again.

CHANGING CONDITIONS ON MOVING WATER

On most fast rivers, the flow can alter quite surprisingly during the day, and it's easy to carry on fishing without realising that the current is now only half the speed compared to half an hour ago. So keep an eye on the water level. It's a good idea to put a bank stick on the edge of the water, or to note the water level against the bank, so you get some idea of whether more water is coming down. If the level drops, it's odds-on that the current is slackening, and if it comes up it's likely the flow has increased. A change in current speed can also change the character of the swim, and may push the fish from one spot to another as the flow takes different courses.

Unfortunately, an increase in flow often means that cold water is coming down the river, and this can put fish off the feed. Luckily on fast waters the fish are used to temperature changes, so they're likely to return to feeding as soon as the flow eases. This also applies to the slower-moving rivers, although here you are much more likely to notice a change in flow speed.

KEEP NETS

You'll need to pay special attention to the position of the keep net in this type of fast water. The first priority is to make it stable, and this may mean using two or three bank sticks. Also, you must have it pointing downstream, and not across the current, because fish in the net will face into the current, and a big fish is unable to do this if the net is across the current. Also, it may not be able to move round. Correctly positioned, the net will allow the fish to line up behind each other. Be warned, though, that chub have a habit of launching themselves out of the mouth of the net, so place it well above the surface. One trick is to float a groundbait bowl in the top, allowing enough room at the edge to place a fish in the net when you catch one.

SECTION FOUR

BAITS

by John Wilson

In our prepacked world, where the convenience factor continues to affect even the baits we use for fishing, there is more reason than ever for 'going back to nature' and, where possible, exploring some of the old values. For instance, simply gathering your own baits is one of the true delights of fishing, providing through a valuable learning curve a greater knowledge of natural history and even increased catches of difficult species.

They say there is nothing new in fishing, and taking the bait scene as a whole, there is much truth in this adage. For instance, even boilies, which, together with shop-bought maggots, are by far the most commonly used of all freshwater baits today, evolved as a replacement for parboiled potatoes, the skin of which protects them from nuisance species pecking away until a carp happens along. But potatoes will still catch, and are especially worth a try in waters where the carp have never seen them, because they will have no reason to treat them with suspicion, as they do all the more common offerings.

This is what bait selection is really all about: choosing one which is readily available, yet of which the fish are not already suspicious. So be adventurous and always willing to experiment.

John Wilson
Great Witchingham, 1993

From his own well stocked, lily-clad lakes in deepest Norfolk, John practises what he preaches, catching carp on a variety of natural and manufactured baits.

CHAPTER TWENTY

Natural Baits

Because many natural baits are either part of a river's ecosystem, or live close by and therefore often find their way into the water, as worms do during floods, for instance, fish come to accept them as part of their natural diet and show far less caution than they do to manufactured baits.

Varying little in format from their freshwater counterparts, even natural baits from the sea, such as cockles, prawns and shrimps, are devoured with equal relish, while the shop-bought maggot closely resembles the grub-like larvae of countless species of aquatic insects which live out their yearly cycle on the bottom of lakes and rivers everywhere as the staple diet of most fish of the carp family, or cyprinids. Many natural baits, both terrestrial and water-borne, also have the benefit of being entirely free. Gathering them vastly increases the angler's awareness of natural history, and he can only be a better all-round fisherman with such knowledge.

By collecting lobworms during periods of wet weather and storing them in his wormery, John can go perch fishing anytime — even during high summer when the ground has been dry for weeks.

There is also a greater sense of achievement from catching fish on naturals which have been collected solely for use as fishing bait. Permanently kept in the boot of my car is a strong, rectangular-framed, micromesh net (available from any aquarium shop) with a 24-in handle; a one-gallon plastic bucket with a pull–off lid with plenty of air holes, which will hold anything from caddis grubs to slugs; and a torch. All three items, which together cost less than three pints of maggots, have frequently provided me with natural baits when far from civilization and even purchasing a loaf of bread was out of the question. The point is, if you always restrict yourself to shop-bought maggots, casters or boilies, you could find yourself at a loss should the chance of an impromptu session suddenly present itself.

For certain species, chub in particular, heavy natural baits such as a big, fat slug or a lobworm simply have no equal for both casting and catching during the summer and autumn. I personally would feel at a great disadvantage if I did not collect these and many other natural baits for use on a regular basis when river fishing.

TERRESTRIAL BAITS

Lobworms

I can't think of a freshwater species that I haven't caught on lobworms, not only in Britain but in freshwater the world over. It is probably the closest thing there is to a universal bait. Barbel, tench, perch, eels, catfish, chub and big bream all bolt lobs down greedily, and under certain circumstances there is no finer bait for specimen roach. Wait until the river has been over the banks for a few days and is running like strong tea, then leger or stret-peg a lobworm on a size 8 hook close into the bank, and you could prove the point.

Lobworms are also a superb bait for carp, which react rapidly to the gyrating movements of a lob freelined among lily pads, into a scum line or beneath overhanging willow branches. Wherever dense bottom weeds prove troublesome with other baits, try injecting a little air from a hypodermic syringe into the head of the lob and adjust the hooklength to the weed's height so that the bait floats easily visible, above the weed. Tench and big bream fall for this technique too.

You must, of course, first collect your lobs. Freshly dug vegetable and flower beds are an excellent source of worms. So is, for those of you who live in the country, a newly ploughed field. Hundreds of seagulls seem to appear from nowhere when in mild, damp weather worms by the thousand are turned over in this way. A few polite words to the farmer could result in a tinful within minutes. But don't simply go marching across the field; always ask first.

My favourite method of collecting worms by the hundred is to visit the local cricket pitch after dark (as night falls worms start to come up out of their holes) following a good downpour. If rain has been falling steadily for a few days, all the better. Wait until it has stopped or reduced to a fine drizzle — these are the best worm-collecting conditions of all — and worms will be lying there, most of them out of their holes, just waiting to be picked up with the aid of a wide-beam torch of medium power. Don't use a powerful spot-beam torch, or they will disappear in a flash. Try not to engage in a tug of war with every worm whose tail is firmly down its hole when you grip hold of the head. Pulled or stretched lobworms are fine for the next day's fishing only, but should not be kept for future use in case they die and contaminate the others.

For ease of collecting lobs, hang a one-gallon plastic bucket on a strap around your neck at chest height. Also, don't scrape your feet when walking, as the vibrations will have the worms scurrying down their holes long before the torch beam catches them. Creep along, raising each foot like a strutting cockerel. It may look stupid, but if you want a bucketful of worms, it is worth the effort of being stealthy.

For fishing sessions I like to pack lobworms into fresh sphagnum moss with plenty of room to spare inside a two-pint bait box. Another excellent medium for transporting them in is sopping-wet, shredded newspaper. This was a tip passed on to me by my old mate, Fred J. Taylor after one of his many trips to the USA, where they call worms 'night crawlers' and keep them in hotel-like comfort. To 'condition' lobs, as the Americans say, put freshly gathered worms (a dozen to a bait box on the assumption that if one dies you can lose no more than another 11) into a two-pint bait box containing strips of wet newspaper. Tear the paper into 1-in strips and soak it thoroughly in a bowl of cold water before squeezing out some (not all) of the water. When all the bait boxes have their dozen or so worms in wet newsprint, simply leave them in the fridge (if you have an understanding partner) until required. They may be left for several weeks, but after a week their 'conditioning' is usually complete and inside will be the fattest, most superb lobworms you have ever seen.

An important part of keeping lobworms is not allowing them to become hot. Below 0°C (32°F) they freeze, while above 10°C (50°F) they will deteriorate quite quickly. A

Lobworm storage box.

temperature somewhere in between — hence the fridge — is ideal. Something you might like to try is making a lobworm storage box for holding up to several hundred worms at a time (see diagram). This is constructed from $\frac{1}{2}$-in marine ply cut into four squares of 20 x 20 in (the sides) and two pieces of 21 x 20 in (the lids). Air holes of $\frac{1}{8}$ in in diameter are drilled through the sides of the box and an inside rim of 1 x $\frac{1}{2}$-in softwood is nailed and glued to the inside of both lids to form a seal.

Inside the box put masses of newspaper strips (you need lots of old papers) well-soaked and wrung out, followed immediately by the fresh lobworms. I can't overstress the word 'fresh' here, for dead worms all too rapidly contaminate the others. Keep the box on a concrete or stone floor, in the garage for instance, and in subdued light. Every three or four days simply turn the entire box over carefully and the worms, now at the top, will work their way through the wet newspaper down to the bottom again. Provided it is kept cool, this 'lobwormery' will keep worms fresh and ready for use for many weeks.

Wet shredded newspaper is an excellent

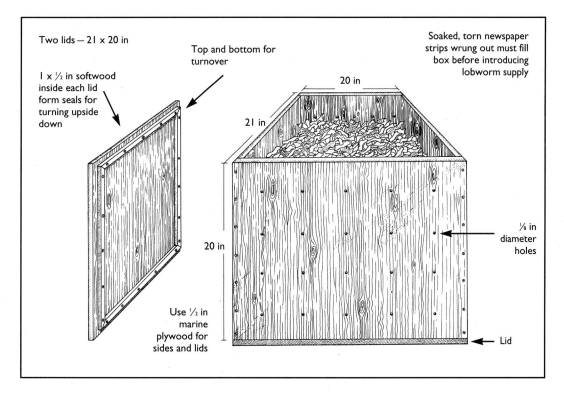

Two lids — 21 x 20 in

1 x $\frac{1}{2}$ in softwood inside each lid form seals for turning upside down

Top and bottom for turnover

Soaked, torn newspaper strips wrung out must fill box before introducing lobworm supply

20 in

21 in

20 in

Use $\frac{1}{2}$ in marine plywood for sides and lids

$\frac{1}{8}$ in diameter holes

Lid

Carp working their way through submerged marginal sedges and reeds or lilies are absolute suckers for a freelined lobworm. And if you cannot achieve the distance with one worm, then put two up on a size 4 hook tied direct to the reel line.

medium for transporting any kind of worm when travelling abroad, should Customs prohibit taking peat, soil or moss into the country. Anyone travelling to the Republic of Ireland, for instance, could have their entire stock of worms confiscated if they are packed in an organic medium.

Dendrobenas

The next worm down in size from the lobworm is the Dendrobena, a chunky 3-in red worm imported to Britain from the Netherlands, where it is very common. These worms are just the right size for perch, tench and bream, and are available from most good tackle shops ready packed in plastic boxes with around 15 worms in each. This may not seem many, but since they are at least twice as thick as brandlings, just one worm on the

hook offers the fish a good mouthful. I am sure I have occasionally come across exactly the same species of worm when moving old, rotten logs and the like, but never in great enough quantity to guarantee a supply of them for bait.

Brandlings

This lively, gyrating worm, easily recognizable by the yellowy-orange rings around its tail and the pungent yellow fluid which seeps out as you hook it, can be obtained in three ways. The cheapest is to politely ask a farmer if you can collect a supply by turning over his manure heaps. If this turns out to be a regular occurrence, saving you many pounds over a season, don't forget to drop him off a bottle of Christmas cheer.

Brandlings are also readily available from most tackle shops and usually come packed in peat at around 50 to a tub. But you might prefer to make your own wormery cum compost heap at the bottom of the garden from both garden and household waste, so as to have a supply of worms readily available

Pack a dozen or so to each two pint bait box filled with sopping wet torn newspaper strips and leave them to chill for a week in the fridge for lobworms conditioned to absolute perfection.

It may seem strange but king ragworms and lugworms from saltwater make a great change bait for freshwater species like eels, perch, chub and pike.

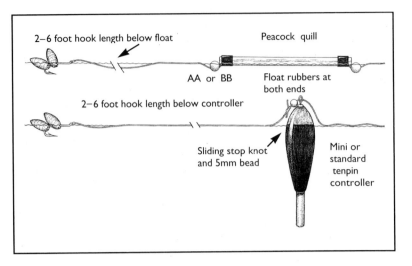

2–6 foot hook length below float

Peacock quill

AA or BB

Float rubbers at both ends

2–6 foot hook length below controller

Sliding stop knot and 5mm bead

Mini or standard tenpin controller

Presenting casters with a tenpin or flat float rig.

throughout the season. If so, start it off with two tubs of brandlings from the tackle shop.

Present one or two brandlings on a size 12 hook or a bunch on a size 10. To stop them wriggling over the barb and off the hook, tip it with a single maggot, caster or kernel of sweetcorn. Alternatively, after the worms, slip on a small section cut from a wide rubber band. Perch, tench, bream, rudd, grayling and especially crucian carp all love brandlings.

Redworms

These short, slow-moving worms are lovers of compost heaps consisting mainly of rotting leaves rather than manure. Wherever piles of leaves have been stacked and left to break down, forming a rich leaf-mould, redworms provide a regular source of bait. All cyprinids love them, especially tench, bream, dace and chub. And for long-trotting for grayling there is no finer bait. Present one on a size 14 hook, two on a 12 and so on, or offer them as a cocktail in conjunction with corn, casters, maggots or a crust cube, for instance. Because these worms do not wriggle off the hook, they are ideal for use in combination with spinners.

Lugworms and Ragworms

If you live near the coast and can obtain a fresh supply of either lugworms or ragworms, or your inland tackle dealer stocks them, don't assume that only sea fish love them.

Expensive they may be, but as an entirely different change bait for species such as carp, tench, chub and bream, both worms produce results.

Use lugworms as you would a big lobworm, freelined on a size 6 or 4 hook — chub devour them greedily. Ragworms, especially the thick-bodied 'king rag' (watch out for its pincers) are best cut into 1–1½ in segments with even smaller bits thrown in as loose feed. I haven't tried them, but as other sea baits such as squid produce well, these worms could prove effective for catfish. Both worms are best kept in the fridge (if possible, wrapped individually in clean newspaper) and you should change the paper daily. Of the two, ragworms will last much longer – up to a week or so.

Mealworms

This popular live food source, bred specifically for rearing birds, reptiles and mammals, has been available to the pet trade for many years, and is now being marketed for the fisherman. Mealworms make a super bait. The largest supplier is the Mealworm Company, which channels its products through specialist tackle shops, offering British-bred mealworms in four sizes, from 'minis' to the 'super giant'. The latter, presented two up on a size 8 hook, is heavy enough for freelining to chub.

Buff-coloured, looking like a cross between a caterpillar and a maggot — in fact not unlike a caddis grub — mealworms are actually the larvae of a beetle, and are extremely active. The larger ones have a similar thrashing action to brandlings, making them attractive to all cyprinids.

Mealworms last much longer than unrefrigerated maggots: at least for several weeks if kept in the bran-filled plastic containers in which they are sold. Alternatively, transfer them to a large, open, smooth-sided bucket or tray with around ½ in of fresh bran in the bottom. Don't bother with a lid for tall containers. A temperature of around 10°C (50°F) seems to suit them perfectly, although the 'super giant' mealworm requires a higher temperature of between 16 and 21°C (60–70°F).

Being little larger than a fat bloodworm, the 'mini' mealworm is ideal for very light float fishing and size 18–20 hooks, in conjunction with loose-fed pinkies or squatts. The standard mealworm as hookbait couples nicely with loose-fed maggots or casters and size 16 or 14 hooks. The two largest mealworms have all sorts of possibilities when presented on hooks in sizes from 12 to 6: for perch, carp, barbel and tench. They are a marvellous natural bait, and well worth a try.

Wasp Grubs and Nests

While wasp grubs readily catch dace, roach, grayling and even the occasional barbel, chub are driven absolutely wild, sometimes into an unbelievable feeding frenzy (through careful loose-feeding) by the sweet and sickly aroma of both grubs and the grub-laden cakes which make up the football-sized nest. These cakes, around ¾ in thick and exactly the size of a round two-pint bait box, may even be frozen until needed. When defrosted (as opposed to fresh), the grubs will be next to useless as hookbaits, but you can feed in mashed-up cake and use this in conjunction with a waxworm or a tebo on the hook (see Waxworms and Tebos). Alternatively, for enticing chub to the surface during the summer, carefully break the cake, frozen or fresh, into 1½-in squares and freeline it on a size 6 hook.

Wasp cake is far better used fresh, so to enjoy this superb bait, which has truly magical qualities for chub, you must find a source of freshly killed nests. Throughout July and August the cakes are more liable to be packed full of grubs and so they are best harvested at this time. Most good hardware shops stock special preparations, such as Rentokil products, for effectively killing the nest. The directions for use must be followed to the letter.

When fishing, keep your eyes open for wasps which disappear into the bank. Or you may see them in your garden, since rockeries and any other quiet piece of bank are prime locations. But if you don't fancy killing your own nests, make a polite request to fruit farmers in July, when, in the process of reducing the wasp population while the cakes are heavily laden with fat grubs, numerous nests are destroyed. Local councils may also hold the key to obtaining a supply of nests. Simply ring the Pest Control Department.

Waxworms

Waxworms are the larvae of the waxmoth, which infests beehives to lay its eggs in the honeycombs. A fat, juicy, fairly buoyant, creamy-white grub similar in size to a wasp grub, the waxworm fits nicely on a size 14 or 12 hook (hook it carefully through the tail end). This makes it especially effective when trotting for grayling, dace, roach and chub in conjunction with loose-fed maggots or with mashed-up wasp cake when good grubs are in short supply. Waxworms keep well in the tub provided, at a temperature of between 13 and 16°C (55–60°F). It is worth checking regularly and removing any dead ones so that the rest do not spoil. Bred specifically for the live pet-food trade, waxworms are also available through specialist tackle shops.

Tebos

If you catch fish on 'super giant' mealworms, then you will love these even larger grubs. They are the larvae of a moth imported from Chile, which feeds on the fibrous soft wood beneath the bark of the tebo tree. Tebos come packed in bran and will last up to three weeks if stored at between 7 and 10°C (45–50°F). Being larger than a wasp grub, they are a superb hookbait for long-trotting when

loose-feeding with maggots or mashed-up wasp cake, and are best presented singly on a size 12 hook or two up on a 10. Chub adore them.

Grubs and Caterpillars

Any large, weighty caterpillar of either moths or butterflies — and there are dozens — makes a superb freelining bait for chub. Hook it very carefully through the head on a size 10 or 8 hook and cast gently. If distance is required, use in conjunction with a mini floating controller such as the tenpin (see diagram, page 160).

Beetle Larvae

One of the largest, fattest, most succulent and more importantly, when weight is required for freelining for carp or chub, one of the heaviest of larvae, is that of both the stag beetle and the lesser stag beetle. Up to 2 in long and $\frac{1}{2}$-in thick, these white larvae have a distinctive, orange-chestnut head and front legs and lie in a curled-up position for up to three years during the second stage of metamorphosis, the first stage being the eggs laid by the adult beetle. In the third stage the larva changes

Above: Available at most pet shops, and even specialist tackle centres, mealworms come in various sizes to suit any situation, be it trotting for roach and dace or freelining for chub.

Opposite: Looking to all intents and purposes like giant, succulent maggots, it is small wonder that tench turn on quickly to mealworms, whether legered or presented on a lift-method float rig.

into a pupa during the autumn, but does not complete the cycle until the following spring, when the adult beetle emerges by chewing its way out of the rotten wood.

Stag beetles lay their eggs in rotting fallen trees and in old fungi-covered tree stumps, particularly of ash, elm, oak and silver birch. Prise the rotten outer layers of wood away carefully to reveal the huge grubs curled up in their separate chambers. When you find one, there could be up to a couple of dozen baits in the same log. So that the internal juices do not burst, hook the grub once only through the head with a size 8 hook tied direct, and cast gently.

Another useful large white grub is that of

the nocturnal cockchafer, found by pulling up turfs or simply digging over the garden. It feeds on plant roots for two or three years during the larva stage, and, like stag-beetle grubs, sports a chestnut-coloured head and lies in a curled-up position. Present it on a size 8 hook, gently nicked through the head.

Leatherjackets

Feeding just beneath the surface of the ground on the roots of many plants and grasses, leatherjackets are the grey, maggot-like larvae of the long-legged crane-fly (better known as the daddy-long-legs) and hatch by the thousand during the autumn. Leatherjackets can be used for roach, dace and chub on float tackle, presented singly on a size 14 hook or two up on a size 12. Alternatively, catch the live daddy-long-legs and carefully mount it on a size 14 or 12 hook, presenting it with a surface controller float to obtain distance. Grease the line between the hook and controller (see diagram, page 176).

Grasshoppers, House Crickets and Locusts

For chub enthusiasts, whether dapping at close range from an entanglement of marginal cover or floating them downstream on the surface with a greased line and controller float such as the tenpin (see diagram, page 176), grasshoppers, house crickets and locusts are wonderful natural baits for use during the warmer months, especially in high summer, when weed growth makes legering almost impossible.

If you don't want to run about chasing grasshoppers, or there are never any in the field beside the river when you want them, invest in some medium-sized locusts or large house crickets, both of which are available from pet shops which specialize in live foods. They are bred to feed spiders, lizards, frogs and certain large birds, and may easily be kept in an old aquarium until required. Make sure that the lid is well ventilated (gauze is perfect) and fits tightly and, with locusts especially, that the temperature remains at around 27°C (80°F). Large house crickets will tolerate lower temperatures, so for both the

kitchen is the ideal place.

Feed locusts with fresh grass daily and house crickets with fresh potato or other vegetable peelings, from which they extract liquid. Your local live-food stockist will give you further advice.

The best way to present these baits so that they remain alive and active, thus luring chub out from even the darkest hide-out, is to gently ease the hook through the rear end, directly opposite the back legs. Locusts sit nicely on a size 8 hook, and house crickets on a size 10, as does the average-sized grasshopper.

Slugs

While I have purposely caught specimen dace on small white slugs, and had the occasional perch or pike lunge into a large slug being twitched back upstream through the swim, slugs are really the prime bait for one species and one species only: that ever-friendly glutton, the chub. During the summer and autumn I put slugs at the very top of the chub's natural bait list, since they are heavy enough to freeline quite a long way (at least 20 yards) without additional shotting. In addition, the slug often slips conveniently up the line during the fight, so that it can be used for a second or even third chub.

I particularly like slugs for summer chubbing when overhanging foliage is dense, because they can be skate-cast – like flat pebbles at the seaside – into the most awkward spots, where the largest chub always love to lie, and invariably respond instantly. But you need to be on your toes, and heaving against that chub with a forgiving 'Avon' – action rod and 6-lb line before it even considers wrapping the hook around a snag. Slugging provides wonderful sport, and is the most exciting of all the mobile freelining techniques available to the summer chubber.

Slugs will also take chub if legered into deep runs or pools where the water is too turbulent or too deep for freelining. But either way, always use a large hook such as a size 4, preferably a long-shank, tied direct to the reel line. Nick the slug once only through one end, just through the leathery outer skin so that the juices do not seep out and shrink

NATURAL BAITS • 165

it to half its original size.

Most British slugs are vegetarians, as gardeners know only too well, but there is a carnivorous species which sports a tiny shell on its rear end (proving its ancestry with snails) that lives underground, where it feeds on earthworms.

For the chub fisherman, however, there are three species of large slugs (2–4 in long) which are particularly suited to freelining. The common red slug is easily identified by an orange frill to the underside of its brown body. The great grey slug, a most distinctive creature, is flecked with dark-brown markings over a pale grey body. But everyone's favourite is the black slug, although I doubt whether the colour makes any real difference. Provided the slug is heavy enough to cast easily and makes a resounding 'dinner is served' plop on the surface, chub come a-running.

If slugs have a drawback, it is trying to find them just when you want them. They are certainly creatures of the night, although during heavy rain among thick vegetation they can be found away from their crevice hide-outs in reasonable numbers. The secret (as with lobworms) is to gather a whole batch of slugs when conditions are suitable and they are plentiful, and keep them in an old aquarium until required.

Search in compost heaps, beneath damp sacking (leave a pile of old sacks in a quiet, dark corner of the garden for this purpose) beneath large rockery stones, in damp cellars or under piles of old logs. In fact, any damp, rotting hidey-hole can prove fruitful. Ensure that the aquarium is fitted with a tight, well-ventilated lid, and introduce a batch of slugs, along with an amount of fresh vegetation for them to eat. Keep it in a cool, dark spot such as the garage, cellar, garden shed or outhouse, and you will always have a superb supply of chubbing baits to hand.

Snails

Just about everything I have said about slugs as bait applies equally to the larger land snails, of which there are over 80 British species. As with slugs, you can even keep snails you have gathered in an old aquarium.

The only difference is that immediately before use you crack the shell and peel it off, allowing the hook to be nicked once only through the outer skin.

True, snails lack the casting weight of slugs once the shell has gone, but this can be remedied by presenting two, or even three, on a size 8 or 6 hook tied direct to 5 or 6–lb line.

I doubt whether chub can really tell the difference between snails and slugs, and certainly snails have on numerous occasions provided me with a chubbing bait when slugs were in short supply.

MAGGOTS

Because they are readily available from all tackle shops at a reasonable price and are instantly attractive to all species of cyprinids, maggots are easily the most popular of all natural, land-borne baits for use in freshwater.

Standard Maggots as Hookbait

The standard maggot stocked by tackle shops are bred specifically from the second most common European bluebottle, and come already coloured either mixed or in single colours: yellow, pink, green, red, bronze and, of course, plain white. Many breeders introduce colour to the fish, chicken or turkey carcasses on which maggots are fed, but colouring white, shop-bought maggots yourself is easy with non-carcinogenic liquid dyes such as the Spectra range.

Riddle off any bran, sawdust or maize meal and dead maggots using a ⅛ -in riddle and put the maggots in a shallow tray. Sprinkle a capful of dye over them and wait for half an hour for the maggots to work their way in and spread the colour evenly. Finally, add half a pint of maize meal to each pint of maggots to stop them sweating, and use them straight away or store them. Maggots are best kept in an old fridge (not the family fridge) in the garage or on the cool concrete floor of the garage itself, or in a garden shed or outhouse in open tins rather than plastic bait boxes.

If you use maggots regularly, an old fridge,

Left: Once you have located the wasps' nest, a liberal coating of the special 'killing' dust should be squirted deep inside each entrance hole after dark, when all the wasps have retired.

Below: When digging out a 'killed' nest, try to remove it in its whole state, which is about the size of a football, comprising several 'cakes' ¾ in thick. Unfortunately, this nest was situated below a thick tree root and had to be removed in chunks.

Above: The hornets' nest is chub bait supreme — much rarer and even better than wasps' nests because the succulent grubs are considerably larger. Use grub-laden chunks on the surface, freelined through the swim, or present a single grub on trotting tackle while loose feeding with the same.

Left: Heavy enough for freelining to chub or carp, and presented one or two up on a size 8 or 6 hook, these fat, juicy stag beetle larvae are found amongst the crumbling wood of fallen and rotten trees.

which will use a minimal amount of electricity soon pays for itself. Without a fridge, however, continuing metamorphosis will rapidly turn the maggots into bluebottles. When buying maggots, look for a dark spot beneath the skin, which proves that they have been off the feed for only a few days and are

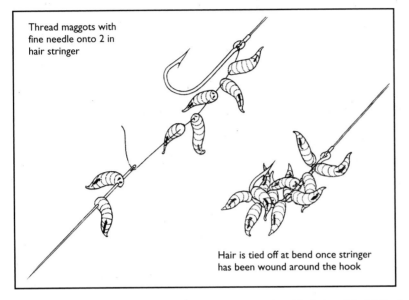

Thread maggots with fine needle onto 2 in hair stringer

Hair is tied off at bend once stringer has been wound around the hook

Presenting maggots on a stringer.

really fresh. Those without a 'feed line' spot will soon be useless as a live bait, their metabolic rate rapidly decreasing as they approach the formation of the chrysalis or pupa. Anglers call this form the 'caster'.

For transporting maggots abroad, or when they could end up crammed in standard bait boxes for a couple of days in warm weather before use, follow this simple procedure. Riddle off the maggots as described above and put the healthy ones in an open tray in the fridge, reducing the temperature to just a few degrees above freezing so that they are hardly moving. Then pack them into a muslin bag (up to two gallons at a time) and place in a polystyrene cold-box to which has been added six standard freezer packs of the flat type, which contain a special fluid and remain frozen for a long time. In this way, maggots will last for up to four days. On arriving at your final destination, remove the maggots and transfer them to a large, open tray, adding maize meal after an hour or so, once their metabolic rate starts to increase.

To ensure maximum attraction, it is imperative that the maggots' inner juices and lifeblood do not drain out when you hook them on. Carefully nick the point of the hook through the tough, blunt end between the two tiny dots. Present one standard maggot on a size 18 or 20 hook, two on a size 16 or 14 and bunches of four to six on sizes 12 and

10. It is a bit fiddly, but when you are carp or barbel fishing with hooks that are really thick in the wire (which burst the maggots) use a 2-in stringer of, say, ½-lb monofilament or fly-tying thread tied to the eye, and with the aid of a needle, sleeve on a dozen or so maggots and tie the hair off at the bend of the hook after winding the string of maggots firmly around the shank. This arrangement looks very tempting (see above diagram).

Maggots make great cocktails: maggots and brandlings or redworms, maggots and corn or stewed wheat, maggots and casters, for instance. The permutations are many. Incidentally, there may well be occasions when maggots are just too lively for their own good and wriggle quickly into the bottom sediment of silty waters such as estate lakes and meres. To counteract this when I intend swimfeedering for bream and tench, for instance, I simply scald in boiling hot water for a few seconds all the maggots to be used as loose feed, which kills and 'stretches' them instantly. Tench and bream never seem to mind, and the loose feed sits there on the bottom, along with the explosion of crumb groundbait, in full view of passing fish.

During a heatwave, when fridges often break down, everything dries and becomes stretched if you are not careful, from maggots left in your box to those stored by the gallon in huge trays by tackle dealers. But don't automatically discard dead, stretched, or even putrid, stinking maggots, because en masse they are a magical carp attractor.

Fortunately the cold room in my tackle shop has not overheated on many occasions over the years, but when it has, hundreds of pounds worth of maggots have been ruined. I have arrived on a Monday morning to find the cold-room motor iced up and most of the stock roasted to death and completely unsaleable after a weekend of suffocating heat. And doesn't it always occur over the weekend?

The first time this happened, rather than completely waste the stock (which, after all, dead or alive, is a protein food source) I took the entire batch home and emptied two trays each (about eight gallons) into several marginal swims in the two shallow lakes close to my house, much to the enjoyment of the syndicate members.

Within an hour, each of those swims was packed full of gorging carp, their tails literally sticking out above the surface while they stood on their heads sucking in the maggot feast. Such was their feeding frenzy, they immediately pounced on almost any bait offered. This is food for thought, because it has since been my experience that this routine works on most fisheries, even those stuffed full of small nuisance species. But you do need a vast quantity of maggots to fill everything up before the carp move in, as they eventually will.

When loose-feeding with maggots, in all but the most extreme close-range, windless conditions opt for the accuracy of a loose-feed catapult or throwing stick rather than chucking them out by hand. There is no easier way to ruin your fishing than inviting fish to chase loose feed indiscriminately hurled in well away from the swim.

Colour is a topic guaranteed to get everyone arguing over the tackle-shop counter. Some prefer plain white maggots, some simply wouldn't tackle up if bronze ones were not available, while others swear by maggots dyed red, or even fluorescent colours. Over the years I must confess to a preference for bronze maggots in cold, clear water, and dark red when fishing in peaty-coloured water — the rivers of Denmark, Sweden and Ireland, for instance. In the end I suppose it's all down to how confident you are, and if a particular colour makes you fish with greater confidence, you will undoubtedly catch.

Sucked or skinned maggots are one of the problems suffered when using this bait. Despite their having been sucked back to the cyprinids' pharyngeal (throat) teeth and crushed to pulp, you can still miss the bite. If you simply did not see a bite, try shotting the float tip down more, moving the bottom shot closer to the hook, reducing tail length between hook and leger or striking earlier, hopefully between the maggots' inner juices being sucked out and the skins spat out.

There are occasions, with the swim full of feeding bream and size 10 or 8 hooks the order of the day, when leaving four 'skins' on the hook and replacing just one or two maggots every other cast can save all the bother of rebaiting. The bream never seem to mind.

Gozzers

These maggots, noticeably softer than those you buy from the tackle shop, are the larvae of the common European bluebottle. Because it does not fare happily indoors, this is not bred commercially and available over the counter.

Some fishermen swear by gozzers, since bream in particular hold on to them longer because of their soft skin. So if you wish to give them a try, you need to breed enough to provide a hookbait. But it is rather a rigmarole. Wrap a chicken breast or a pig's heart loosely in newspaper and leave it in a dark, dry, cool spot in a quiet corner of the garden and wait for the fly to lay its eggs. Once the meat has a blow on it, put it into an open tin covered in gauze (protected from the rain) so that no other flies can lay on it, and leave the eggs to hatch.

Within several days the 'gozzer' maggots will have had their fill and be ready to leave the meat, which should be shaken over a $\frac{1}{8}$ in riddle into a tray containing bran or maize meal. Colour your gozzers pale bronze or golden yellow, and you have the bream maggot *par excellence*.

Wherever small species do not prove troublesome, there is no finer bait for barbel than a bunch of a dozen or so maggots gently sleeved on to a size 8 or 6 hook, as John proves with this splendid River Wensum specimen.

Pinkies

We have the shiny-backed 'greenbottle' to thank for this considerably smaller maggot, which gets its name from turning a very pale pink within hours of being taken off the feed. Many fishermen nevertheless still prefer to colour their pinkies either red or bronze, and use them as loose feed or mixed in with the groundbait while presenting a standard-sized maggot or maggots on the hook.

Being much smaller, pinkies are ideal with tiny hooks or when you are fishing in really cold, clear water during the winter for dace, roach and bream. One pinkie fits perfectly on a size 22 or 24 hook, or two on a size 20. Remember to use only fine-wire hooks, which puncture the skin easily without bursting it, and allow the bait to behave as naturally as possible. Heavy, forged hooks weight the pinkie down, making it sink too quickly. A pinkie 'caster' and pinkie maggot together on a size 20 hook are a deadly combination over a weedy or debris-covered bottom.

Squatts

This tiny maggot, bred from the common housefly, is usually only available from tackle shops during the summer, when it is put to bream fishing. Nowhere near so active as other maggots, it will not burrow into the bottom sediment before the bream locate it. Nowadays most bream enthusiasts prefer to lace their groundbait with casters instead of squatts, so that this tiny maggot, always difficult to keep, has slipped down the popularity ladder.

The squatt is the obvious match fisherman's hookbait choice wherever bloodworms are banned, and is best presented singly on a tiny size 24 fine-wire hook, or two up on a 22.

Along with pinkies, squatts are great for catching tiny fish such as gudgeon, sticklebacks, minnows and the like when you require a few small live or deadbaits for chub, perch and the like.

One small piece of advice when buying maggots over the counter, be they pinkies, squatts or standard hookbaits. Never cram into a bait box exactly what it will hold. Two pints of maggots crammed into a two-pint box, for instance, will not allow sufficient space and air for them to breathe, resulting in spoiled bait and wasted money unless they are used within hours. An excellent rule of thumb is to use a bait box which holds a pint of air, plus fresh maize meal to stop them from sweating, for each pint of maggots bought. Into a pint-sized box, therefore, put no more than half a pint of maggots. In the long run, extra bait boxes are far cheaper than suffocated maggots.

Casters

Once referred to as the 'chrysalis', just as before the 1960s, maggots were called 'gentles', the caster is the pupa stage of the bluebottle, during which time the maggot is eventually transformed by metamorphosis into an air-borne fly.

It is best to catch the caster during the early stages, while it is a golden yellow and the inside juices are still heavy, which ensures that it sinks. this is most easily achieved by regularly putting a batch of slow-moving maggots through an $\frac{1}{8}$ in riddle at low room temperatures during the summer. Outside, in the garage or garden shed, is ideal. In the winter, dare I suggest, unless you have a heated outhouse, doing this inside the house is best as there is an even temperature in which maggots will continue to 'turn'.

The sinking casters can be kept in two ways. The first is to put them into a bucket of water to ensure they all sink (skim off any floaters) and leave them for a few minutes, which kills the creature forming inside and so completely halts its advancement. Pack them into a polythene bag and store in the fridge for up to three or four days, during which time they should be used, otherwise, as the animal inside decays, they will start to stink.

The second method is to put the golden sinkers straight from the riddle into a bait box covered in dampened newspaper or a piece of damp towelling, and pop them straight into the coldest part of the fridge, where further metamorphosis is greatly retarded. Again, ideally they should be used within a few days before the colour darkens as the fly forms inside and they all turn into floaters.

All cyprinids love casters: dace, roach, rudd, bream, chub, barbel, tench and carp, even perch and grayling. In clear, cold water conditions, casters invariably produce a better stamp of dace, roach and chub, particularly when used with loose-fed hempseed. When they are mixed in with hempseed and deposited on the bottom with a large block-end feeder (enlarge the holes for a swift delivery) barbel soon acquire a great liking for casters. Use a bunch on a size 10 hook tipped with a brandling or redworm, or for shy barbel, two casters and a bronze maggot on a size 14 hook.

Caster cocktails in conjunction with brandlings, sweetcorn, maggots and bread are great catchers. Because of the buoyancy of dark (floating) casters, it is possible to offer both a maggot and a dark-red caster on the hook, which rises conveniently above dense bottom weeds.

Floating casters are superb surface baits. During the warmer months dace, rudd, chub and carp will all rise freely to the surface for loose-fed floaters. Present them on a flat float peacock rig or in conjunction with a mini tenpin floating controller (see diagram, page 160).

For roach, dace and chub, present standard sinking casters singly on a fine-wire

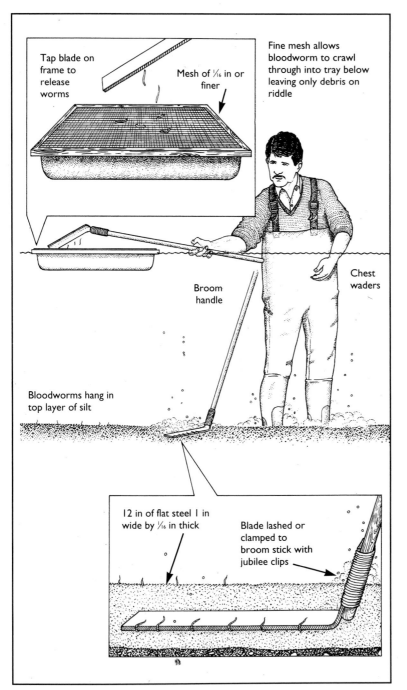

Collecting bloodworms.

Tap blade on frame to release worms

Mesh of ⅟₁₆ in or finer

Fine mesh allows bloodworm to crawl through into tray below leaving only debris on riddle

Broom handle

Chest waders

Bloodworms hang in top layer of silt

12 in of flat steel 1 in wide by ⅟₁₆ in thick

Blade lashed or clamped to broom stick with jubilee clips

size 18 or 20 hook, piercing one end with the point and gently burying the entire hook inside. With larger hooks pierce the shell carefully or it will shatter.

To stop golden casters from turning into floaters when fishing in warm weather, cover them with water in the bait box. Casters are great for mixing in with groundbait for tench and for bream.

Bloodworms

Wherever you spot the feeding bubbles of tench or carp exploding in the surface film of still waters, it is odds-on they are syphoning through the bottom detritus for the little red bloodworm, the larva of the midge.

While there are hundreds of bloodworm variants, either living in the silt on the bottom of still waters, in plant tissue, in little tubes which they construct, or even swimming freely, it is the bright-red (because of the haemoglobin in the blood) segmented larva of some of the larger species which match fishermen, in particular, use for bait. Some species of midge have a yearly cycle like most other aquatic flies, while others produce two or three generations during a season. This makes them about the most prolific source of natural food to all bottom feeders, because the greater part of their cycle is spent in larval form and so they are always readily available, summer and winter.

Most cyprinids share a love of bloodworms (as do perch and ruffe) and in both clear and really cold water they are by far the most effective bait for smaller species such as gudgeon and roach. The trouble is, their size alone calls for a very delicate presentation demanding the use of gossamer hooklengths and tiny, fine-wire hooks. The bloodworm is then best nicked gently through the darker, more bulbous head end so that it hangs straight.

Obtaining bloodworms yourself is a laborious, messy job requiring chest waders and the construction of a scraper for obtaining them from shallow, silty ponds and lakes. To a long broomstick add a 12 in length of flat-steel of around 1 in wide and

$1/16$ in thick (see diagram). It should be set at a right angle so that when scraped just beneath the top layer of silt, where the greatest concentration of bloodworms live, they 'fold' and are held against the blade edge.

As you lift the scraper out of the water, a quick sideways turn of the wrist will ensure that the worms do not immediately fall off. Then tap the scraper on the side of a floating riddle or sieve, to knock off both debris and bloodworms. The worms crawl through the top riddle into the chamber below, leaving behind all the debris.

Much smaller species of midge, referred to as jokers and used purely as loose feed when bloodworms are presented on the hook, are most commonly found in semi-polluted streams, particularly below sewage outfalls. Collect them by disturbing the bottom sediment and netting them en masse in a large, extremely fine-mesh net when the float up. They can be separated from all the unwanted bits of weed and debris by putting the whole lot into a fine-weave sack and lowering it into a bucket of water, then waiting for the jokers to crawl through the mesh into clear water.

But the fact is, most of us just haven't the time for lengthy bait-collecting sessions, and the easiest way of obtaining bloodworms, if rather expensive – though now you know why – is by the pint from your nearest specialist tackle shop. To ensure bloodworms keep for as long as possible, put them in peat wrapped in newspaper and store them in the fridge.

CHAPTER TWENTY-ONE

Manufactured Baits

BREAD

Breadflake

Because the polythene bag encourages moisture, which makes the bread last longer, I much prefer to buy ready-sliced white loaves. And to ensure breadflake stays on and you are not simply sitting there with a bare hook, insist on fresh, doughy white bread. If you shop around and try various brands you will no doubt notice a difference between loaves. As second choice, a large, freshly baked tin loaf makes good breadflake. Either way, it pays to keep one or two loaves in reserve in the freezer just in case.

In addition to using only the fresh, doughy white bread of a new loaf, the secret of ensuring that flake stays on the hook is to compress it really hard between thumb and forefinger around the shank of the hook while masking the point and barb with the other thumb. It then swells to twice the size when it becomes wet, with an attractive, fluffy (unpressed) part hiding the hook point, which easily finds a purchase on the strike.

I rate breadflake among the better standard baits for good-sized dace, rudd, roach, bream and tench, whether freelined, presented 'on the lift' or legered. A lump of flake the size of a 2p piece, for instance, hiding a size 8 or 6 hook, will, because of its size, put you straight through a shoal of rudd or roach of mixed sizes to the whoppers.

A cocktail of flake on the hook shank, with

Left: Though considered by many as 'old hat' bait, breadcrust can still tempt carp. This beautiful orange koi accepted a small cube of brown breadcrust freelined into a tiny gap in a large bed of lilies.

Opposite: As a change bait from using plain bread on the hook, why not try flake or crust cocktails. Sometimes that little extra difference can really switch spooky fish on – especially bream, rudd and tench.

either maggot, corn, caster, wheat or worm on the bend, provides yet another trick up your sleeve when fish are wary. A balanced bait (excellent for presenting over thick bottom weed) of crust on the shank with a pinch of flake round the bend is also worth trying.

Breadcrust

Although the crust has nowhere near the durability of breadflake as far as staying on the hook is concerned, because of its buoyancy, presenting a cube of crust on the hook often scores over most other baits. A situation which immediately springs to mind is legering or float-fishing over a weedy or debris-covered bottom. This applies not only to stillwaters but also to long-trotting in swift-flowing rivers for roach, chub or barbel. Bear in mind that crust swells to around twice its size when saturated, and cut the cubes accordingly.

If you are using reasonably small hooks, say size 16 to 10, then the crust from the edge

of a sliced white loaf is perfect. Large hooks demand bigger crusts and then I much prefer to buy small tin loaves because there is little white bread wastage once the crusts have been removed. I also like the rubbery crust of a fresh – and I stress 'fresh' – French loaf. Again, because the loaf is narrow, not much white bread is wasted.

As with flake, crust cocktails are very effective, particularly for presenting 'on the drop'. Try an oblong of crust on the hook shank, with a maggot, caster, corn, worm or even a piece of flake on the bend, for a truly balanced bait. A balanced crust and flake trick, which carp fall for time and time again if they are attracted by surface crusts, is to slide a small piece of crust up over the eye of the hook, then squeeze on a large piece of breadflake, which, if presented on its own, would immediately start to sink. However, if you gently pinch a corner of the flake together with the white bread on the crust, the crust holds the flake until a carp inspects the bait, knocking it with its lips, the top of its

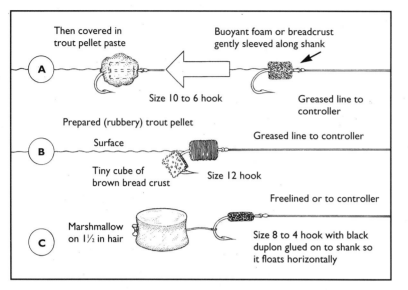

Presenting floaters.

A — Then covered in trout pellet paste — Buoyant foam or breadcrust gently sleeved along shank — Size 10 to 6 hook — Greased line to controller

B — Prepared (rubbery) trout pellet — Surface — Greased line to controller — Tiny cube of brown bread crust — Size 12 hook

C — Marshmallow on 1½ in hair — Freelined or to controller — Size 8 to 4 hook with black duplon glued on to shank so it floats horizontally

head, or even with a swish of the tail, as carp often do.

Once separated, the waterlogged flake suddenly starts to sink, and wham, the carp sucks it in greedily with complete confidence because it is behaving naturally. Great fun.

At close range, use simple freeline tactics (remember to grease the line) and for distances in excess of 20 yards, use the added weight of a small floating controller such as a tenpin to place the crust or crust and flake combination accurately (see above diagram).

Breadpaste *(see page179)*

Punched Bread
When a fish's metabolism slows right down and conditions are difficult – the water is clear or cold or both – offering a tiny pellet of punched bread on the hook is an excellent alternative to maggots or casters. Dace, rudd and roach, in particular, readily respond to it.

Use a really fresh, sliced white loaf and rest a slice on a hard board so that a neat pellet is formed when you press the punch into it.

Making Your Own Coloured Bread
If the situation arises, as it does in carp fishing for instance, where fish quickly wise up to bread and particularly its stark whiteness, one answer is to change the bait's colour. This occurred to me many years ago

and I have since had considerable success when, for instance, surface fishing 'black' breadcrust. This has nowhere near the shock effect on carp that have previously succumbed too many times to crust from an untreated white loaf.

Black breadflake, orange breadflake, pink breadflake and so on may sound strange, but do give them a try, and you will find other species, such as tench, bream and chub, will also respond favourably.

To make your own 2lb loaf exactly the colour of your choice could not be easier. You will need a 1¼ -lb packet of white bread mix, powder colouring, hot water and an appropriately sized baking tin.

First dissolve a level teaspoon of powder colouring (two spoonfuls of black) into ¾ pint of hand-hot water. Then put the bread mix in a large bowl and slowly add the coloured water, stirring thoroughly. Knead the dough with your hands for a timed five minutes, and then place it in the baking tin, which should be slightly greased and floured. Put clingfilm over the tin and leave it in a warm place for half an hour until the dough doubles in size.

Place the tin in the middle of a preheated oven set on gas mark 8 (230°C) for 45 minutes. And hey presto, your very own loaf in exactly the colour you want.

GROUNDBAITS

Mashed Bread

Hanging from a nail in my garage (so that the mice cannot reach it) is an old keepnet full of dried bread scraps, which I use to make mashed-bread groundbait. To stop bread scraps from going mouldy, pop a batch in the oven on a large tray for a few minutes.

The secret of making mashed-bread groundbait is to use stale bread at least five or six days old. While it really doesn't matter how old the bread is, never use new bread. Start by soaking a batch of scraps in a bucket of water for a couple of hours and then straining off the excess water, before squeezing and mashing the bread between your fingers into a fine pulp. The success of mashed bread can be attributed to its make-up of thousands of tiny, separate, fluffy particles which attract more than they overfeed.

When you are using mashed bread during the winter in running water, for instance, if it is not quickly eaten, the cloud of mash soon passes on downstream through the swim and disintegrates without overfeeding the intended quarry of quality roach or chub. By the way, rather than freeze my hands off squeezing out mash in sub-zero temperatures at the river, I make it up in the kitchen sink in warm water the night before an early-morning stint, and after squeezing out the excess water pop it into a polythene bag.

Alternatively, if you store bags of ready-made and squeezed mash in the freezer, just take one out and leave it in the sink overnight so that by dawn it will have defrosted sufficiently for throwing in. Immediately before baiting up I like to squeeze the mash again into golf balls, and the tighter it is squeezed the longer it holds together before breaking up.

To obtain a nice 'cloud' for use with, say, punched bread, make your mash sloppy and squeeze it into tiny balls. But if you are seeking bream, which form huge shoals, stiffen a sloppy mash with bran, maize meal, dry breadcrumbs or even a proprietary groundbait, plus hookbait fragments of corn, worms, casters or wheat, and so on (if you are not using flake or paste as hookbait) and mould it into firm cricket balls. In really deep, fast rivers, the best binders for mashed bread are flaked maize, which looks like heavy-duty cornflakes (you can use ordinary cornflakes) and pearl barley. Both help take your mash straight down to the bottom, regardless of depth.

Breadcrumbs

Breadcrumbs, plus additives such as crushed hempseed or maize meal, are the universal base for most prepacked 'special' groundbaits. But you can easily make your own from crunching up toasted bread scraps kept in an old keepnet, as I do, or buy plain brown or white breadcrumbs in 2 or 3-lb bags, or in bulk, which is by far the cheapest way.

To dampened crumbs various binders may be added. For bream fishing in deep, fast rivers and in stillwaters where you want the bait to go straight to the bottom, add either pearl barley or flaked maize, plus hookbait samples. Whether using them on the hook or not, casters are a most valuable inclusion, and far better than maggots, which tend to wriggle and break up the ball even before it is thrown, and then quickly disappear into the bottom sediment if not eaten immediately. By contrast, casters lay there on the bottom in full view among the cereal carpet and make nice firm balls for throwing or catapulting.

Incidentally, if your maggots turn into 'floating' casters, don't throw them away in disgust, whatever the amount. For adding to breadcrumbs, there is nothing more attractive. With your fingers, crush a handful at a time into a pulp over the tub of crumbs, so that the juices and the millions of shell fragments all go in. Add a little water if necessary, and the resulting 'cloud' from the casters' juices creates a mix to which bream respond eagerly. It is particularly effective in lakes and canals which are difficult because of their clear water.

When tench fishing, I add to the breadcrumbs a pint of fine, granulated trout-pellet feed or salmon fry crumbs plus, when obtainable, a pint of fresh blood from the butcher's. Crushed hempseed is another

Whether dyed black or orange, coloured bread provides a most interesting and effective change bait to surface feeders like rudd, chub and particularly carp. And it is so easy to make.

excellent additive. I also mix in a few hookbait samples such as corn, casters, chopped worms or maggots.

To make a much lighter breadcrumb groundbait for rudd, roach and bream hybrids, use fine breadcrumbs and mix them in a shallow bowl or tray by fluffing the crumbs about with your free hand while trickling in water from a spare bait box with the other. To ensure the mix will break up quickly into a cloud, or will go straight down when squeezed tightly, put it through an $\frac{1}{8}$-in riddle to eradicate any hard, stodgy lumps. Finally, add a handful of the hookbait.

For feeder fishing with either plastic open-ended or metal-cage feeders, I prefer really coarse breadcrumbs since these, if only lightly dampened, hold together well yet explode instantly the feeder touches bottom. When using plastic open-ended feeders, it is a simple matter to fill the middle with hookbait fragments and plug each end with slightly dampened coarse crumbs.

Prebaiting and Swim Clearance

Simply heaving in a bucketful of free nosh is not always the key to instant success. It will undoubtedly make shoal fish, bream in particular, congregate within a chosen area,

following several days of prebaiting wherever shoals are large, but there are side-effects to consider. For instance, try to prebait only as dusk falls, since this not only coincides with a part of the day when bream feed more aggressively, but will also attract the attention of neither waterfowl such as swans, mallards and coots, nor opportunist anglers who could very well reap the rewards of your efforts.

While prebaiting is going on, it pays to visit in the morning to look for visual signs of bream activity in the swim: streams of bubbles, heavily discoloured water or rolling bream. If the swim is in a distant area reachable only by boat or a long walk, then take your binoculars. Whether prebaiting, fish spotting or actually fishing, I never leave mine at home.

In flowing water that is really heavily populated with bream – for instance, many rivers in Denmark and Ireland – a good helping of groundbait at dusk is invariably enough to ensure hectic sport at dawn. But the bream in huge stillwater fisheries are known to take their time, especially in summer, when pickings are rich, and so prebaiting for two or three days could be useful.

Much of the above also applies to tench,

Dried breadscraps, which are thoroughtly soaked and then squeezed into a mash, are a superb groundbait for chub and bream. To stiffen this mash for throwing long distances, and so it sinks quickly through fast, deep water down to the bottom, various ingredients must be added.

For species like bream, aim to prebait as dusk falls on the evening prior to the morning's fishing (unless you intend fishing throughout the night) so that water birds and other anglers do not show interest in your chosen swim.

which likewise respond to a good stirring up of the bottom and actual weed clearance before the bait is presented. I have even caught good-sized tench while a friend has been in the process of throwing out a heavy weed rake. Tench rarely seem perturbed about the commotion; on the contrary, I'm certain it attracts them. Once they locate the disturbed bottom silt with the mountain of tiny, natural items of food it contains in suspension, plus fragments of your hookbaits and cereal base, they might well root about in the swim for several hours.

PASTES

Breadpaste

Plain breadpaste is a bait I often use in preference to breadflake on the hook when bream fishing. They hang on to paste just that much longer in order for a strike to be

If you are a chub addict, then it is well worth taking the time to ensure your cheesepaste is of a smooth consistency without any nasty lumps to impair hook penetration on the strike.

made before the bait disintegrates. For the same reason, although to a much lesser extent, plain white breadpaste also works effectively with quality dace, rudd and roach. Tench and chub too succumb to paste when it is used in conjunction with mashed-bread groundbait.

To make a super creamy breadpaste simply soak several slices of four to five day-old bread (or a chunk from a tin loaf with the crust removed) under the cold tap and knead it with clean hands until it reaches a firm consistency. Like cheese paste, it can be frozen for future use.

Cat-food Paste
Just about every brand of tinned cat food will, if sufficiently stiffened, make an excellent paste for tench, carp and catfish. Most chub won't refuse it either.

The secret is to bind the paste together so that it does not break up on the hook. Mix it with cornflour (or plain flour) and wheatgerm (or Beemax) until it is firm. Wheat gluten, boilie gel and egg albumen are also binders well worth trying, with a sticky base, so experiment until a lump of paste will stay on the hook in a bucket of water for at least 20 minutes without disintegrating. A spoonful of powder colouring may also be kneaded in.

Cheese Paste
To make a cheese paste that will not go rock-hard in cold water and possibly impair hook preparation, simply mix together equal parts of finely grated Cheddar (Danish blue or Gorgonzola if your prefer, and can handle the pong) and mashed bread. Start by soaking under the cold tap several slices of white bread or a chunk (with the crust removed) from a tin loaf. Bread at least four or five days old is best and should be kneaded until creamy. Now add the grated cheese and continue kneading the mix until it is of a fairly stiff consistency. I don't think adding colour is necessary, but any powder dye may be added and kneaded in at almost any stage. To simply intensify the yellow, add a teaspoonful of turmeric.

Cheese paste is a superb bait for chub, barbel, carp and even tench. It can easily be spiced up a little once carp, for instance, start to wise up to the basic cheese and bread base, by adding a teaspoon of either Marmite, Bovril, curry powder or Phillips' yeast mixture, which is a cage-bird tonic that really pongs. For immediate use, wrap the ball of paste in a square of clean cloth, or put it into a polythene bag and freeze it until needed.

Flour and Water Paste
During my childhood immediately after the Second World War, fancy adhesives for sticking cuttings and pictures into scrapbooks were not available, and so everyone used a runny paste made from flour and water. It is the natural gluten in flour which binds a simple flour and water paste together and stops it coming off the hook. So if you suddenly find yourself without a loaf of bread in the cupboard or freezer, don't despair. There is bound to be a bag of flour in the kitchen.

Put three cupfuls of flour into a bowl and slowly add cold water while stirring briskly with a spoon until the mix is of a firm enough consistency for kneading. Although well-kneaded plain white dough will readily catch roach, bream, tench, chub and carp, you can spice it up by adding a large spoonful of either custard or blancmange powder to the flour before adding water. This results in a large ball of bright-yellow or pink (pink is the best of the blancmange colours) paste with a really distinctive aroma.

MEAT IN TINS
That time-honoured tip of always keeping a tin of luncheon meat in your tackle bag or car boot remains as sound as ever. For tench, chub, barbel and, of course, carp, tinned meats are not only readily accepted, often with unbelievable aggression, but are also cheap, easy to use, last almost indefinitely unless opened and are readily available. What more can you ask of a manufactured bait?

Under this heading I put first and foremost good old luncheon meat in its dozens of different brands, followed closely by tinned

Presenting tinned meat (luncheon meat etc.) in cubes or oblongs.

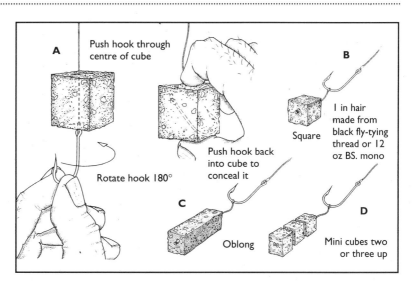

ham, chopped pork roll, bacon grill and so on, the only exception being corned beef, which is just too crumbly as a hookbait. As a paste, though, kneaded with cornflour and bound together with the help of a raw egg, corned beef might well be a winner. I haven't tried it, but go on, prove me wrong!

For me, the main advantages of tinned meat are that it can be cubed or cut into oblongs (or triangles) with a sharp knife and it remains firm on the hook. Some types and brands are rather fattier, and thus far more buoyant, than others, which makes them extremely useful for presenting over thick bottom weed or debris. Others are more dense, and so stay on the hook longer in strong currents, or are more resistant to the attentions of small nuisance species such as gudgeon, roach or rudd. Experiment with various brands until you find one to suit the particular situation.

As for presentation, the secret of using meat is to be confident that your cube does not fly off the hook on a firm cast. Cut it into cubes of equal size (with a sharp, long-bladed knife) no longer than the shank of the hook being used. This is imperative, as can be seen from the diagram. Gently push the hook downwards through the top of the cube and pull it through at the bottom by gripping the bend with thumbnail and forefinger. Now rotate the hook and ease it into one corner of the cube, pulling gently on the line so that it becomes completely embedded in the meat

and hidden from view without the eye of the hook protruding from the top of the cube. The hook, will, however, slice neatly through the meat and into the fish on the strike (see above diagram).

When barbel or carp in hard-fished waters refuse meat presented on the hook, rig it on to a 1-in fine hair, to give them greater confidence (see above diagram). Alternatively, change the shape to an oblong and present it on a hair if it appears that fish have become scared by a square bait (see diagram). Another ruse is to dice the meat into mini cubes and present two or three on a hair (see above diagram).

Why it should be, I have never been able to fathom, but cubed meat presented over a carpet of stewed hempseed – whether you are legering or float-fishing the lift method for carp, or quivertipping or stret-pegging for barbel and chub – must be the all-time-best combination of loose feed and hookbait. It does no harm to dice a block of meat up into tiny hempseed-sized cubes for mixing in with the loose feed.

MEAT IN SKINS

Everything I have said about the presentation of tinned meat also applies to meat in skins once it is cubed or cut into oblongs. A wonderful choice is available from the local delicatessen or supermarket's chilled meat counter, and tench, barbel,

Left: Whatever the make, whatever the brand, and regardless of their density, meat cubes always work better for species like chub, barbel and carp if presented in conjunction with a carpet of loose-fed stewed hempseed. Don't stick to large squares only. Dice them into mini cubes, oblongs, and offer on a hair rig for more confident bites. (See diagram on page 181.)

Right: Rigged 'off the hook', on a fine-hair made from black fly-tying thread, with a short, fixed paternoster swan shot leger is, without question, the most effective way of presenting baits such as luncheon meat to wary barbel and chub.

chub, carp and even catfish simply adore it. The trouble is, I also love spicy sausage meats and invariably wolf down far more than the fish I am after.

Among meats in skins I include ordinary pork or beef bangers (cooked and left to cool), chipolatas precooked in tins, tinned cocktail mini sausages, saveloys, garlic-based German sausage, black pudding, Pepperami, salami and the like. The list is as varied as you want it to be, and so there is always a change bait available should carp, for instance, start to wise up to a particular type or brand.

You have the option of dicing the sausage (in some instances it is best to remove the skin, in others, leave it on) into tiny cubes and using a large one either on the hook or presented on a fine hair. Or you can offer it over a bed of attractor particles such as stewed hempseed or red dari seeds (see page 196).

Opposite: Relaxed yet expectant, a barbel enthusiast legers a cube of luncheon meat among the shallow, weedy gravel runs on the Dorset Stour at the famous Throop Fishery near Holdenhurst.

Another attractor I regularly use when presenting meat cubes is extra-fine sinking trout pellets in granular form. A handful scattered into the swim or around the bait every so often works wonders.

RAW MEAT

When I was a nipper living in Enfield in North London, I regularly fished the local ponds with my grandad, who would always insist on taking along, in addition to our carefully prepared breadpaste and tin of 'gentles', a piece of fresh calf's or pig's liver for bait. I thought he was barmy, of course. But every now and again 'Pops' would whack into a sizeable common carp.

I'm not suggesting that liver and raw steak are anything more than just alternative options worth trying on occasion. But the fact remains, fish are really attracted to the blood, and I have regularly used raw steak successfully as a stand-by when in remote parts of the world, for both fresh and saltwater species. Catfish, especially, quickly home in on liver and raw steak, but it is imperative to change the bait regularly, since the blood dissipates, leaving the meat pale and unattractive.

Cut steak into suitable strips or chunks and hook it as with a lobworm, once only, with all the point and barb of the hook exposed. A cube of liver is best presented on a fine hair rig off the hook. Try raw meat for carp, chub, eels and catfish. You won't be disappointed. For eels and catfish, make up a few balls of groundbait (to deposit around the hookbait) from a mixture of brown breadcrumbs and fresh blood. Your local butcher will oblige.

CHEESE

Traditional hard and processed cheeses, as opposed to the soft ones which are spread straight from the tub, make great baits for chub, barbel and carp. It is well worth exploring the cheese counter in your supermarket, because in addition to cheeses such as Cheddar, Red Leicester and Double Gloucester, which don't crumble when cut, there are many smoked and processed cheeses, all of a suitable consistency for cutting, using a really sharp, thin-bladed knife, into $^{1}/_{2}$-in cubes or oblongs for presentation on a fine-hair rig (see diagram, page 181).

In waters where small species continually peck away at most baits, go for the rubbery cheeses, which are just as effective as boilies, I can thoroughly recommend Subenhard and Danbo from Denmark, Maasdan, Edam and Gouda from the Netherlands, Swiss Emmental and Gruyère and Jarlsberg from Norway. Also from Norway, the somewhat softer Gjetost is made from goats' milk and has a sweet, caramelized flavour.

For use as loose feed, dice a block into hundreds of mini cubes and scatter these into stillwater swims by hand or with a catapult. For barbel and chub in fast, deep swims, mini cubes can either be deposited by bait dropper, at close range, or at longer range with a large, heavy block-end feeder with the holes enlarged. Give a hefty pull on the feeder as it touches bottom, to ensure instant dispersal of the cubes.

CHAPTER TWENTY-TWO
Particle Baits

The secret of presenting 'particles', which by the handful number in their dozens of even hundreds, as opposed to single baits such as a lump of breadflake or paste, is that bottom-feeding fish become so confident grubbing about and hoovering up numerous small food items (because this is the way they feed naturally) that they are consequently far less suspicious of sucking in the hookbait.

Moreover, once they have been 'drawn' to a particular area by a particle attractor and start feeding aggressively, they will even gulp down much larger offerings without hesitation. For instance, one of the most successful combinations for carp, chub and barbel is a meat cube presented over a bed of stewed hempseed or tares. And surely there isn't a bream or tench living that won't suck up a big, juicy lobworm or a bunch of brandlings once attracted to the swim with either stewed wheat or casters mixed into a cereal-based groundbait. The opportunities for experimenting are immense.

It is worth pointing out that while baits such as casters and maggots are, of course, particle baits, the word 'particles' has over the years become synonymous with grains, peas, beans, nuts and seeds, most of which are cheap, easy to prepare and readily available from many sources. Visit your local pet shop, corn chandler, Indian food shops and health food shops, where you will be amazed at just how many potential fishing baits there are waiting to be tried. Most specialist tackle shops also stock many of the more popular particles in dried form, prepared and ready to use in vacuum packs – even ready-coloured.

The only word of warning I would issue about fishing particles is that you should always ensure they are properly soaked and stewed before use. Not only are they then more manageable for presentation both on and off the hook (as with a hair rig), loose seeds finding their way along the margins will not germinate and sprout, thus introducing alien plants to our indigenous stock of wild flowers. But very much more serious is the accidental damage and possible premature death which could occur in certain species through the expansion of uncooked nuts or grains inside the stomach. Indeed, on some of my local Norfolk tench and carp fisheries, particle baits of any kind, except sweetcorn, have been banned. This is a great pity and a sad reflection of attitudes and the state of coarse fishing in the 1990s.

Over the years all kinds of stories about particles have emanated from waters where fish, and carp in particular, are found dead, their bellies unnaturally bloated. As a fishery owner, I have always listened with great interest. After all, carp of a desirable, catchable size are certainly not cheap to purchase. And yet, having fished with stewed peanuts, for instance, for well over a decade, using them regularly on both my own two stillwater fisheries and local club lakes and pits, I have yet to come across a single carp death caused by them. I have even learnt to recognize certain distinctive individual carp stocked into my own two lakes which are repeatedly caught on peanuts by my syndicate members year after year. Therefore as far as I am concerned – and as I said previously, so long as they are pre-soaked and stewed properly – all particles, including peanuts, are extremely effective baits and no cause for concern.

Sweetcorn
I take my hat off to whoever first tried sweetcorn as a bait and passed the tip on. It is now common knowledge that this hybrid of the maize plant, which is harvested while young and tender, is an instant winner with non-predatory freshwater species all over the world in both running and stillwaters. Even

A feast of particle baits: first row, (left to right): peanuts, tiger nuts, maize; (second row): blue peas, hempseed, black beans, soya beans; (third row): red dari seeds, maples, buckwheat, malting barley, mung beans, black lentils; (fourth row): red sweetcorn, yellow sweetcorn, stewed wheat, black tares, yellow rice, aduki beans.

estuarine sea species, such as the grey mullet, readily accept corn.

Sweetcorn is among the top baits for carp, including crucians, tench, barbel, bream, chub and rudd, roach and dace. And while it is most often used in the summer, the majority of anglers thinking of it as an exclusively warm-weather bait, it can sometimes produce excellent results during cold water conditions, for chub in particular.

Even grayling love sweetcorn's bright-yellow colour. Or is it that unique sweet smell and succulent insides? Unfortunately, wherever small perch abound in sizeable shoals, they too will gobble up the yellow kernels fished static on or off the bottom and even on the retrieve.

For tench and bream, sweetcorn is certainly a fine change bait to breadflake, worms or maggots. Present a single kernel on

a size 14 hook, two on a size 12, or three or four up on a size 10. In practice, how many you use depends on the size of the individual kernels. If you economize by buying sweetcorn in bulk freezer packs, the kernels are noticeably larger and very much firmer than those in tins. To really fill up a size 8 or 6 hook when after carp, barbel or chub, for instance, slip three of four kernels on the hook and slide them over the eye and up the line. Then slip another three or four on to the bend and shank before sliding the others down against them. Another way of creating a good mouthful is to rig up several large kernels on a separate hair, tied direct to the bend of the hook. This creates a real mouthful – useful for crafty specimen fish in clear waters which repeatedly refuse corn slipped directly on to the hook.

Sweetcorn is also very effective as a 'cocktail' bait. Try presenting it on the bend of the hook with a liberal pinch of flake along the shank. Or experiment with maggots and corn, redworms or brandlings and corn, or casters and corn. How about corn plus a cube of luncheon meat? Simply sleeve two or three kernels up the line and down again after burying the hook in a meat cube (see

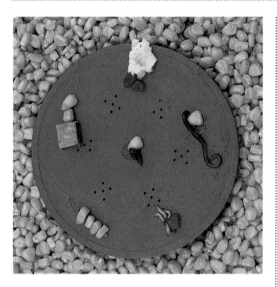

Plain yellow sweetcorn is a great particle bait, but so is red sweetcorn. Or how about trying sweetcorn cocktails, adding worms, breadflake, meat cubes or maggots? When fish are extra shy and spooky you can also hair rig corn most effectively.

A cupful of wheat put into a vacuum flask with boiling water and left overnight, will provide you with more than enough hookbaits for the following morning.

Meat in Tins, page 180). The permutations are limited only by your imagination.

Another ruse worth trying once fish wise up to plain yellow sweetcorn, is to change its colour. This is easily done by dissolving a teaspoon of powder dye (as used for colouring carp baits) into a cupful of hot water and pouring it over the sweetcorn (strain off the juices if it is tinned) placed into a clean bait box. Stir the mix gently until all the kernels are evenly coloured, and then drain the excess fluid off. Red, purple, orange and brown are worth trying. At the same time, incidentally, flavouring may be added. Or, to give yellow sweetcorn a different flavour, strain off any liquid and pop it into a clean polythene bag, adding a tablespoon of, say, oil of anis (the choice is yours) and shake vigorously. After a couple of hours most of the flavour will have been absorbed and the bait is ready to be used straight from the bag, or popped into the freezer.

Stewed Wheat

After returning a catch of tench or bream caught during the summer, you may notice lying in the bottom of the keepnet a residue of regurgitated natural foods in addition to your own hookbait and groundbait fragments. If you look carefully you will notice the seeds of natural grasses, blown into the water by the wind. My point is that many summer species are already tuned into feeding on the swollen grains of grasses as part of their natural daily diet, in addition to eating aquatic insect larvae and crustaceans. This is why stewed wheat is one of the most natural, but underrated and indeed most underused of all particle baits. I urge you to give it a try, whether for prebaiting a new location for carp, or as a bulk groundbait for bream, because wheat is amazingly cheap. You can buy from a farmer or corn chandler a 50-kg (hundredweight) sack of wheat for little more than the cost of a bag of shelf-life boilies or three pints of maggots.

Many of the ponds and estate lakes I fish in Norfolk for tench, carp and bream are most conveniently prebaited with regular sackfuls of wheat, as it is spread along the margins by farmers and wildfowlers to attract mallard and teal in readiness for the shooting

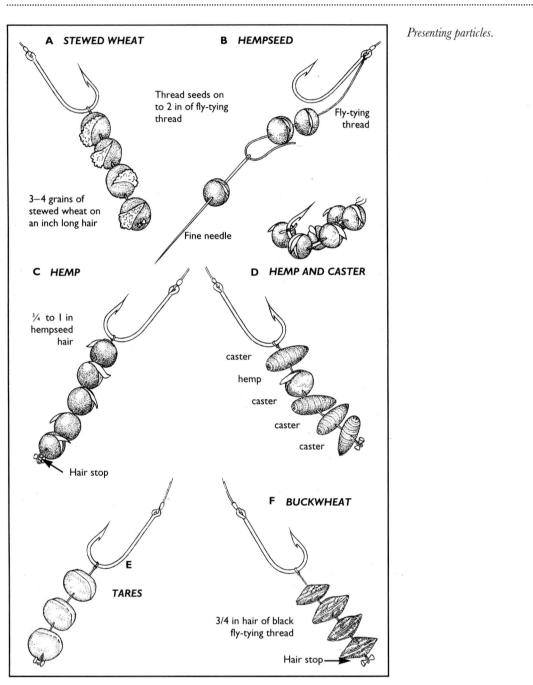

Presenting particles.

A STEWED WHEAT

3–4 grains of stewed wheat on an inch long hair

B HEMPSEED

Thread seeds on to 2 in of fly-tying thread

Fly-tying thread

Fine needle

C HEMP

¾ to 1 in hempseed hair

Hair stop

D HEMP AND CASTER

caster

hemp

caster

caster

caster

E TARES

F BUCKWHEAT

3/4 in hair of black fly-tying thread

Hair stop

season. The benefits to the angler of this common countryside practice are worth bearing in mind.

Wheat is an exceptionally clean bait, easy to prepare and easy to use, and works in both still and running water throughout the summer and autumn. To prepare just enough for a day's roach, rudd or dace fishing (chub love it too) on the evening before, pop a cupful of wheat into a large vacuum flask and top it up with boiling water, leaving space at the top for expansion of the grains. In the morning simply pour the wheat into a bait box. Incidentally, wheat swells to three times its size when stewed — a phenomenon my long-suffering mother regularly experienced, with exploding vacuum flasks and blackened saucepans full of wheat and hemp left on the cooker by her irresponsible, fishing-mad teenage son, long after all the water had boiled away. How I never set fire to the kitchen, I don't know.

To prepare large batches of wheat – it is a most effective tench, bream and carp particle – use three times the volume of water to wheat and bring it to the boil in an old saucepan (remember to open the kitchen windows) and leave it simmering for 10 minutes before turning off the heat. Leave it to stew overnight with the lid on.

Alternatively, leave a batch of wheat to soak in cold water for two days, then put it into a plastic bucket with a pull-off lid and cover with boiling water (twice as much by volume).

If you fancy having some fun by colouring wheat, this is the time to add a tablespoon of powder dye and stir in. Red and yellow provide the greatest contrast to its natural buff colour, but the choice is all yours. Press the lid firmly on and leave it, preferably for 48 hours, after which the excess water should be strained off. The grains may not have swelled quite to the size achieved by boiling and simmering or the 'flask' method, but for prebaiting or mixing with a cereal-based groundbait for bream or tench, they will be fine.

Freshly stewed wheat has a wonderful, highly distinctive nutty aroma, and a triangle-shaped split reveals the soft white (flour) inside. For the best results use it immediately. The aroma, I am certain, is part of this bait's very special magic. Alternatively, as with all particles, after preparation stewed wheat may be divided up and stored in polythene bags in the freezer for future use.

Using stewed wheat rather than, say, maggots or casters for roach or rudd, automatically (because of its size) sorts out a better stamp of fish. In fact, my first-ever roach over 2 lb, way back in 1957, caught by trotting a deep weirpool on the River Waveney in Suffolk, accepted stewed wheat.

Bites on wheat are invariably much slower too. But be careful not to overfeed the shoal. Wheat is a heavy, very filling bait. As with sweetcorn, one grain fits nicely on to a size 14 hook, three on a size 10, and so on. Alternatively, for finicky carp or barbel, string several grains on a fine-hair rig off the hook (see opposite diagram).

Maize

Yellowy-orange with a lovely popcorn smell (popcorn is simply exploded maize) and swelling to twice the size of even a large kernel of sweetcorn, properly prepared maize is a superb carp bait, totally impervious to the attentions of small nuisance species.

The only drawback is that preparation does take time, although in my opinion it is well worth the effort. Start by soaking the maize for a few days. It will still be rock-hard afterwards, but marginally more receptive to subsequent pressure cooking for a good 20 minutes. Pressure cooking is imperative. Simply boiling it and leaving it to simmer is usually not enough to expand this extremely resilient grain, although I have noticed really fresh maize swells much quicker than old stock, with which you stand no chance. I have left old maize in a tub of water for several weeks, until it stinks to high heaven, yet even in this putrid state it still refuses to swell. Mind you, in the USA, stinking, hard maize is a favourite bait among carp addicts. But not, I hasten to add, with this fisherman.

Once prepared, maize can be put in the freezer in polythene bags until needed. A single grain of maize is none too large for a size 8 hook, which makes it an ideal bait for tench, chub and barbel in addition to carp, whether float-fished or legered. Maize works effectively on a hair rig to overcome the problem of hook-shy fish and, unlike sweetcorn, will stay on when cast long distances.

Pearl Barley

Used in stews and country soups, pearl barley is also a useful fisherman's particle, not only as a binder for making fast-sinking groundbaits (see Groundbaits, page 177) but also as a hookbait and particle attractor. Off-white and smaller than wheat, barley is prepared in exactly the same way. It can also be coloured and/or flavoured during the expansion period, which culminates in a swollen, oval grain around the size of an AAA shot.

During the first half of the century pearl barley was a favourite trotting bait for roach and dace in southern England on rivers such as the Thames. And while today's favourites, such as casters, reign supreme, since shoal fish eventually wise up to the more commonly used offerings, there is good reason for turning the clock back and giving pearl barley a try.

Pearl barley is best presented singly on a size 16 or 14 hook while introducing a dozen or so loose grains every other trot down. Used as a stillwater attractor feed, it is excellent for most cyprinids, particularly tench, bream and carp.

Malting Barley

Being similar in size and colour to wheat, malting barley is best prepared in exactly the same way. When properly stewed, it swells to twice its dried form, splitting lengthways to reveal an off-white inside. It may be coloured with the addition of a teaspoon of powder dye during stewing (yellow, orange and red look terrific) and even flavoured. Present two grains on a size 14 hook, four or five on a size 8, or string half a dozen on to a fine hair tied to the bend of the hook. Like carp and tench, bream too hoover up malting barley, so it can be used like wheat as a bulk additive to cereal-based groundbaits. Even so, in my opinion it is a poor second to wheat.

Rice

Much underrated and rarely used by the vast majority of fishermen, boiled rice is in fact a great bulk additive for making tench and bream groundbaits (see Groundbaits, page 177) and an inexpensive mass-particle attractor for carp. It is virtually impossible to present on the hook, however.

Rice is easy to colour. My preference is for a deep golden-yellow, simply achieved by adding a teaspoon of turmeric to the water when boiling. The powder dyes used for making carp baits also work well. Because rice expands, always add treble the volume of water and leave it to simmer for 15 minutes after it starts to boil. Finally, tip the contents

into a colander and leave for a while to drain away the excess water.

Hempseed

Were I limited to the use of just one particle for all my freshwater fishing, not as hookbait but as a loose-feed attractor, then without hesitation I would choose hempseed, which I truly believe has almost magical qualities. Some say that because of its mussel-like shape and because the stewed seeds sprout tiny white shoots, hempseed is mistaken by fish for tiny pea shell cockles, on which they feed naturally. Others put more importance on its unique aroma and oil content, which permeate the water once it is lying on the bottom. Either way, its pulling powers are without equal, for no other particle attractor puts barbel and carp into a feeding frenzy as quickly as stewed hempseed. In addition, it has the benefit that small nuisance fish tend to leave it alone, which is a godsend when you are fishing in a gin-clear summer river for chub and barbel. Also, while casters and maggots, if not attacked by minnows, bleak or dace, instantly get washed downstream and out of the swim, hempseed settles attractively on the bottom among the sand and gravel, remaining there until barbel or chub find it.

Because hempseed proved so effective in barbel rivers, anglers started gross overfeeding, which led to this fine bait being banned on fisheries such as Throop on the Dorset Stour and the Hampshire Avon's famous Royalty, which is a great pity. There is no need to overfeed: simply attract the fish — two pints is quite sufficient for a day's sport on all but the largest of rivers — and then use a different bait on the hook.

Although hempseed works best purely as an attractor for barbel, carp and chub in conjunction with a cube of meat, casters, maggots, peanuts, corn, tares, maple peas or tiger nuts on the hook, there are occasions when it is worth trying as a hookbait. This can be achieved in two ways

Opposite: Well stewed peanuts are a fabulous carp bait, whether legered or float-fished 'lift style', the method John employed to lure this lean double-figure fish.

(see diagram, page 188). Either wind a string of seeds around a long shank hook, or simply hang a short hair of seeds from the bend of the hook. Other small particles such as casters, tares, buckwheat or maggots can be threaded on along with the seeds (see diagram, page 188), but because these rigs take time to arrange, it is not necessary when bites are fast and furious. Keep it as a trick up your sleeve for when fishing is hard.

When you are using hempseed for smaller species, dace and roach in particular, beware of overfeeding, which encourages super-fast bites that are almost impossible to hit. In clear water during the summer, dace and roach can actually be seen 'flashing' as they rise close to the surface, competing for the loose seeds thrown in, and this results in many false bites as they peck mistakenly at the split shot. To overcome this problem wind a length of lead wire around the line a foot from the hook and secure it by bending it over at each end. Fix all additional shots around the base of the float.

For roach and dace, a size 16 or 14 hook is perfect for presenting a single seed. Simply press the bend of the hook into the split. What also invariably improves results is to loose-feed with hemp, just a half dozen seeds every other trot down, while presenting an elderberry, tare or caster on the hook. In cold water conditions a single caster or bronze maggot trotted close to the bottom over loose-fed hemp is a deadly combination for roach and chub.

Preparing Hempseed

To prepare a batch of hempseed (and most other particles) is simplicity itself. You can boil and simmer it in an old saucepan (with the emphasis on 'old') on the cooker for 30 minutes – and completely stink the kitchen out. But far easier is to leave the seeds in cold water to soak for two to three days, then drain the water off, put them into a bucket with a pull-off lid and cover them with boiling water to a depth of 2 in. Press the lid down firmly, and simply leave them to stew and swell in their own juices for a minimum of 24 hours, during which time they will split and darken, almost to black. If you can wait 48 hours, so much the better. For carp fishing I prefer to leave hemp in the bucket for several days, almost until it starts fermenting, when I am sure it has even greater pulling power.

Once the seeds are ready, the surplus water can be strained off and the bait used immediately. Or it can be popped into the freezer, a pint or two to a polythene bag, until required. As it is a bait I use regularly throughout the season for carp, barbel, roach, dace and chub, I prefer to prepare hempseed a gallon or two at a time, as I do with several other particles. This way, it is less time-consuming and very much cheaper.

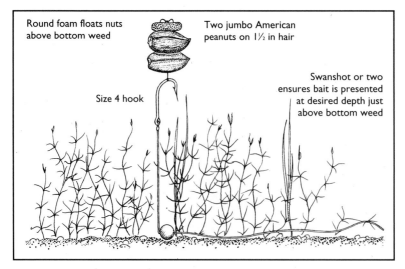

Round foam floats nuts above bottom weed

Two jumbo American peanuts on 1½ in hair

Size 4 hook

Swanshot or two ensures bait is presented at desired depth just above bottom weed

Presenting peanuts.

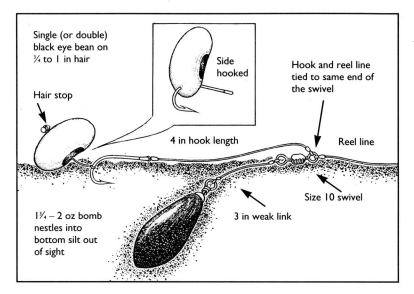

Single (or double) black eye bean on ¾ to 1 in hair

Hair stop

Side hooked

Hook and reel line tied to same end of the swivel

4 in hook length

Reel line

1¾ – 2 oz bomb nestles into bottom silt out of sight

3 in weak link

Size 10 swivel

Simple shock rig for particles and boilies.

Tares

As either loose feed or hookbaits or both, tares are preferable to hempseed for some anglers. The preparation of tares is exactly the same as for hemp, and I like to leave tares in the bucket for 48 hours before straining the excess water off and bagging them up for the freezer or immediate use.

Naturally dark brown, tares often work more effectively for trotting if coloured black. Simply add a tablespoon of powder dye (the carp bait kind) in with the boiling water and stir gently to mix well in. To allow for expansion (with one gallon of tares) ensure the boiling water covers them by at least 3 in. For legering and loose-feeding tares for chub, barbel or carp, fix tares three or four up on a short hair (see diagram). Alternatively, simply rely on the tares as loose feed, using a change bait on the hook such as a mini boilie, cube of meat or tiger nuts. For trotting for roach, dace and chub, a single tare fits nicely on a size 14 hook. A winning combination is to feed with tares while using a caster or an elderberry on the hook. Experimenting with hookbait alternatives invariably produces results.

Buckwheat

In its curious angled and dried form, this unusual particle from the Middle East looks incredibly like the shell of a minute Brazil nut and would seem to be anything but a fishing bait. However, being small and dark, it is yet another 'change' particle that can be effectively used for carp, chub or barbel that have been bombarded with all the more popular offerings. Preparation is the same as for wheat, and while two or three grains fit neatly on a size 8 hook, once softened and split, buckwheat is also very effectively presented on the hair rig, whether legered or float-fished (see diagram). Try a single grain on a size 14 hook when loose-feeding hempseed or tares for roach, dace and chub.

Tick Beans

Prepared in exactly the same way as wheat, this large, shiny, dark-brown bean is deadly for carp as both loose feed and hookbait, or simply as a hookbait presented over a bed of hemp, tares, buckwheat or maple peas. It is certainly among the top six particle baits for carp.

Tick beans can be legered and/or float-fished beneath a 'lift rig', either side-hooked or offered two up on a hair. They are a most reliable bait for casting long distances, totally impervious to the attentions of small nuisance species which rip softies and wheat to bits in minutes. Try them for barbel when loose-feeding with tares or hempseed.

Maple Peas

I once reared a squab (fledgling pigeon) by having to chew into pulp and then

Float-fishing particles such as tiger nuts at close quarters demands the utmost stealth and concentration. John prefers to kneel so that he is close to the water, holding the rod throughout for an instant strike.

regurgitate twice a day an entire mouthful of softened maple peas. They are certainly not my idea of food, but like most small, dark particles, maple peas are adored by carp. Preparation is exactly the same as for wheat, and the results may be frozen if not used immediately.

Once softened, maples may be side-hooked two up on a size 8 hook or threaded on to a hair with a baiting needle, three or even four up. Use both as loose feed and hookbait, or as a change hookbait only, presented over a bed of tares or hempseed. They are well worth trying for barbel and chub.

Blue Peas
Years ago blue peas (a pale greenish-blue version of maples) were soaked and mixed into soups and stews. Perhaps they still are, but it is mostly pigeon fanciers who buy them nowadays – and carp fishermen. Preparation and presentation are exactly the same as for maples, though blue peas are generally much less effective, probably because of their lighter colour.

Peanuts
I have to admit that I am a peanut addict. I also rate them very highly indeed as a carp bait, or simply as a hookbait presented over a bed of much smaller particles such as hemp, buckwheat, maples, tares or red dari seeds. Better still, in my opinion, is to loose feed with standard-sized nuts and on the hook offer giant American peanuts. These, once swollen, may be side-hooked singly on a size 6 hook or two up on a size 4, but ensure that the point and barb are exposed for clean hooking. Alternatively, whether legering with a bolt rig or presenting peanuts beneath a simple lift rig – my favourite method with this bait – sleeve two nuts on to a 1 in hair.

Their tremendous buoyancy makes

Left: Colouring white particles such as black-eyed beans could not be easier. All you need is a bucket with a rip-off lid, a spoonful of powder dye, a spoonful of flavouring, and boiling water.

Below: It is sensible and very much cheaper to colour and flavour particles in bulk. Then pack them into polythene bags and store them in the freezer for future use.

peanuts ideal for presenting over a weedy or snaggy bottom (see diagram). Where soft weeds prove troublesome, however, use a similar length piece of round, buoyant foam on the hair with the two nuts so that they float well within the carp's vision above the bottom crud. This ruse works with most particles.

In still waters that are extensively baited with peanuts for carp, tench quickly learn to get in on the act and acquire a liking for them. And so do the quality roach. Moreover, if you are attracting barbel or chub into a particular swim by prebaiting with loose-fed hempseed or tares, give peanut hookbaits a try. Simply dice up a few nuts and mix them in with the loose feed so that the fish get used to the taste.

Ready-shelled (unroasted) standard-sized peanuts are perfect for loose-feeding and prebaiting and can be bought from corn merchants, pet shops and even specialist tackle shops by the pint or in 25-kg (half-hundredweight) sacks. The jumbo American peanuts are available from health food shops

and specialist tackle shops.

The method of preparation which swells the peanuts to at least half as big again and makes them rubbery for easy hooking without the two halves coming apart. Like hempseed, nuts are best prepared in bulk in a large plastic bucket with a pull-off lid. To allow for expansion, cover them with boiling water to a depth of several inches and leave them for 48 hours after pressing the lid down firmly. They will be nicely swollen and ready for immediate use or for bagging up and storing in the freezer once any excess water has been strained off.

Tiger Nuts

For carp, I rate these crunchy vegetarian treats as having almost the same pulling power as peanuts. Tiger nuts can be bought from health food shops or specialist tackle shops in bulk or in pint packs already prepared. Care must be taken with their preparation, which is similar to that of maize. Soaking them for a full 48 hours in a bucket of cold water and then pressure cooking them for 20 minutes really softens them up. Alternatively, after the initial soaking, put half a pint at a time (barely covered with water) into a cereal bowl and microwave them on the high setting for 15 minutes.

I love to float-fish tigers on a lift rig along the margins, having loose-fed with them or hempseed. I side-hook the nuts, or where cautious carp are a problem, present them on a hair rig. One nut fits nicely on a size 8 hook, two on a 6 or a size 4. Tiger nuts vary considerably in size and shape, and I have a habit of sorting through and selecting the long ones for hookbaits. They are a great long-distance legering bait as they rarely fly off on the cast.

Sometimes it takes carp several sessions of prebaiting to switch on to this curious-looking new food source. But when they acquire a liking for tiger nuts, action is assured. They also make a good change hookbait for barbel and chub in conjunction with loose-fed buckwheat, tares or hempseed.

Red Dari Seeds

These interesting little seeds, which come from the Middle East, once prepared (as for wheat) make an exceptionally fine particle attractor for carp. Like wheat, they benefit from being left to slightly ferment in their own juices for a few days. Colour alone sets them apart from other mass particles in that they are of mixed colours, from buff to dark brown, and so a carpet of daris is not instantly frightening to an approaching carp. As they are small, the seeds are best presented several at a time on a fine-hair rig and a size 8 or 6 hook. This is an effective bait when fished over a bed of tares or hemp, or used as both loose feed and hookbait.

Mung Beans

Small and pale green, mung beans are prepared exactly the same way as wheat. As with most particles, if you have the time, soaking them beforehand in cold water for 48 hours will produce maximum expansion during stewing. Present three or four beans on a fine hair and a size 8 hook, whether float fishing or legering in conjunction with a bolt rig.

Mung beans are not in the same league as hempseed as an attractor, but carp do respond to them in well-stocked waters, whether used purely as a hookbait over a bed of hemp or as both loose feed and hookbait.

Black-eyed Beans

These beans, widely available from health food stores, can also be bought in specialist tackle shops, which sell them by the sack, by the pint, and even ready-prepared. Black-eyes can also be purchased in tins, but it is far better and considerably cheaper to buy them in dried form in bulk and prepare them yourself.

This off-white salad bean with a distinctive black 'eye' can easily be stewed, coloured and flavoured to suit any purpose. It is therefore one of the most versatile of all particles for carp, which, in the vast majority of fisheries, respond quickly to prebaiting with it.

Preparation is the same as for peanuts, with the addition of a tablespoon each of powder colouring and flavouring. Be sure to cover the beans with at least half their own volume of boiling water, because their expansion is massive. The permutations of colours and flavours are endless and very much part of the fun gained from preparing these and other particle baits. Colours I have used to good effect are orange, yellow, brown and red, while successful flavours are aniseed, maple, caramel and butterscotch. Experiment for yourself. Why not, for instance, dye the beans jet-black and get them to reek to high heaven with squid extract?

One bean fits nicely when side-hooked on a size 8 and two work well on a size 6 or 4. Make sure that the point and barb go right through and are fully exposed, or penetration on the strike could be impaired. Black-eyes also thread nicely on to a fine-hair rig with the aid of a baiting needle, and, like most particles, work well in conjunction with a simple bolt rig (see diagram).

In waters where black-eyes are extensively used for carp, other species, tench in particular, soon learn to appreciate them, and it is not uncommon to account for the occasional quality roach or rudd, especially when presenting these beans on a lift rig.

Black Beans

I suspect that anyone who enjoys Chinese food will be acquainted with the flavour of this shiny black bean, which is about the same size as a black-eye, and can be prepared, presented, and even flavoured in exactly the same manner. Strangely, though, I have not experienced the same kind of success with this particular bean as I have with black-eyes.

Soya Beans

These creamy-white beans, an important food source all over the world, are halfway in shape between round and oval, and the size of a swan shot. They swell considerably if prepared in the same way as wheat, turning pale yellow. If this colour is not to your liking, simply add a spoonful of powder dye to the boiling water plus the flavouring of your choice.

Soya beans can be side-hooked for float fishing and legering at reasonably close range, one up on a size 8 or two on a size 6.

But for distances beyond 25 yards, because of their softness they are best threaded on to a hair rig, say three up on a size 6 hook. They are a very effective particle for carp, and tench also accept them readily.

Chick Peas

These round, creamy-coloured peas are a firm salad favourite throughout Europe and are gaining in popularity in Britain as people turn towards healthier food. Chick peas are available ready-prepared in cans in most supermarkets, but this is a very expensive way to buy them. It is far better to buy them in bulk from health food stores and prepare them yourself, using the same method as for wheat. Chick peas accept colours and flavours readily, which makes them an extremely versatile particle that carp soon latch on to after a little prebaiting.

Since chick peas are almost round, once coloured – deep red is my choice – they look very similar to medium-sized boilies and are presented in the same way. They can be either side-hooked or threaded on a fine-hair rig, with hooks in sizes 8 and 6.

Haricot Beans

In their familiar form as baked beans, haricots are an instant particle in a can, effective both for carp and tench. Although somewhat soft to present, baked beans may be carefully side-hooked for close range float fishing, but are best hair-rigged for legering and presented up to medium range only. Hooks in size 10 and 8 complement this bait nicely. Plain haricot beans are also available in tins, but frankly they are not worth the bother.

Borlotti Beans

These beans are another convenient carp bait available ready-cooked and in a rich sauce in a tin. I find borlottis far superior to baked beans and, since they are slightly larger and firmer, easier to present. Side-hook them for float fishing or thread them on a hair for legering. They work especially well in heavily coloured water as both loose feed and hookbait, or as hookbait only when presented in conjunction with a mass-particle attractor such as hempseed.

Mounted using a fine baiting needle and a Gardner V hairstop, here are a selection of particles some hair-rigged and others side-hooked, ready for action. (First row, left to right): peanuts, blue peas, aduki beans; (second row): soya beans, black beans, maize; (third row): tiger nuts, maples, black tares.

Red Kidney Beans

One of the biggest beans available, red kidney beans do not require colouring, but, in their dried form, must be prepared in exactly the same manner as wheat. They are available in bulk packs from health food shops and from supermarkets precooked in cans ready to be mixed with a salad or chilli con carne. Incidentally, unless these particular beans have been thoroughly stewed, it is dangerous to eat them. Red kidneys are a fine carp bait when presented over a carpet of maples, tick beans or hemp, and when used as both hookbait and loose feed. Side-hook them on a size 6 or use two on a fine-hair rig tied to a size 4.

Butter Beans

By far the largest bean, and flat in cross-section, butter beans seem almost designed for fishing over-dense weed or thick silt, where small particles soon disappear. On

Used in conjunction with loosefed hempseed, long trotting elderberries is a superb technique for taking dace, roach and chub throughout the autumn and winter months.

some waters they produce carp, on others nothing at all.

Butter beans can be bought precooked in tins or in bulk from health food stores. Stew them in the same way as hempseed, adding powder colouring and flavouring if you prefer. Being large, butter beans permit the use of large hooks, and though soft, are heavy enough to be freelined into lily pads on weightless tackle, just like a lump of paste, if you cast with care. They are a good particle for hair-rigging and offering with a 'lift rig'.

Elderberries

Though elderberries are not generally considered a particle bait, I have included them in this chapter because when trotted in conjunction with loose-fed tares and especially stewed hempseed, they are a cracking bait for dace, roach and chub, and I have even caught barbel on them.

The secret is to harvest the berries in the autumn before they become overripe, and bottle them for use at any time throughout the season. If you try to pull them from the stalks they will spoil, so simply cut off little bunches containing 20 or 30 berries and let them drop straight into a preserving jar containing a solution of dilute formalin or glycerine. When required, simply give the berries a good rinse in cold water and present them on a size 16 or 14 hook.

The finest spots for trotting with elderberries are where elder trees hang out over the river and provide the occupants with an autumnal windfall of these juicy purple-black fruits.

Aduki Beans

These mahogany-coloured beans possess a strong but pleasantly nutty aroma, and once prepared, reach double the size of a swan shot, though oval and typically bean-shaped. Simply bring them to the boil in twice their volume of water, to allow for expansion, and simmer for 30 minutes. Then rinse them in cold water or leave to cool. Store them in the freezer in a polythene bag if they are not for immediate use.

An effective particle for carp, aduki beans can be side-hooked singly on a size 10 or three to a 6, or hair-rigged three or four up, and presented over a bed of hempseed or as both loose-fed attractor and hookbait.

Black Lentils

Also called urid whole or black matpe, black lentils, which because of their protruding white shoot look rather like stewed hempseed even before preparation, are readily available from Indian food shops. Some of my carp-fishing friends even rate them on a par with stewed hempseed both as attractor and hookbait, although in my opinion their aroma is not as penetrating. Nevertheless, black lentils, which turn a khaki colour when stewed, are well worth trying in fisheries where the carp are suspicious of all the more commonly used small attractor particles, purely as an attractor or as both attractor and hookbait.

Black lentils can be side-hooked singly on a size 10, two up on a size 8 or 5 up on a hair. To prepare them, bring to the boil in twice their volume of water and simmer for just 10 minutes – any longer and they go mushy. They may then be used straight away or frozen for future sessions. Like hempseed, black lentils prove more effective if left in the water in which they were stewed for a few days before use.

SPECIMEN HUNTING

Just why the pursuit of specimen fish has provided me, and countless other anglers, with so much pleasure. is difficult to explain, especially to the uninitiated. All I know is that ever since experiencing the thrill of that first quivering roach, extracted from Barnes Pond on a makeshift rod and line not long after World War II, I have been a hunter of big fish. Initially, any fish over 1 lb in weight would suffice, no matter what the species. Then particular species were targeted: perch, roach, pike, chub, barbel, tench and, finally, the mighty carp, in that order. This, in turn, led to the quest for bigger specimens; and, more than 40 years after the capture of that first roach, the enthusiasm still remains.

My search for big fish has led me around some of the most delightful, exciting and exclusive waters in England. Redmire Pool: the home of giant carp and haunt of all those famous names of the past like Dick Walker, Peter Thomas, Fred J. Taylor, Maurice Ingham. The Royalty Fishery on the Hampshire Avon: this was where F. W. K. Wallis and the Hon. A. D. Tryon caught their record-equalling barbel, not to mention the record chub caught respectively by F. W. Smith, G. F. Smith, and Bill Warren, the doyen of this country's barbel anglers in the 1950s and 60s. Throop Fishery on the Dorset Stour: still the home of some of the most impressive river fish. The pits of the Colne Valley, Longfield, where I saw the biggest common carp of my life; Savay, Wraysbury, the Long Life pits, the River Kennet, the Longford syndicate waters on the upper Hampshire Avon...the list goes on.

Big-fish angling has also brought me some of the finest friends a fellow could wish for, anglers like Bob Buteux and Bill Quinlan, two of the finest fishermen of my generation. Then there is Ron Chant, without whose help my 14 lb barbel would not have been landed; Kevin Clifford, who first encouraged me to write of my fishing experiences; Jack Hilton and the late Tom Mintram, who allowed me to join the Redmire syndicate in 1973; fellow Carp Catchers' Club members like 'BB', Fred J. Taylor and Maurice Ingham, all of whom have indulged my passion for angling memorabilia, as have angling legend Peter Stone, and Chris Sandford, Bob James, Chris Yates and Hugh Miles, the stars and makers of the best angling series yet filmed 'A Passion for Angling'; and, finally, Peter Drennan without whose help and trust these words would never have been penned.

If the pursuit of specimen fish brings you only half the blessings it has brought me, you will still be very fortunate indeed. So enjoy this book, learn, and then go out and catch that big fish. With a little patience and persistence eventually it will happen.

Best wishes to you all,

Len Arbery
Captor of a 14 lb barbel and winner of the Drennan Cup in 1990.

*The angler puts the
pressure on and wins
another hard fought
battle*

CHAPTER TWENTY-THREE

Start with Carp

If you are thinking of taking up specimen hunting, why not start with carp? A species that has gained in popularity over the past few years, carp will give you a real taste for the big-fish scene. However, as you start out on the road to becoming a carp angler, don't set your sights too high. Remember that carp do not start at 20 lb. Although there are lots of pictures of fish over this size published in the angling press, it would be wrong to believe they are easy to catch.

Start with a water that is heavily stocked with fish running right through the range from real babies of 2 lb to 10 lb. This type of fishery is a good grooming ground. Here you will be able to learn how to play and land fair-sized fish, and get an insight into the different baits and rigs.

Fishing the smaller carp waters will also help you to understand the movements of fish, how they react to wind, temperature changes and, of course, angling pressure. It is no good buying all the fancy gear if you do not know the first thing about the species.

The heavily stocked water will give you a good foundation on which to build. Lessons learned at this stage will help you in the future.

TACKLING UP

Most tackle shops will have a vast array of carp rods from 10 ft to 13 ft, and test curves ranging from 1½ lb to 3½ lb. It's best to start with an 11-ft or 12-ft rod with a test curve of 2 lb, which will be heavy enough to cast a 2 oz leger a good distance and still be forgiving when it comes to playing a decent carp under the rod-tip.

Big-fish anglers often select rods by test curves, but exactly what does this mean? The test curve is a guide to a rod's power; traditionally it was the weight that had to be suspended from the rod-tip to pull it into a 90-degree arc. Test curves are always given in

The helicopter rig – a superb method for catching carp.

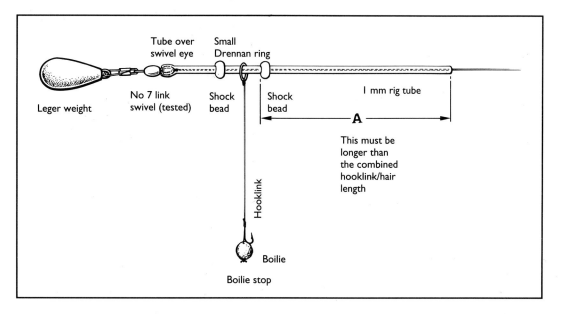

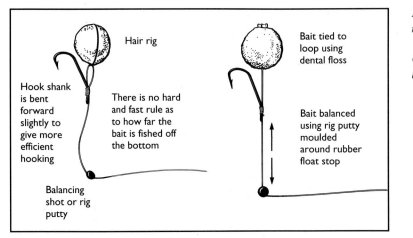

Hair rig

Hook shank is bent forward slightly to give more efficient hooking

There is no hard and fast rule as to how far the bait is fished off the bottom

Balancing shot or rig putty

Bait tied to loop using dental floss

Bait balanced using rig putty moulded around rubber float stop

Left: Two methods of making a 'pop-up' bait.

Opposite: A good anti-tangle rig.

pounds and fractions of pounds, and specialist big-fish rods usually start at around 1½ lb. You are unlikely to need a rod in the UK with a test curve of more than 2½ lb.

Despite all the advances in modern rod technology, the test curve probably remains the safest way of choosing a rod for specimen fishing. As a simple guide, multiply the test curve of a rod by five to give yourself an idea of the best breaking strain of line to use with it. For example, if a rod has a test curve of 2 lb, the ideal line strength will be 10 lb. Of course, it is never quite as simple as that. Cost, material and action as well as length will all be determining factors in your rod choice. Do not feel you have to use a certain breaking strain of line with a rod of a certain test curve. Good rods will handle large fish even if you are not using a line with the 'ideal' breaking strain. Similarly, an experienced hand can use a higher breaking strain line than the ideal one.

Buy a rod with lined rings, especially the butt and tip rings, and a screw-type reel fitting. Big reels tend to work loose on the fittings on match rods. Most modern-day carp rods seem to be fitted with abbreviated duplon handles, which are fine. They may look a little strange compared to a standard match rod, but they are good enough for the job in hand. Some carp anglers will use only black rods with black whippings because of a belief that they will catch more fish with them. That is nonsense. There are many good rods with colourful cosmetic finishes.

Most reels over £20 are of an excellent standard nowadays so you do not have to pay the earth. There are various situations where specialist rods and reels costing a lot of money will be needed, but do not be too adventurous when you are starting out. Buy a reel that will hold at least 150 yd of 10 lb line with a gear ratio of 4:1 or 5:1. Do not get one of those super-fast ratio match reels for playing big carp because they will lose you fish. Some anglers back-wind when playing carp while others prefer to use the clutch. Nowadays, you have a choice of reels, some with the clutch at the front of the spool some with a rear drag. It is wise to find out which suits you before actually paying out your hard-earned cash. Spare spools are cheap to buy so get several. Then you can load them up with 4 lb line (for floatfishing), 6 lb (for open water fishing) and 10 lb to 12 lb (for use in snaggy swims). Use the knowledge you have built up from general coarse fishing to decide the right line strength. It is all very well getting plenty of takes, but it worth nothing if you are broken by a big fish. Make sure you have the right breaking strain for the job.

Choice of hooks is very much a personal decision, but not every pattern in the bigger sizes makes a good carp hook. You may swear by a hook you have been using for maggots but in a size 2 it may be useless for fishing with boilies. Carp have thick rubbery lips so your hookpoint needs to be sharp. The first thing you should do after buying a

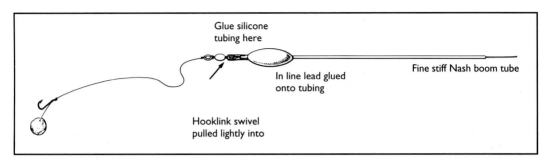

Glue silicone
tubing here

In line lead glued
onto tubing

Fine stiff Nash boom tube

Hooklink swivel
pulled lightly into

packet of hooks is to check them with a magnifying glass. Check for a good barb, correctly shaped eye or spade, and sharpness of point. Put the good hooks in an appropriate box and throw the others away. A hook costs pennies, but it could make or break your day's sport.

The list of accessories is endless. Take a trip to your tackle shop and you will be amazed at the number of carp knives, baiting needles, chairs, bite alarms, stainless-steel buzzer bars and rod-rests on sale. However, be careful, because you can spend so much money on looking the part that you cannot afford to go fishing. Most important, you will need a landing net with 36-in arms and a strong handle. The pan nets used by match and pleasure anglers are unsuitable both in size and strength. Bite alarms – more commonly called buzzers or optonics – cost anything from £10 to £70 each. You can catch carp without them, but if you expect a long wait between 'runs' they can be invaluable. Even on those small-carp waters, the fish can sometimes take a little time before picking up the bait.

BAITS

Do not get carried away with the idea that carp can only be caught on boilies. Maggots, casters, meat, sweetcorn, pastes of various flavours and bread will all take their fair share of carp. However, boilies are the most favoured bait, and many thousands are used by Britain's carp anglers every year in their quest for a specimen fish. The majority of baits used are bought off the shelf, and are so popular because of their convenience.

The top fishermen will most likely use their own baits, prepared in advance at home. They will experiment with mixes, additives and colourings to find a bait that will make the difference between catching a 20-pounder or leaving the lakeside fishless. There is nothing complicated about boilie-making. With a little practice you will be preparing your own baits quickly and efficiently, and the satisfaction you will get from catching fish on them will make the effort worthwhile.

If you have already done some carp fishing you will know that a boilie is a small, round bait. But why is it so called? The simple answer lies in the bait-making process. After being rolled into a small ball, the boilie is placed in boiling water for a short time to give it a hard outer skin and to help the eggs in the mix to congeal quickly.

You will find that it is a lot more economical to make your own baits than to buy shelf-life boilies, and you should eventually enjoy experimenting with different mixes. However, do not run before you can walk. Start by using one of the many boilie base mixes that are commercially produced in powdered form, and do not go overboard with exotic flavourings or additives. Ask your local tackle dealer which are the most popular brands of mixes because you can be sure these are very effective.

In the beginning you do not need many tools for boilie production, but after a time you might like to buy specialist bait-making systems that will save you time. However, your wife or girlfriend may not like you using their favourite mixing bowl or non-stick saucepan, so you may need to invest in both before you start. A deep mixing bowl is best.

When it comes to ingredients the first thing to buy is your boilie base mix. Mixes such as bird food or fish food come in bags of

The angler's pulses are racing as he lands a hard-fighting fish.

around 4 lb. Many companies sell products for boilie-making – the majority are excellent – so it is a case of choosing one of the leading brands. Next, you need eggs. As a general rule, six per lb of mix is the right amount. In the beginning flavourings and dyes are optional, but a vegetable oil like sesame seed oil helps to add essential fats and make the bait roll out smoother.

Put a saucepan of water on the stove to come to the boil. Crack three eggs into a mixing bowl. Use a pipette to add flavouring (if used) to the eggs – 1 ml of flavouring per egg is the ideal amount. The vegetable oil should also be added at this stage – 10 ml for three eggs – plus a small sprinkling of colouring powder. Whisk the flavourings, dye and eggs together and then add the base mix. You want a sticky texture so make sure you do not add too much powder or the mixture will go stiff and be difficult to roll out. Mix the contents together and then knead into a ball of paste.

Break the paste into smaller balls and roll out with both hands into sausages. With a knife, chop the sausages into bait-sized pieces,

Carp should be handled with care and quickly returned to the water after capture.

and then roll each one into a ball between both hands. By now the saucepan of water should be boiling. Put about 20 balls in a cooking basket and immerse in the water. Depending on how hard you want them to be, the baits should be left in the boiling water between 30 seconds and 3 minutes. The longer you leave them, the harder they will get. Shake off the water before dropping the baits on to a piece of cardboard to cool.

RIGS

As carp fishing has become more popular in recent years, pressure on fisheries has obviously increased. This has led to greater developments in rigs and terminal tackle as fish have become harder to catch. Consequently, owing to the popularity and effectiveness of ultra-supple hooklink materials, it has now become necessary to use end rigs that help to eliminate any tangles. There is nothing worse than sitting by the side of a lake worrying whether or not your end tackle is tangled. It does your confidence no good at all when you reel in at the end of

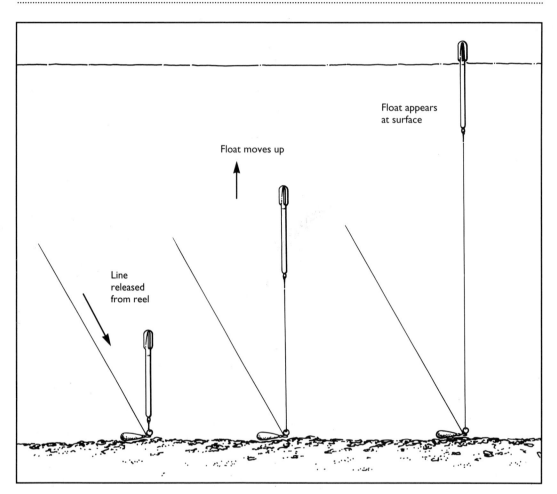

Float appears at surface

Float moves up

Line released from reel

a night session, only to find that your hooklink is wrapped tightly around your leger weight. It will have been a complete waste of time.

To a certain extent it is possible to eliminate tangles by feathering the line on your cast. This means that you are slowing down the leger weight, and the hooklink is generally held further forward during flight, and as a result enters the water straighter. One disadvantage with feathering the line is that casting distance is cut down. That's no problem if you are fishing at close or medium range, but puts constraints on distance fishing.

For all-round efficiency you will find the best way to eliminate tangles is to incorporate some kind of anti-tangle tubing into your set-up, and this will give the added advantage of protecting your main line from getting roughed up or broken on sharp gravel bars.

There are a number of different permutations on rigs using tubing and all of the ones shown in the diagrams should hold you in good stead. All the necessary bits and pieces to make up these rigs are available from most good tackle shops. For the helicopter-type rigs shown, use $\frac{1}{2}$ mm black PVC tubing; for the other rigs, fine stiff boom tube is ideal. The stiff tubing will improve your casting distance because it adds extra lift and more stability to the leger weight in flight. As an example, imagine throwing a javelin without its long tail section – it would not go very far.

Having decided which anti-tangle rig to use, you next have to decide how to present your hookbait. The 'in' thing over the past few years has been to use popped-up hookbaits – floating boilies fished anything

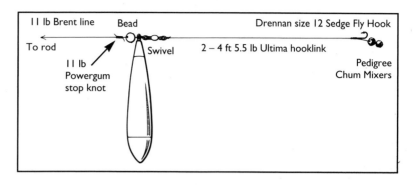

Opposite: After casting, release line from the reel 12 in at a time until the float appears at the surface.

Right: A good rig for surface fishing for carp.

from 1 inch to 1 ft off the bottom of the lake. Pop-ups are a very effective method because they are clearly visible to the fish and waft about enticingly should a fish swim nearby. Carp, being generally inquisitive creatures, sometimes can't resist sampling them whether they're interested in feeding or not. There are a number of different methods that can be used to make pop-ups. The most common is to cook boilies in a microwave oven for three to four minutes. You can also bake them in an ordinary oven, grill them or simply roll polystyrene inserts into baits before boiling them.

A recent innovation that has come about because of the use of pop-ups is the bent hook. When used correctly, the bent hook can lead to extra fish on the bank because the hook turns more easily when a carp ejects the bait and catches inside the mouth. One problem, though, is that bent hooks inflict more damage to the fish's mouth than normal hooks, therefore it is unwise to advocate their use. You should stick with the more normal hooks because if your bait presentation is right you will still catch lots of fish.

SURFACE FISHING

Surface fishing for carp is one of the most enjoyable and successful ways to catch fish, and yet too few anglers take it very seriously. Especially on warm and sunny days, it is worth giving it a try, probably before all other methods. The sight of surface-feeding carp taking floating baits can set the pulses racing as you wait in anticipation for a fish to pick out your hookbait. The beauty of this method

is that you don't need much tackle. You can walk around a lake with one made-up rod, a landing net, a bag of bait, and a catapult. It cuts out those long sessions on the bank; in fact it's ideal for those short early morning or evening fishing trips.

It is not necessary to have special rods and reels for surface fishing. However, it is probably better to use a softer-actioned rod because you will sometimes be fishing with lighter breaking strain hooklinks. Therefore, the softer action of the rod will provide a buffer against the sudden lunges of a hard-fighting fish.

The rig should be a fairly simple but effective set-up. Thread your main line – 11 lb would be sufficient – through a bead and then a surface controller float before tying it to a size 10 swivel with a five-turn grinner knot. For surface fishing use a nylon hooklink with the lightest breaking strain you can get away with – 5 lb is about right. However, if you intend fishing a fairly snaggy water then you should use a stronger line.

A size 12, lightweight and extremely sharp hook should be tied to the hooklink with a knot shown in the diagram, which also forms the hair for your hookbaits. The other end of the line is attached to the swivel mentioned earlier. To complete the rig, tie a Powergum stop knot above the bead, which obviously prevents the controller float from sliding up the line. With the float fixed in position it sometimes helps to prick the fish into bolting.

When it comes to a floating carp bait you can't beat Pedigree Chum Mixers. Drill your hookbait samples with a special drill available from tackle shops before mounting them on the hair rig. Once the hole has been made

Left: The carp-angler's set-up with two rods waiting and ready for action.

Opposite: A plump carp in the net. Don't set yourself too high targets because fish like this common carp will give you an exciting battle.

Below: Many anglers prefer to roll their own boilies, using specially-made machines.

Below: Boilies have become the staple diet of carp in many waters. A throwing stick is often used to fire them out into the swim.

use a baiting needle to thread the Pedigree Chum Mixer on to the hair. Use two for the hookbait and keep them on the hair with a hair stop.

All you need now is a catapult to fire loose offerings of Chum Mixers into the swim. Initially, spread the feed over a fairly large area, and then wait for at least half-an-hour to allow the carp to build up confidence. When you are about ready to fish, begin to concentrate the feed and this should gradually pull the carp into a smaller area where you intend to fish your hookbait.

It is best to cast beyond the baited area and then draw the tackle back. Casting among the floaters could easily spook the feeding fish. Try to make sure that your hookbait is left at the edge of the floaters because carp usually take these samples first. A pair of good-quality polarising glasses are an essential item for surface fishing because they help to take the glare of the sun off the

water as you watch for movements around your controller float.

You can fish a controller float at long range, but it is a far better method at shorter distances of around 30 to 40 yd, where the top of the float can be seen fairly easily. More often than not, a fish that takes a bait will hook itself with the set-up described. The line between rod-top and float will tighten dramatically, and a scrap with a hard-fighting fish will begin immediately. Try to spot any signs of fish near your controller, and strike at any sudden movement of the float. Usually, you'll soon know when a fish has taken the bait. Always hold the rod because of the violent nature of any takes.

More often than not, you will catch two or three fish quickly and then notice a lull in the action. This is the time to give the swim a rest and allow the fish to gain confidence again. Keep introducing loose offerings and you will soon find the fish back on the feed. However, carp are a very suspicious species and if you start fishing again too soon they will ignore your baited hook.

Plumbing the depth

Finding the depth of your swim is of paramount importance if you want to be successful at catching carp. It's no use just casting out your baits and hoping, yet far too many of today's anglers do just that. You need to find the contours of the swim and any features like gravel bars that aren't visible even if you have the most expensive polarising glasses. Time spent discovering possible fish-holding or fish-patrolling areas will pay handsome dividends later in the session. It only takes a few minutes to find the deeper and shallower areas of your swim.

Use any normal rod, but mark the butt section 12 in from the reel mount. This mark, made with Tipp-Ex, will help you to estimate the depth of the swim. As well as a reel loaded with good-quality line, you will need a float. There are various floats on the market that are ideal for the job although a vaned drift float – used in pike fishing – is preferable. It has a slim, pencil design with vanes on the tip, which certainly helps to cast long distances and is very visible. The slimness of the float makes it very aerodynamic both in flight and also underwater. As you pull it through the water you can feel for features, unlike most bulky floats, which do not give you the same kind of touch. Other bits and pieces required are a 2 oz or 2½ oz leger weight, two link clips, a bead and a run ring.

The rig used for depth-finding is simplicity itself. First, attach the link clip to the run-ring before clipping it to your leger weight. Then thread your reel line through the ring and bead before tying it to the other link clip, which is attached to the bottom of the pike float. You will need a leger ring of some sort to allow the float to rise in the water after casting – an ordinary swivel would easily get clogged up with weed and prevent line from running through smoothly.

It is best to cast to the furthermost point, and then keep drawing the tackle back as you find the depth of swims at different distances. After casting out, tighten up the line immediately and sink it. The float and leger weight will now be on the bottom of the lake. Open the bail arm of your reel and feed off line with your left hand until you reach the 12-in mark on your rod. This process is continued until the float appears on the surface. If you have fed line off the reel four times to the required mark you will know the depth of the swim is 4 ft – 12 in multiplied by four equals 48 in. Easy, isn't it? Keep repeating this process until you have a clear picture of your swim – the deeper drop-off areas, gravel bars and other, shallower marks.

Once you have decided at what range you want to fish, it is best to cast out your depth-finding rig, checking once again how much water you will be fishing in. Leave the float in the water because it is a good marker for your loose offerings of bait. Using your catapult or throwing stick, you can feed with great accuracy around the float. Then cast your actual fishing tackle to the marker before retrieving the float. You will be certain of the depth of water and also that your hookbait is near your loose offerings.

Finding features

What do you do after finding the depth of your swim? Good question, and one which often confuses a vast number of anglers. It has to be borne in mind that a lake is like a fish's house. There are areas for playing, areas for sleeping and areas for feeding. The latter is obviously the place you are most interested in finding. For instance, a slight deviation in the lake bed may signal the dining-room table. However, you may be able to create a feeding spot by groundbaiting with a few free offerings of the chosen bait in and around the area.

Bear in mind your reason for choosing a particular swim. If you have seen some evidence of fish, you may spook them by casting around with a plumbing rod and firing out free offerings of bait. In this case, a softly, softly approach is needed; tackle up as quietly as you can and then cast out your tackle with as little disturbance as possible.

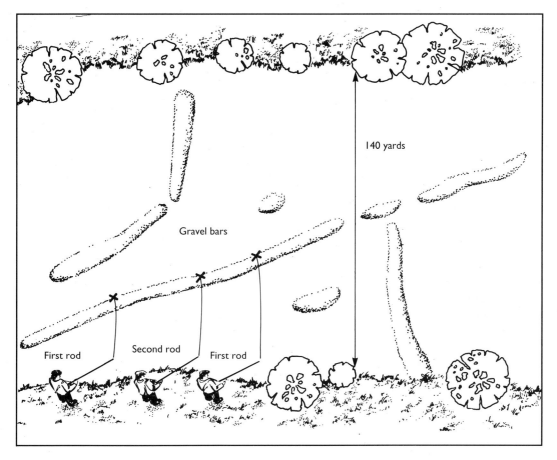

140 yards

Gravel bars

First rod   Second rod   First rod

Here's how to find gravel bars in a water. Note the leapfrogging effect of the two rods to find the direction of the bar.

Then sit back and see what happens. Prior knowledge of a few swims will be invaluable in situations like this. It is very worth while forfeiting a day's fishing for a day's plumbing. One day's fishing is a small price if it pays dividends in the future.

A walk round the lake on a hot sunny day – when the fishing probably wouldn't be any good anyway – with a bottle of cold drink to quench the thirst, a plumbing rod, a few spare leads, some floats and a notebook, will prove invaluable in future. Note down all you find and keep it for future reference. Despite the fact you won't actually catch anything, you should really enjoy your day out.

So what are you looking for? It's all very well knowing that one particular area is 1 ft

deeper than the surrounding water, but what relevance will this have? When feature finding, the angler should be trying to form a picture of the lake bed. This has to be done by not only finding depths but also 'feeling' the lake bed – something you get better at the more you do it.

After casting out, keep your plumbing rod fairly low, almost parallel to the water. Slowly drag your leger weight along the lake bed by bringing the rod round by your side, at the same time watching the tip. If the area is silty, you will feel a fair bit of resistance on the rod-tip as the leger is obviously sinking into the silt. If this resistance then disappears, it could be that you have pulled over an area where the bottom is made of a firmer material such as clay or sand. It is preferable to fish on these areas as your hookbait and free offerings will be more visible and accessible to the fish. If you feel a series of short taps on the rod-tip, you are probably pulling the weight over a clean, gravelly patch. This is another favoured area because it is usually kept clean by the regular attentions of feeding fish. On the other hand, if the tip locks up and it suddenly becomes fairly difficult to pull your leger along, then this could be because you have pulled up against a gravel bar. This can be confirmed by letting your marker float up to the surface, at the same time measuring the depth. Reel it back down again, drawing in your leger weight a fraction, then checking the depth again. If it is a gravel bar, obviously you will get shallower readings until your leger drops off the nearside of the bar.

Fishing on the slopes or tops of gravel bars can be very productive as the fish use them as roadways to swim around the lake. As these bars are often covered with mussels and snails they can be productive natural feeding areas. You may need to make quite a lot of casts around the same area to confirm your findings. In order to find the direction a bar follows, it is preferable to have another rod set up in the same manner – with the same weight of leger and same type of float.

Once you have cast the first marker float onto the bar and it has popped up to the surface, cast the second rod out to either the right or left of the first but further out. Draw back the tackle on this rod until you feel the bar again, at which time let the float rise to the surface. Once you have noted the second float's position, you can retrieve the first rod and cast back out to either the right or left of the second float. By following this leap-frog procedure with the two rods, you can fairly quickly determine the direction of the bar. Obviously, at the point where you cannot feel the bar, it has either ended or there is a gap in it. If you cannot feel it with your second cast it, could be because it runs directly away from you; either that, or it is not a bar at all but a gravel hump or plateau.

SETTING UP

Having done your homework on a few swims – plumbing the depth and feature finding –the next task is to set up your tackle. Ideally, you should make up your rods at home and carry them to the water in a rod holdall. The main advantage of carrying your rods ready made-up is that it will save a little time when you get to your swim, and you can start fishing a little quicker. This can be very beneficial because sometimes you do catch within a few minutes of casting out, especially in high summer when the most productive period is often first thing in the morning. And in winter, when temperatures around the lake are hovering around freezing point, your tackle will be much easier to set up in the warmth of your living-room.

One thing you should do before casting your tackle into the water is to roughly set the clutch on your reel so that it gives line should your rod be pulled down past its test curve by a powerful carp on its first run. Often, when a run occurs, it comes out of the blue and can take you by surprise. If the fish takes off at a rapid rate, and you are not prepared, you can often lose the fish either because your line breaks or, what is more common, because your hook pulls out of the fish. To set the clutch, thread the line through the rings of your rod, and pull the tip down by way of the line until it arcs round to its approximate test curve. Keep loosening the clutch until it just starts to give line. Don't pull the rod-tip round at too sharp an angle because this might compress the material, causing it to snap.

You are now ready to cast out. Usually, you have the rods pointing in the direction that you intend to cast. Although this is not absolutely necessary it just means that in doing so your bite detection system – monkey climbers – will work more efficiently.

After casting out, it is entirely up to you whether you fish with your line tight or slack from the rod-tip to leger. On some of the more intensively fished waters carp have become wary of tight lines, therefore it may be preferable to fish with them slack. There is one disadvantage with this, however, which is that you will not spot 'drop-back' bites very easily. Drop-backs come about when you are using a fixed leger rig. With conventional running-leger set-ups there is no problem, because in whatever direction the fish moves after picking up the bait, you will get a registration on your indicators. If, however,

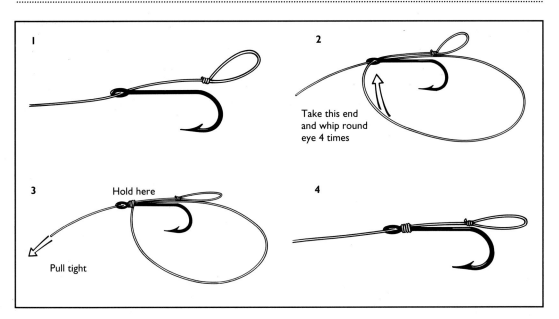

1	**2** Take this end and whip round eye 4 times
3 Hold here / Pull tight	**4**

How to tie a hair rig:

Step 1: Tie a loop in one end of your hooklink. Thread the other end through the back of the eye of the hook, leaving enough line between the eye and the loop to form the hair.

Step 2: Bring the end of the line round into a loop and thread the end through the back of the eye again.

Step 3: Take hold of the line, forming the large loop just in front of the hook eye and make four turns around the shank, moving towards the bend of the hook.

Step 4: Holding the turns in place, moisten the knot and pull on the other end of the hook length to tighten.

you are using fixed legers and a fish picks up the bait and moves towards you, this will only usually register if you are fishing with fairly tight lines in conjunction with heavy monkey climbers.

There are many different types of monkey climber available, but the principle behind all of them is the same and involves a nylon or PTFE body that slides up and down a stainless-steel needle. It is preferable to fish all types of monkey climbers in conjunction with bite alarms because then you have an audible as well as a visual indication of a bite. As a result, you can sit back and relax once the baits are cast out and scan the water for signs of fish, read a book or whatever.

The most popular type of bite alarm is the optonic. This involves a wheel, a paddle plus a clever bit of circuitry, all nicely packaged together into what looks like a little black box. Once cast out, the rod is placed on the rod-rests, and the line rests on the wheel of the optonic. Any movement of the line, whether forwards or backwards, turns the wheel, which is attached to a paddle that runs between a light circuit inside the alarm. Every time the paddle breaks the light beam, it causes a beep. Obviously, the faster the wheel turns, the faster the beeps, hence the saying 'a screamer'.

Your reel has to be set so that it can give line should a fast run occur, otherwise your rod could be pulled into the water, even by a relatively small carp. Some anglers set the rod on the rod-rests with the bail arm open so that a running fish is free to take line. Others have their reels set in order that they can turn the handle backwards, bringing about more sayings like 'reel spinners' or 'churners'. Nowadays, however, a better system is available to the carp angler by way of a baitrunner system.

With a baitrunner-type reel you disengage the spool of the reel by way of a lever found on the top and back of the reel. The reel is able to give line on a run without any fuss or the possibility of any tangles. Then, with a slight turn of the handle, the baitrunner facility is engaged, leaving you to play your fish.

Ideally, you should put your chair close to your rods so that you can strike a bite easily from a seated position. Knowing when to strike should a bite occur will come with experience. If, as is often the case with modern-day rigs, it is a real screamer, then it will be obvious. Usually the fish is hooked before you even pick up the rod, and as a result all you need to do is lift the rod out of the rest and bend into the fish. A violent swiping strike could result in your snapping your line on the strike.

If you are getting a series of short lifts on the monkey climbers, these could be either bites from finicky fish or line bites. The thing to do, if you are fishing with slack lines, is to watch your line where it enters the water. If it flicks forward quickly and then back, forget it. If it flicks forward and then holds, it might be worth striking. If you are fishing with tight lines, watch your rod-tip. If it nods, then stops quickly, don't bother. If it continues to nod, however slightly, strike. It could be that a fish is already hooked.

Once a fish is hooked, try to keep your cool. Take your time and apply steady pressure. This is a moment to enjoy, and provided your tackle is sound and you don't make any mistakes, the fish should be yours. If you play it properly using adequate tackle and don't make any mistakes, but lose it through the hook pulling out, don't be too disappointed. The moment to savour, however, is when you pull the fish over the waiting net. The anxiety ends, your heartbeat slows and you've achieved what you set out to do – catch a carp.

CHAPTER TWENTY-FOUR

Handle Pike with Care

The modern, thinking pike angler cares for his prey. His tackle and approach reflect this attitude. He selects rigs and baits with conservation in mind and, he is aware that his behaviour in handling the fish on the bank is critical to its well being and his future sport. Such skills are not learned overnight, but are the result of long-term use of correct procedures. The condition in which a pike is returned to the water is often a measure of the ability of its captor.

Good handling does not start when the pike is on the bank. The use of sensible tackle and tactics in catching the fish will reduce the complications at the unhooking stage to a minimum. Tackle should be suited to the water fished. Ideally it needs to be strong enough for the job of landing pike from that water, but not so heavy that it takes away the pleasure of playing and landing them. Fishing deadbaits on a small gravel pit, for example, demands entirely different tackle to that for drifting baits across a huge reservoir. No rods and reels will be suitable for all applications. An ideal compromise that suits most piking situations is a 12 ft, $2\frac{1}{4}$ lb test curve carbon rod with a reel capable of holding 150 metres of 11 lb line. Pike left with broken traces in their mouths – caused by their being played on inadequate tackle – should be a thing of the past.

The end rig should be strong enough to land the pike and be simple to remove from a hooked fish. The use of quality hooks, swivels and wire is vital. Breakages can lead to rigs being left in the pike's jaw, or even worse, in its throat if poorly hooked. Barbless or semi-barbless hooks make unhooking a very simple procedure.

Bite indication must be positive. The angler must know the instant that a pike has picked up his bait. It takes only seconds for a pike to swallow a bait and become at risk of damage. Pike fishing is often a waiting game, so bite indication should preferably be both audible and visual to allow the angler time to relax and look away from his tackle for a while. Drop-off type run indicators fitted with alarms are an ideal choice.

The best run indication system in the world is a waste of time if the angler has not got the mind to strike straight away. A positive attitude is necessary. Most serious pike anglers agree that a sensible-sized bait, correctly rigged, can be struck as soon as a run is detected with near certainty that the pike will be cleanly hooked. Any delay will worsen the hooking position and increase the problem of unhooking and risk of damaging the pike.

UNHOOKING

A degree of firmness and confidence is required and certain items of equipment are essential. A pair of artery forceps are vital for removing hooks from the awesome jaws of the pike. Choose a size – an ideal length is 8-10 in – and style that you feel comfortable with. Some have straight ends and some are curved. Ensure that they grip well and do not spring open when you twist them. Never leave a fish unattended on the bank while you rummage through your tackle looking for them. Pike can damage themselves considerably, simply by jumping and flapping about on the bank. On occasions you may

The pike is an awesome-looking fish but it can provide some spectacular action.

need to cut wire or a hook at the unhooking stage, so it is advisable to have a pair of wire-cutters ready just in case.

Pike should never be laid on a surface that can damage them, such as gravel banks and concrete-sided reservoirs. They are often laid on wet sacks but an unhooking mat is preferable. In a boat, line the bottom with old carpet or underlay.

Many smaller pike can be unhooked at the water's edge with a quick twist of the forceps if the hooks are exposed. Do this, if possible, to avoid handling them. Where this is not possible, place the fish on a suitable surface and apply the technique now adopted as standard by pike anglers. Kneel astride the pike – putting no weight on it, of course. Slide the first two fingers of one hand up under the gill towards the snout, taking great care not to touch the rakers, and grip the bottom jaw with these two fingers and the thumb. Slowly lift the pike's head off the ground and the jaws will open to expose the hooks. If you have used barbless or semi-barbless hooks and proper bite indication, and struck straight away, you will find the hooks easy to remove with a couple of twists of the forceps. If you have a companion, ask them to tension the trace while you are unhooking. If you are alone, grip the trace with your teeth and pull it tight. If this procedure takes more than a few seconds, you are doing something wrong and should analyse your approach to find out what.

RECORDING THE CATCH

The ritual of weighing and photographing the catch is part of the modern pike-fishing scene, but it extends the handling process and can expose the fish to as much risk as unhooking does. Reduce this risk by working to a set procedure. Never hook the scales under the pike's gills to weigh it. Place it in a large sling and only lift it as far from the ground as is necessary, in case you should drop it. Do the same when you return the pike to the water.

Great care should be taken when unhooking pike.
Inexperienced anglers should ask the advice of experts.

Carry it close to the ground in the sling and lower the sling into the water. Be ready for the unexpected with a big, lively pike.

Photography is simple with a friend to help you, but make sure he is getting the camera ready while you are unhooking to save time. Never put pike in keepnets, and only in a sack as a last resort. If you are alone and want a photograph, you will need to use a tripod and remote shutter release. There are endless ways of setting this up. Most anglers set up two rod-rests and frame the picture around them. Then it is simply a matter of holding the fish between the rests and

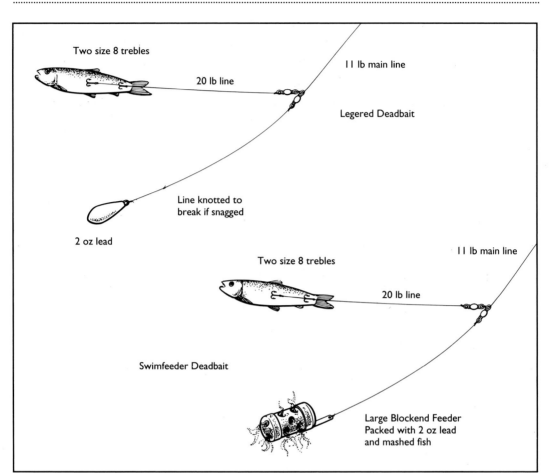

Two size 8 trebles

20 lb line

11 lb main line

Legered Deadbait

Line knotted to
break if snagged

2 oz lead

Two size 8 trebles

11 lb main line

20 lb line

Swimfeeder Deadbait

Large Blockend Feeder
Packed with 2 oz lead
and mashed fish

treading on the shutter release. It takes a lot of experience to get good results, so practise with small pike until you get it right. The thing to remember is that the fish should be held safely in the sack or landing net, and only come out of the water for a very short time for the photographs. Perfect composition and exposure is wasted if the fish has split fins and scales missing. The photographs will testify to the way that you have cared for your catch.

DEADBAITING

It is a well-established fact that pike scavenge for dead or dying fish, quite readily taking them from the bottom, mid-water or even from the surface. By presenting a suitable bait, the pike angler has a very good chance of catching them. But what constitutes a

Two rigs for a static deadbait. The diagram above is a simple legering rig while the bottom diagram shows how to use a swimfeeder for attracting pike.

suitable bait? A pike will, if hungry enough, take anything that fits into its jaws. Huge pike can swallow fish of 4 lb or 5 lb in weight, or more! On other occasions they will pick up quite tiny fish only a few inches long. The angler selects his bait size between these extremes and has to consider the practicalities of mounting and casting them and striking at runs, and needs to achieve a sensible compromise.

Experienced pike anglers tend to use deadbaits of approximately 4-8 in long, occasionally going slightly bigger or smaller if circumstances dictate. Such baits are easy to mount on standard rigs and will cast a good distance on suitable, balanced tackle. An

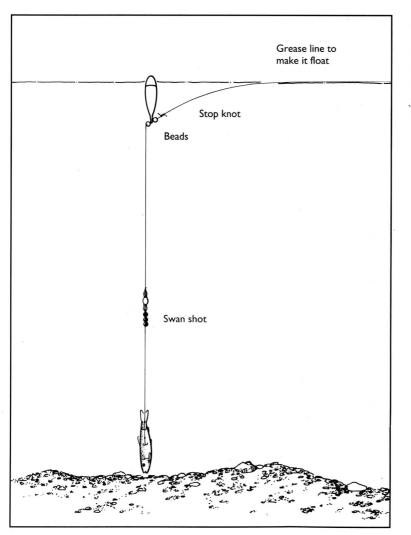

Grease line to
make it float

Stop knot

Beads

Swan shot

A suspended bait. When using this rig it is possible to experiment with the depth by using a sliding step knot. If bites are not forthcoming, alter the depth accordingly.

immediate strike can then be applied without fear of missing a run or deep-hooking a good fish. Very hungry pike will pick up quite stale baits. Most often, though, this is not the case and they can afford to be choosy. By aiming for maximum freshness, you reduce the chances of rejection.

Deadbaits can be considered in two groups: freshwater fish and sea fish. Some waters may show a preference for one or the other, and this may need to be established with a certain amount of trial and error.

The taking of coarse fish from a water for bait may be subject to regulations and local club restrictions, and this needs to be investigated before doing so. Sometimes, such fish can be found in fish markets, and these

are generally imported from Europe. Pike will pick up any type of coarse fish. On rare occasions they might show a preference for a particularly abundant species or conversely something completely alien to the water. The more sizeable 'silver' fish are readily accepted by most pike, with roach and rudd being the most popular. For long-distance casting, slim fish like small chub and dace take some beating, whereas bream make excellent baits but do not cast well. Do not neglect perch either because, contrary to popular belief, the pike is not at all bothered by its spikey dorsal fin.

The minor species like gudgeon and ruffe work well but, by virtue of their size, generally attract a smaller class of pike. If you can get them, small pike and zander are readily taken, too. In fact, all the coarse fish species work as deadbaits. There are no hard and fast rules, so experiment!

Convenience, cheapness and availability have made sea-fish baits the most popular choice among pike anglers. The variety is considerable, although quality varies immensely from source to source. Freshness dictates just how long they will last on the hook, so buying them in the right condition and storing them correctly are vital considerations for economical and effective use.

Here are the more popular sea baits and their individual characteristics. The herring is an oily, clearly visible, soft fish with a strong, distinct smell. It casts extremely well when semi-frozen, but not so well when thawed out. Large herrings are just as effective when cut in half. The mackerel is another extremely popular and effective bait. It is ideal for long casting as its tough skin allows a really good hookhold when a powerful cast is used. Larger mackerel are generally used as half-baits, with the tail section being the most popular as it casts so well.

The sprat is a small, yet surprisingly effective bait, possibly due to its strong smell and very bright appearance. It is very soft fish and difficult to cast unless used with a leger rig, in which case it is best to tie the bait to the trace to prevent it from flying off on the cast. Sardines are extremely soft and need tying on for other than close-range work. They are best cast when semi-frozen, and are a very oily fish that soon become unusable due to their soft skin. Smelts, with their unique cucumber-like smell, have gained great popularity in recent years, but they need to be very fresh to retain their effectiveness and to prevent them from falling apart. Use semi-frozen for long-range casting.

A visit to a large market will often reveal all sorts of strange-looking fish on the slabs. They will all catch pike. Don't be afraid to try them if they are a suitable size, and in particular look for goat fish, snappers, whiting and scad. Small trout make excellent deadbaits, although they tend not to stay fresh for long. Their tough skin is very suitable for hooking, and they will withstand quite a powerful cast.

Finally, sections from a small eel or a whole sand-eel make ideal baits and are readily accepted by the pike. The tough skin enables a good hookhold and by virtue of this, they can be re-used several times over.

BUYING AND STORING DEADBAITS

How and where you obtain your sea baits depends on how much piking you intend to do. There are three main options: pre-packed bait; fish from a stall or market; and bulk buying.

For the angler who intends to have an occasional session at short notice, the most convenient way of acquiring bait is to pop into a tackle shop and purchase a couple of packs of blast-frozen, vacuum-packed baits. You can store them in your freezer at home until you need them.

More serious pike anglers make use of pre-packed baits, but will need to reduce costs if they are getting through a lot of bait. Regular trips to a fish-stall or market will eventually produce baits of the desired size and type at the right price. Snap them up while they are available and freeze them as soon as possible in readiness for the months ahead.

The ultra-keen piker, who gets through vast quantities of bait, will need to buy in bulk from a wholesaler, preferably at a fishing port where prices are lowest. This might be the only practical way of obtaining large quantities of the rarer species such as smelts. By special arrangement wholesalers will sometimes supply small fish of a suitable size, like joey mackerel, which are too small for retail sale. Delivery can sometimes be arranged, but be prepared to go and collect your bait and have a large freezer ready for it to go into. Bulk-buying with friends can make this a cheaper exercise.

When it comes to storing baits the

Opposite: Deadbaits are probably the most effective bait for catching pike.

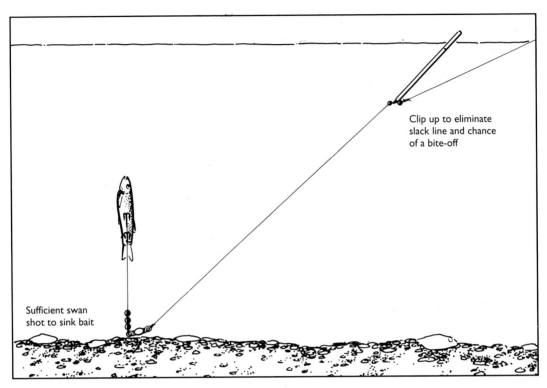

Clip up to eliminate
slack line and chance
of a bite-off

Sufficient swan
shot to sink bait

How to present a buoyant deadbait.

occasional pike angler can simply pop his pre-packed baits into the ice-box of his fridge. The more serious angler with more baits to store might just get away with taking up space in the family deep-freeze. The fanatics usually have their own dedicated bait-freezer out in the garage. Small, 4-6 cu. ft, models are ideal and have sufficient capacity for a good bulk purchase. Any spare capacity should be taken up with bulky items such as bread to reduce running costs. All baits should be individually frozen, bagged and clearly labelled. The more bait you store, the more carefully you need to manage your stocks.

STATIC DEADBAITING RIGS

Armed with the knowledge required to select baits and handle pike, it is now time to move on to the exciting part – catching them! The static deadbait is a good way to start and can be rigged to catch pike in a variety of situations. You will be confronted with endless rigs for deadbaiting, but don't become confused. They are all variations on

simple principles. Learn about these basic methods first, and then vary the details to suit your own particular situation.

Freelining is a commonly used method because it is so simple. All you do is tie a trace to the main line, attach a bait and you are ready to cast out. Behind the simplicity of this approach lies a great danger, however, and one that you may fail to appreciate at first. Never forget that a pike can pick up and swallow a bait in a few seconds. Any delay in indicating a run or striking a run is irresponsible and leads to deep-hooked pike. They will be difficult to unhook and be damaged in the process. When freelining, it is possible for the pike to move a considerable distance before any run indication is given. The further the range that you have cast, the greater the possibility of this delay.

If you must use this method – and serious anglers are rapidly moving away from it – ensure that you tighten right up to the bait and set the rod on rests to show drop-back runs as well as conventional ones. If you do not do this, you will not know for quite a while that your bait has been taken. A drop-back run is indicated by the line going slack as the pike moves towards the rod. This is more difficult to achieve than one would think, and requires a bait that is quite heavy and a bottom that does not drag on the bait as you tighten up. A great degree of vigilance is required when freelining and, other than at very close range, is not recommended.

Legering is a much better way to fish if you are considering the pike's welfare. It is highly suited for long-range work although it can be used at any range with equal effect. Use a heavy leger of about 2 oz, which will not be dragged by the pike provided the line runs

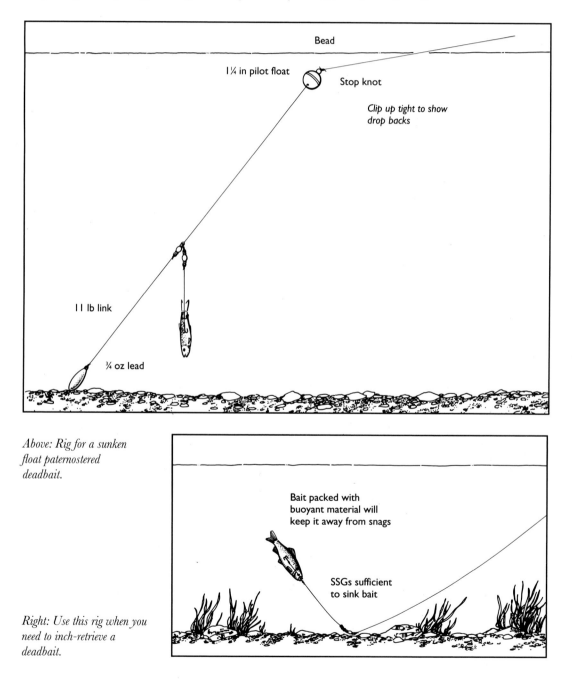

Bead

1¼ in pilot float

Stop knot

Clip up tight to show drop backs

11 lb link

¾ oz lead

Above: Rig for a sunken float paternostered deadbait.

Bait packed with buoyant material will keep it away from snags

SSGs sufficient to sink bait

Right: Use this rig when you need to inch-retrieve a deadbait.

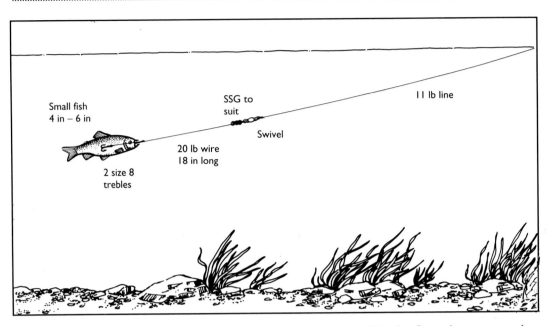

Small fish
4 in – 6 in

SSG to
suit

11 lb line

Swivel

20 lb wire
18 in long

2 size 8
trebles

freely through the lead-link swivel.

As soon as the pike moves with the bait you will get an indication at the rod-tip provided you have set the rod on rests and clipped them up tightly with no slack line. It is best to set your tackle up to show drop-backs just in case of the unexpected. For example, the swivels may tangle or become clogged with weed, preventing the line from running freely. Silicone rubber tubing over the swivels reduces this problem.

A very effective way of tempting pike into feeding is to make use of a swimfeeder packed with chopped fish on the line. Put a 2 oz leger in the feeder to increase your casting range and reduce the chances of the pike dragging it, which could increase the run-indication delay time. The juices and scent given off by the chopped fish will attract pike into the swim.

A lot of anglers prefer to watch a float, and there is certainly a lot more excitement in seeing a run develop in this way than just waiting for bobbins to drop off. In theory, this approach should give the best indication of a run and enable the angler to strike right away. This is only true, however, if you are watching your floats constantly. If you cannot concentrate, use a different method. If not carried out in a responsible way, floatfishing has the same dangers as freelining – deep-

hooked pike. Fish the float about one-and-a-half times the depth of the water and tighten up after casting to cock it slightly and to eliminate any slack line, hence keeping the main line away from the pike's teeth. With a non-self-cocking float, the first indication of a bite is usually the float lying flat as the pike picks up the bait. Floatfishing is most often the boat-angler's choice because rod-rests and electronic bite indicators are often difficult to set up.

On some days pike want the bait presented off the bottom. Where there are snags or dense weed, this may be the only way to proceed anyway. The easiest way of achieving this is to simply suspend a bait under a float. This has an inherent problem in that the bait will start to drift away from the desired spot if there is any breeze at all. This can, of course, be used to the angler's advantage, for covering more water, but may otherwise cause frustration. A sliding stop knot will give you the scope to change depths. Always grease the main line to prevent it sinking and becoming tangled up with the bait, leading to a bite-off.

Paternostering is the best way of suspending a bait off the bottom and preventing it from drifting away. The pike will now also have to drag the paternoster leger but unless they are particularly small

Right: More experienced pikers prefer to hand-line their catch into the bank. But this should only be attempted by confident anglers.

Opposite: A rig for a wobbled deadbait.

Below: The action of a sink-and-draw deadbait.

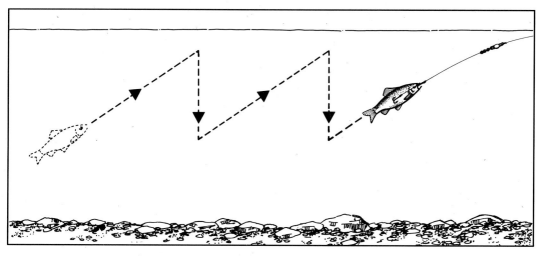

pike or have been well fished for, this will not deter them at all. The length of the paternoster determines the distance from the bottom that the bait is fished. This unlikely looking method catches great numbers of pike. The float is best fished on the surface if possible, but where the bottom of the water is uneven it is often fished sunken to ensure that the main line is kept taught, reducing the possibility of tangles.

Rather than suspending a deadbait, another presentation is to bring the bait up from the bottom by making it buoyant. This is a very effective way of presenting baits over weedy bottoms and assists the pike in finding the bait more quickly. It is equally effective in open water. It can be achieved by packing the bait with a buoyant material such as balsa or polystyrene. This is not a method to be entered into lightly as there is always the possibility of a discarded bait being swallowed by a fish, bird or animal. To prevent this happening, tie your baits to the trace and at the end of the session account for all the pieces of buoyant material that you have used. Take them home and put them straight in the dustbin. The buoyant bait can be used in conjunction with either a leger or float. If floatfishing, ensure that the buoyant bait does not tangle with the main line by tightening up gently after casting which keeps everything in a straight line as the rig sinks.

TRACES

With so many different rigs to consider, the beginner may be a little confused regarding what trace to use with each. At this stage, consider just two traces, the components of which will depend upon where you are fishing. For normal pike fishing situations, a multi-stranded wire of 20 lb breaking strain and standard hooks and swivels will suffice. Where exceptionally large or hard-fighting fish are likely to be encountered or where conditions are rugged, when loch-fishing for example, step up to 30 lb wire and extra-strength hooks and swivels. Barbless or semi-barbless hooks are strongly recommended.

Nothing could be simpler than a one-hook rig. Take a suitable length of wire, and fix a swivel to one end and a treble to the other by crimping or twisting. Use this trace for small baits and select a hook size to suit the bait used. A size 8 covers most eventualities.

The two-hook rig is similar, but in this instance leave sufficient length of wire for tying on a second treble. The only variable to consider is the distance between the trebles. For sensible-sized baits, this should be no more than 3 in and, if anything, somewhat less. Hooks as small as a 10 might be used where runs are finicky or if there are zander about. Size 6 is suitable for larger baits or where a hard cast is required.

MOVING BAITS

Consistent success with pike involves giving them what they want on the day. On many occasions a static deadbait fits this bill. However, there will be days when the pike will react far more positively to movement, and recognition of this fact will lead to more pike in the net. If you prefer not to livebait or if livebaiting is not allowed, you may need to put 'life' into your deadbaits to provoke a response from pike. It is often a more interesting way to fish anyway, involving the angler in much more than just sitting and waiting. Mobile tactics have another major benefit in that they will show the bait to many more pike because they will cover a greater expanse of water.

Deadbaits cast out and retrieved in an enticing manner often spur lethargic pike into action, as well as tempting actively feeding pike. There are several ways of retrieving the bait and it is up to the angler to experiment and decide which one suits the situation in hand. The basic tackle could not be simpler, involving no more than tying a two-hook trace to the main line and adding SSG shot as necessary. It is then just a matter of casting the bait to a likely looking spot and retrieving.

The skill comes in making the fish look like a live one in distress, and also in fishing it at the correct depth and speed. Takes can come either near the bottom, in midwater or even on the surface. If the bait sinks too quickly, insert a buoyant material inside it to slow it

A floatfished retrieved deadbait.

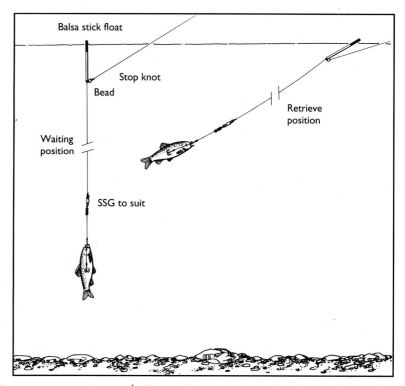

Balsa stick float

Stop knot

Bead

Retrieve position

Waiting position

SSG to suit

down. Although a preference is sometimes shown for coarse fish, which look more natural than sea fish, on most occasions any small fish will suffice. Start with baits of about 4-6 in long, mounted on two size 8 trebles set 3 in apart. Vary the retrieve if takes are not forthcoming. Try a steady midwater retrieve to start with, and if this does not work, inch the bait along near the bottom, stopping occasionally. If this fails to get a take, try to make the bait rise and fall in the water to imitate a fish in trouble.

To really slow down the bait and fish more effectively over snags and weed, try suspending it under a float. This method gives the option of bringing the bait to a stop in midwater and allows time for the pike to inspect it more closely. Snatches often occur just as the retrieve is recommenced after such a stop. The take may vary from a gentle tap on the rod-tip to a violent snatch. If you are rigged correctly, an immediate strike will see the fish cleanly hooked near the front of the jaws. The mobile angler can cover a vast amount of water in a session using this technique.

On those days when nothing appears to be

happening on the static baits, and you feel the pike should be feeding, try the following tactics. Go to each rod, slowly take in two or three turns of line and reset the rod on the rests. Be prepared for a snatch, as a pike will often be watching a bait, or may detect its movement from some distance away. This may be enough to induce it to take. If the water is not too weedy or snaggy you can, over a period of time, work the bait right back to the rod-tip. Even if you do not tempt a pike by moving the bait, you may move the bait closer to a pike lying inactive elsewhere in the swim. Be prepared for a take as you lift the bait from the water at the end of the retrieve. You will be amazed at the number of bonus fish this produces. Whether your bait is floatfished or legered, on or off the bottom, this technique is effective.

Just as a drifted deadbait covers a lot of water on stillwaters, so a trotted deadbait will do the same on a river, but in a much simpler manner due to help from the current. A fairly large, cigar-shaped float is ideal for this technique, and the line should be greased. If you're used to trotting a stick float or waggler down a river for species like roach and chub,

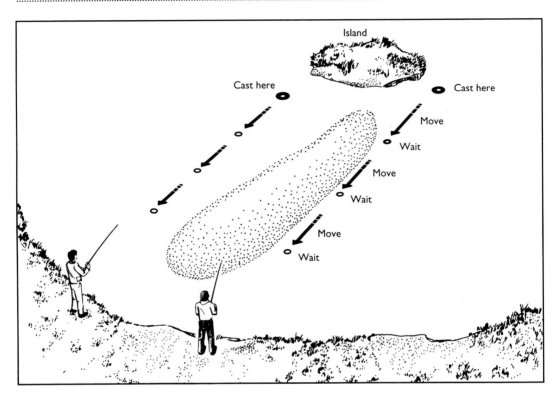

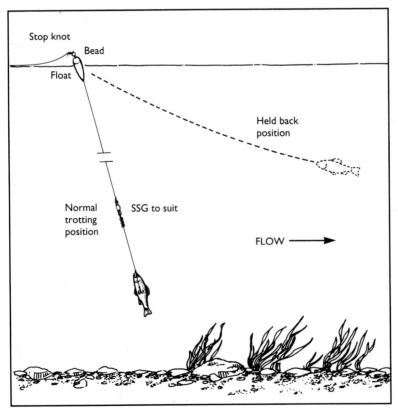

Above: In an attempt to induce a take, retrieve your baits in rotation.

Left: A trotted deadbait is effective on rivers.

This is the set-up to use when drifting a deadbait.

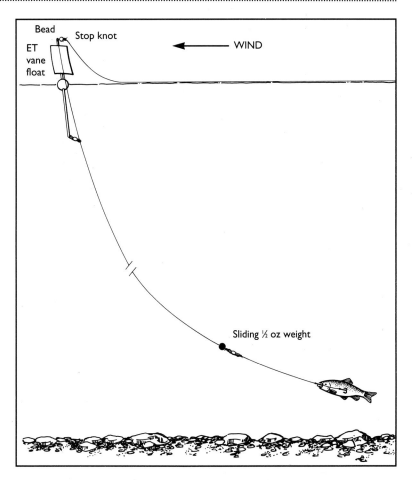

you will find this method familiar. It is best carried out from a boat, so that you are not impeded by trees and bushes. By anchoring in various positions, you can fish vast areas of water. Try holding the bait back occasionally by trapping the line against the reel spool. This will make the bait rise and fall enticingly in the current.

The more water a bait covers, the greater the number of pike you are likely to see. This is part of the thinking behind the drifted deadbait method. In addition, it can be used to take the bait to water beyond your normal casting range. Pike often move out of reach in this way if they are under heavy fishing pressure, or perhaps their feeding grounds are well out from the bank of a gravel pit.

Drifting may be the only way to reach pike if boats are not used on the water you are fishing. And the movement of a drifted bait may just tempt a pike not in a hunting mood

to take a bait passing overhead. A major problem associated with drifting a bait lies in setting the float depth when you are fishing over an uneven bottom. The bait may, for much of the time, be fished too high in the water. When the water is particularly cold, it may not be too easy to tempt a pike to rise too far for a bait, and by employing the drifting method at least you are in with a chance of some action.

As you may be drifting baits to distances in excess of 150 yd, normal striking is out of the question. It is then a matter of taking in line as fast as possible, and perhaps walking backwards at the same time. It may be several seconds before you make contact with the fish, so to avoid deep hooking don't delay. To get any speed out of the drift, and to be able to see it at a distance, a special type of float is required incorporating a large, coloured vane. Use quite a large sliding

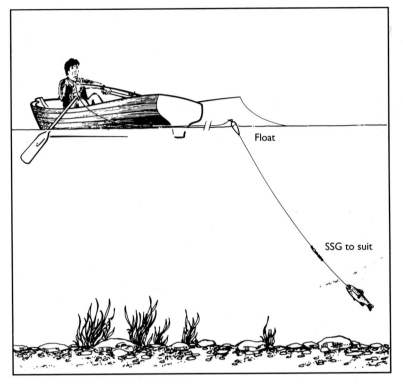

Trolling from a boat can be particularly effective.

Float

SSG to suit

weight just above the trace to keep it upright should the weight of the bait be insufficient to sink to the bottom. Line must be well greased and it is best to use a line greaser that fits into the butt ring of the rod and greases the line as it passes through. After casting, the rod should be positioned on rests, and once the float has travelled a good distance it will start to pull line from the reel, with the bale arm open, without any assistance. A proficient pike angler could have two rigs working at the same time, but this needs extreme vigilance.

Take a pair of polaroid glasses for drifting into bright sunshine. A prerequisite for this technique is a wind of suitable strength and in the right direction. If these are not just right, all your efforts will be frustrated.

In addition to taking pike on the outward drift, never forget that the same amount of water can be covered again on a slow retrieve. By walking 40 or 50 yd along the bank of a fishery, this retrieve can be made to cover previously unfished water.

A boat has definite advantages. It enables you to troll or trail baits over great distances, making them available to many more pike than if you had remained static. The baits are set under floats at a depth just off bottom. In deep water, experiment with this depth as pike will often be active higher up in the water, especially during the warmer months. Grease the line and use sufficient weight to keep the bait well down in the water. Trail the baits 20 yd or so behind the boat and row along at a snail's pace. The lines are held in line clips or rubber bands on the rod butt and are pulled out in the event of a snatch from a pike. Alternatively, set rear drag or baitrunner reels to give line under the minimum pressure. As soon as the take comes, lower the anchor and strike without delay. Play the fish from the back of the boat and it should stay well clear of the anchor if you have plenty of rope out. It's an exciting method for searching vast expanses of water for pike. More specialised trolling techniques are employed for the huge deep waters, but these are beyond the scope of the beginner and should not be attempted.

MATCH FISHING

I suppose my match fishing career started when I was about eight years old, when three of us used to visit a farm pond suitably geared up with garden canes, string and bent pins. We caught rudd on a 'first to 10' basis. Big ones of over 3 oz counted as two. Believe me it was easier winning the World Championships! Things have, of course, changed since then. Match anglers have been responsible for the creation of a multi-million pound industry of which I am proud, in a small way, to have been a part. Whether or not I could have been an achiever in some other sport or occupation, I will never know. What I do know is that, given my time again, I would not change a thing. What started out as an innocent casual hobby grew into an absolute obsession that was carried out at the expense of everything else.

Some of the characters I have met, and some of the experiences I have enjoyed are worth sharing, such as the time in 1961 when Ted Carter opened up his tackle shop in Church Street, Preston. It was to become not only the largest in the immediate area, but one of the first angling mega-stores in England. Then it was only a small shop. Ted was famous not only as a brilliant angler, but also for producing the Ted Carter Match Special, a wonderful 11 ft, Spanish-reed canal rod. I remember paying £6.17s.6d for one – and I was on my way.

The two greatest influences on my match fishing career were without doubt Ivan Marks and Kevin Ashurst. Their contributions over the years were priceless. When I first started fishing the Irish festivals during the early 1970s, Ivan was usually present. He used to take Dave Brogden and me fishing on free days and we learned an enormous amount. On one day on the River Suck, Ivan took half a dozen of my prized, home-made peacock wagglers and made one great big float out of them. He then fished a fixed float 15 feet deep along the middle. I wonder how many of today's matchmen would show such initiative.

Kevin was different. To be honest he frightened me a little. He could achieve more with one look than anybody else I know. On one occasion I was fishing a match at Foulridge Reservoir in Lancashire and I drew on the next peg to Kevin. The whistle went and we all started to feed a long-distance legering swim. I pulled back my catapult elastic with an oversized ball of groundbait and one strand of the elastic snapped. The ball of groundbait shot up into the air and landed right in front of Kevin, 10 yd out into the lake. I can still remember the look on Kevin's face. Since then, of course, I have travelled all over Europe with Kevin and other equally talented match anglers, and to them all I owe a tremendous debt.

Match fishing is a great sport and if you have chosen to concentrate on it in preference to other aspects of angling, I know you won't be disappointed.

Dave Roper

*Former world champion
Dave Roper with bonus
canal bream.*

CHAPTER TWENTY FIVE

The Appeal of Match Fishing

When someone takes up angling for the first time, the main priority is to catch fish. What sort of fish is largely immaterial. As long as the float goes under, they're happy. However, as the angler becomes more proficient, there usually comes a time when he wants to specialise. It might stem from a chance conversation in a fishing tackle shop, a story or a feature he has read in the angling press, or just an inner feeling that one branch of fishing is more interesting, enjoyable or exciting than any other.

For some, the excitement comes in the pursuit of a big fish. The term 'specimen hunter' springs to mind, although most would now prefer to be called 'specialist anglers'. Many such anglers think little of spending a whole season trying to catch a single, known fish – carp, barbel or whatever. Others – and these can equally be called specialists – enjoy pitting their wits against their fellow fishermen as well as against the fish, and it is these who are known as match anglers.

Perhaps their interest has stirred during a trip with friends to the local canal, when as the day progressed it gradually became apparent that there was a sense of competition in the air. The jocular banter was replaced by tense silence as each one tried to catch more than this friends, now his rivals as well. More likely they joined a local club that held matches on a favourite venue, where the angler could pit his wits against others. These club contests are where most of the top match anglers started their 'careers'.

Even impromptu affairs can be regarded as matches, and many anglers, once they have fished a match or two, are hooked for life. Not for them the solitary existence of the specimen hunter or the relaxed deck-chair stints of the out-and-out pleasure anglers. Once the competitive bug has hit, there's no getting away from it.

But perhaps we are running before we can walk. Let's first of all ask one vitally important question. What is match fishing? To an angler who has been fishing matches for years, that might seem a ridiculous question, but what about the one who is still getting to grips with the sport? How could he know what is involved in a fishing match?

It's quite simple really. A fishing match involves a row of anglers placed equal distances apart – usually a little more than 15 m – with each trying to catch a greater weight of fish than the rest during a set time, usually between two and six hours.

The competitors meet at an allotted time and place beforehand, where they pay an entrance fee and sometimes optional pools before making the draw for 'pegs' out of a hat. Ideally, there are the same number of pegs in the hat as there are competitors in the match. Once the angler has drawn his peg, he makes his way along the waterside with his tackle until he reaches the swim tagged with the number he has drawn. This is where he has to fish for the whole of the contest.

Some of the more popular match venues are permanently pegged, meaning that there are permanent markers – concrete posts, for example – placed at equal distances along the bank, to save the match organiser having to peg the stretch before every contest. Once the angler has reached his swim – in match fishing the swim is usually known as the 'peg' – he tackles up and awaits a signal telling him to start to fish. On no account must he fish before the signal, although he can usually mix groundbait, position his keepnet and test the depth of the water in front him with a float and plummet. Plumbing the depth with a swimfeeder is not allowed as it opens the door to cheating if anyone is that way inclined.

At the end of the contest a whistle is blown by the organiser or somebody mandated by him to tell everyone to stop fishing immediately. Stewards then walk along the bank weighing each angler's catch, which they have stored in a keepnet. Special anglers' scales are used, which are often accurate to within ¼ oz. Once all the anglers have been weighed in, the results are calculated and prizes presented to those who have taken the biggest catches.

In general terms, that is how a match works, and from that you might assume that match fishing is a pretty serious business. Of course it is, but ask any match angler why he has chosen this branch of the sport to pursue, and he will answer: because he enjoys it.

From the smallest Sunday morning club contest to the largest 'open' event, there's always a buzz of excitement during the draw as each angler tries to pick out the winning peg. Then there's the anticipation as they wait, tackle at the ready, for the match to start, the enjoyment of catching fish, and the satisfaction of knowing they have beaten their rivals. And usually the winner can feel highly satisfied. After all, match fishing by its very nature puts constraints upon those who pursue it. Who apart from a match angler would choose to be told where he has to fish, at the most difficult time of the day for fishing, and only 20 paces away from two

other anglers?

Of course, there's also the disappointment of choosing the wrong method to fish and knowing you have done so after the event; the frustration of losing that all-important fish at the net; the annoyance of finishing just out of the prize money . . . but that all just makes most match anglers want to go out and do better next time.

A match can take many forms. At its most basic level, it's simply a group of friends fishing in a line to see who catches the most – something to add a little spice to a day's pleasure fishing. Then there are club events, where members of a club meet up and fish a match together. At the end of the season, someone is usually crowned club champion. On the next rung of the ladder are the open events, contests that are available to any angler in the country to fish as long as he buys a ticket in advance.

Team matches are another question altogether. Here, teams of up to 12 anglers compete against each other with the results being decided on a points basis. One member of each team is placed in each section and the anglers are awarded points according to where they finish in that section. The pinnacle of team events are the National Championships, now fishable by many more than just match angling's elite, thanks to the divisional system. At present there are six National Federation of Anglers divisions, each comprising 90 teams of 12 anglers. A lot of people go match fishing!

However seriously you take it, match fishing is ultimately just another branch of angling to be enjoyed, just like specimen hunting and pleasure fishing. Winning is a bonus – but it's great!

CHAPTER TWENTY-SIX

How to Start

So you want to take up match fishing? Welcome to the ranks of thousands of anglers who fish matches every week or every month of the season. For some, three matches a week is not enough. These are the open match anglers, willing to spend a great deal of money in pursuit of glory and prize winnings. They think nothing of travelling the length and breadth of the country in pursuit of good contests, and nothing less than total commitment is enough for them. Others prefer one weekend match, still possibly an open event and to be taken just as seriously, while for many a Sunday morning trip with their local club is the highlight of the week. The beginner to match fishing would do best to start with these club contests, but even this branch of match fishing is not to be taken lightly. Even the smallest, most friendly of contests usually has cash winnings at stake, and wouldn't you rather be walking up to receive the money afterwards than standing clapping the winner?

Many anglers make the mistake of thinking they can run before they have learned to walk. They decide that they know a certain venue like the back of their hands and can take on the world. So they fish an open match against some of the best in the business and are beaten out of sight. They try again. The same thing happens. This is the quickest way to destroy a would-be match angler. You might know a lot about a certain venue, but there's a world of difference between choosing your swim and having it chosen for you. That's the whole essence of match fishing. You can't choose your spot. This has happened to many match fishing beginners, especially youngsters, who decide to fish open matches without graduating through the club ranks first. Most of today's top matchmen served a club apprenticeship. Follow their lead and one day you too could be fishing for your country.

There are several ways of joining a club. Many tackle shops sell membership books for various clubs in their area, especially if they control some fishing of their own. Then there are those clubs that are formed through a pub. These are very common and often offer the best chance of making friends with the other club members. Enjoying a drink after the match is a good time to talk tactics, listening to others about how they fished the match, trying to assess where you went wrong, and even offering advice of your own. As you become increasingly successful, you will find that more and more club members are wanting to buy you drinks and pick your brain! Other clubs are formed purely and simply to hold matches and a call to the secretary will usually bring you membership. Again your local tackle shop can help here. Some limited-member clubs have waiting lists to which you can add your name until being asked to join officially. These are often clubs with good fisheries that hold most if not all of their matches on their own water.

You should think carefully before deciding to join one particular club. Is it right for you? Are some of your friends already members? Does it hold enough matches for you, or too many? Are the matches fished at the most convenient time? Are you familiar with the venues? How good are the other anglers who fish the club matches? The question of venues is a very important one. Many of the country's top match anglers started by joining a club that fished its matches on familiar venues on which they felt proficient.

As an example, an angler might believe, with good reason, that he has mastered his local river. He catches consistently more than others fishing on the same stretch. What better way to test his ability than by joining a local club that holds matches there, because there's only one way to discover just how

Above: Could you handle a 'gallery' like this?

Opposite: You're never too young to start match fishing.

proficient he is – by fishing a match against others on the same venue. There's nothing like a match for bringing an angler down a peg or two, but it can also be a tremendous boost to confidence. It might destroy a budding match angler completely if he was to pick a club that holds many of its matches on a local lake if he has done most of his fishing on the river. Of course, some might want to do this, on the assumption that the best way to learn is to fish against others and probably take a good hiding into the bargain. However, you need a thick skin to do this more than a few times!

Another way in which many anglers approach match fishing is to make their decision. Then before spending valuable time and money fishing matches – and being beaten – they do plenty of watching, perhaps sacrificing a few Sundays to sit behind their favourite anglers and see how they tackle a particular venue. Most matchmen will be delighted to chat about baits and methods . . . after the contest has finished. During the event, it would be far better to keep your distance. Check with the competitor that he doesn't mind you sitting behind him, stay well back, where he suggests you settle, and watch and learn. Don't speak unless you are spoken to. Match anglers are many and varied. Some find that a keen spectator, asking the right sort of questions, is an aid to their concentration. These are the ones who are only too keen to talk to you before, during and after the match. However, others take the opposite view and look upon spectators as unnecessary distractions. You'll soon discover which camp your matchman lies in.

The question of finances is obviously an important one. At the draw for most matches, you'll pay your entry fee and probably have the chance to enter the optional pools. You don't have to enter them, but if you don't and you win the match, you don't win anything from the pools. 'Your' money goes to the runner-up, or the highest-placed angler who entered the pools. However, many club matches are well within the reach of most anglers' pockets and £3 will usually see you 'all the way' in the pools. Even if finances dictate that you cannot afford to enter all the pools, many club and open matches divide up their pools system, allowing you to be selective as to which pools you want to enter. It's worth checking whether your chosen club allows this before you decide to join. For example, you might want to enter the section pool only. This means that you are entering the pool against the others in your section of, say, 10 anglers. Separate pools are run taking in the whole of the match. Don't put too much pressure on yourself by having a full bet. Build up your confidence with a few good section wins and you'll soon be ready to go 'all the way'.

Club matches take several forms. Most will be simple individual events where the angler who catches the biggest weight of fish is the winner. However, there are other types of contest that add a little excitement to the proceedings, such as pairs events where two anglers pair up – either by choice or, more often, by being drawn out of the hat – and fish against other pairs, the pair with the highest aggregate weight being declared the winners. Then there are inter-club events where one club takes on another. These are usually enjoyable days out, with one club travelling to a venue of the other club's choice before returning the favour later on in the season. These events are very popular and some inter-club challenges have been taking place twice a season for many years. It's certainly a way to make new friends and fish new and exciting venues. Handicap matches used to be more popular than they are now. These are events where the match organiser assesses each competitor and issues them with a handicap according to their ability. For example, a beginner might be given a 100 per cent start, in other words his catch is doubled, whereas an expert might have to

fish without the benefit of any help at all.

When you enter your first match, there are a few golden rules to follow. First, arrive at the headquarters early. It might be a pub, or it might be at the venue. If it's at the venue, take a little time to go and have a look at the water. Already you will be forming ideas on how you are going to fish. If the headquarters is a pub, have a cup of tea. Decide whether you want anything to eat before the draw. Most pub headquarters now lay on food, and you might be too busy to eat anything once the match has started. When it comes to the draw, draw early. Don't listen to those anglers who insist on telling you that it's best to draw late. An early draw gives you the best possible chance of a good peg. A late draw obviously means that more of the good pegs will have been taken. Of course, so will more of the bad ones, but you're not interested in those are you? Think positive! After the draw, try to discover as much about your peg as you can by asking friends and local experts, some of whom will be only too pleased to show off their knowledge. Take it all in, but remember that the best anglers are those who listen and then use their own skills and experience to build on what they have been told. Copy an expert and you can only ever be as good as him. Innovate and you'll be better.

Once you have found your peg, place your tackle down beside you gently and take a little time to assess the water. Ask yourself several questions. Have you ever fished your swim, or a neighbouring one, before? If so, what have you learned about it? Even if you haven't fished it, there is a lot to be learned just by looking. Are there any good features like overhanging trees, or places on a river where the flow seems to have picked up. Plumb the depth. Are there any shelves or ledges where the depth suddenly drops off? This can act as a magnet to fish. Places such as these are all potential fish-holding areas so make a mental note of them before the match starts. Even if they produce one or two 'bonus' fish, they were worth fishing, weren't they?

It's all too easy to fish a match in your own little world, totally oblivious to what's going on around you. This is a mistake. If the angler at the next peg suddenly starts catching bream on the swimfeeder while you're polefishing for small fish, you need to know about it. Match fishing success is almost as much about reacting to different situations as it is about angling ability. You'll need to know what your neighbour's up to, especially if he is one of the club experts. Of course, don't spend so much time looking at the anglers either side that you don't concentrate on your job – catching fish. Some matchmen look as if they are tennis-match spectators and end up frustrated also-rans. The ideal situation is when the anglers on either side spend all day watching you – and you're too busy catching fish to notice them!

Once the match is finished, stop fishing immediately, pack your tackle away, taking care to remove any litter, and await the scales. Now here's another important point. When your catch is weighed, watch carefully. Every ounce now is vital. Make sure the scales are 'zeroed' before each angler's catch is weighed. All sets of scales have a small setting wheel at the back that is turned to move the needle to the zero position. As the weight sling becomes wet and slimy with each weighing, it weighs a little more and could give the next angler some advantage unless the scales are zeroed every time. Check the weight as well. If you feel you're being 'done', speak out. It's no use moaning afterwards that you just missed out on a prize and you should have been given $\frac{1}{2}$ oz extra. Finally, make certain that your weight has been correctly recorded on the weigh board, especially that your pounds have been put in the pounds column and your ounces in the ounces column. Fractions of ounces are usually recorded either as fractions or as drams. Sixteen drams weigh 1 oz. Hence, a weight of 6-4-12 on the weigh board means 6lb 4 oz 12 dr ($\frac{3}{4}$ oz).

If possible, walk along with the scalesman while he is weighing to check the catches of other anglers around you. If anyone has obviously fared better than the others, ask him what he did to give him that extra edge and make a mental note, or better still, a written one. It takes much effort, but a diary really is an indispensable aid to the match angler. In it you should record everything you think might be of value about every competition you fish – how you fared, how others fared, winning methods and pegs, time of year, water conditions, weather conditions and the like. It can prove more than helpful in future years. It's amazing what you forget unless you write it down. By offering to help the scalesman, you can ensure that you have a ringside seat when it comes to seeing the catches taken by other anglers.

Let's assume that you have fished many club events and have found yourself reasonably successful. The next step is an important one, and could make or break your match fishing career. You can do one of three things. First, you can stay in the same club, continuing to participate against the same anglers on the same venues and continuing to enjoy success. Or you may feel the time is right to join another club with new venues, new adversaries and new challenges. Finally – and this is the really big step – you might decide that the time is right to join the ranks of the open match anglers.

Your first open match can be a daunting experience. The chances are that many more anglers will be competing in this match than competed in the club matches you're used to. The odds of winning are considerably reduced and you will need to draw a good peg to stand a chance. Most open matches are on venues that have one or two noted pegs. On many occasions, unless you draw one of these, your chances of an overall win are slim. However, you can still win some money in an open event simply by attempting to win your section. Most open matches are split up into sections, often of 10 pegs in a line. The angler who wins his section can go home better off even though he didn't finish among the main prizes.

Others take an all-or-nothing approach. They fish every open match to win as an individual, and often their chances of a section win are eliminated because of that. For example, many rivers in summer are dominated by bream and many open matchmen will fish exclusively for them, even though the nearest feeding bream shoal might be 50 pegs away. These rivers often contain good numbers of eels, certainly

Above: When you hook a bonus fish like a chub, make sure you don't lose it!

Opposite: The weigh-in.

Right: Legering accounts for hundreds of match wins every season.

enough to provide a section-winning weight should the angler so desire. By fishing for eels rather than bream, however, an angler will almost certainly lose his chance of winning the match individually.

This is one of the reasons why the decision to enter your first open is such a big one. If you are serious about it, you will need the bait to cater for every eventuality, but the chances are you will take most of it home again with you. Fishing for your section is really like fishing a club match all over again, but in a team event such as a National Championship that is really all that you are doing. In fact, you might have to sacrifice your chance of individual glory for the sake of ensuring good points for the team.

Only you can decide upon your open-match approach. Knowledge of the venue helps, of course, and you should have some idea of the worth of the peg you have drawn before setting off to fish. Have you a chance of an individual win or even a top-six placing, or will you only be fishing for your section? If you have done your homework, you will have some idea yourself. But if you haven't and are fishing a venue that is relatively unknown to you, ask around after drawing your peg. You'll soon know if you're in with a chance by the looks on other anglers' faces . . . even if they don't tell you the truth. The rest is up to you. Perhaps a method at which you are proficient will be right for your section, but will give you no chance of winning the match from your peg. Then it would be wise to fish for your section and miss on the chance of individual glory. However, if you suspect, or have been told, that the match might be won from your area, it would pay you to throw caution to the winds and go for it. Fish too negatively on a good peg and you might waste your chance. Fish too positively on a bad one and you might miss out on a section win. The decision is yours.

CHAPTER TWENTY–SEVEN

Fishing a National

National Championships remain at the pinnacle of most match anglers' careers. After graduating from pleasure angler to match angler, through club events to open competitions, the time comes when you're given the chance to fish in a National. With six divisions of 90 teams and 12 anglers in a team, more than 6,000 anglers fish Nationals every season. No longer are they the elitist 'All-England' events, and while many top match anglers would bemoan the loss of one big National, they are forgetting about the thousands of anglers who, if that remained the case, would never get the opportunity to compete in an event that offers a real chance of glory and big cash prizes. In truth, there's much more to fishing a National than winning. Taking part is something in itself, for the atmosphere at all Nationals, Division One or Division Six, is very special. Even if you are not an open match angler, the expansion of the divisions has allowed clubs to take part as long as they pay an affiliation fee to the organisers – the National Federation of Anglers. Then, if that club of perhaps only 20 members put in the work required in practice, there's no reason why they shouldn't be called up to the rostrum to receive their winners' medals. There are few greater feelings in angling than to be recognised by your fellow anglers.

Nationals are run like any other team match that is decided on points. One member of each 12-angler team fishes in each section. The sections are given letters A to M (omitting I because of the confusion with the figure 1), and each angler is allocated a section by computer at NFA headquarters in Derby. This section draw is kept secret and nobody knows until the morning of the match in what section he is to fish. When the team captains line up to make the draw, they tell the organisers the name of their team. The captains are then given a sealed envelope containing the pre-determined section draw (team members' names and pools money have to be supplied months in advance, although team changes can be made on the day). Then they draw a peg number, just as in any other match. Each of the team then fishes that peg number in their section.

Then the fun really starts. Instead of over 1,000 anglers making their way to their allotted sections, coaches are laid on for the purpose. Each angler has to find the coach marked with his section – C1-24, for example – load his gear on, and travel to the section. National novices find these trips awe-inspiring. Everyone seems to know everything about their section except you, so all you do is sit quietly saying nothing. Don't worry. They are probably as much in the dark as you are and simply putting on a brave face. Those who really know the score are likely to be sitting as quietly as you, smiling silently to themselves about the comments that are being made. Once the coach arrives at the water, there's something of a free-for-all when all the fishing tackle is unloaded, after which you have to find your way to your peg. Stewards – each team has to provide two – will probably check your tackle for signs of banned bait, and at this point it is worth having a quick chat with them to make friends. Getting the stewards on your side can work to your advantage when it comes to keeping anglers back from the skyline or even finding out what's happening elsewhere in your section. After that, it's just like any other match fished to NFA rules.

When the whistle goes for the end of the contest, do not leave your peg until you have been weighed in. Stewards will do this, but check the scales and check also that your

Above: Get everything right and you could be celebrating like this.

Left: Help from local experts can be invaluable in your preparations.

Opposite, top: Fishing your first national can be a daunting experience.

Opposite, bottom: The crowds gather as Jeff Perrin fishes the John Smith's Championships.

weight has been correctly recorded on the weigh-in cards. Nationals have been won and lost through stewards' errors, although thankfully these are now very rare occurrences. The weigh-in completed, every angler makes his way back to the coach, the register is called, the coach returns to the headquarters and you can relay your tales of success or woe to your team-mates.

It takes only a couple of hours for the results to be announced, during which time the tension can be tremendous, especially if your team is in with a chance of promotion. Each National has 15 teams that are promoted (except Division One) and 15 that are relegated (except the bottom division, unless a new division is to be created because more teams have joined the NFA). Results are worked out on a points basis, with each section winner receiving the same number of points as there are teams competing in the match. With a bookie in attendance, cash is handed out to the victors, although pools winnings are sent later in cheque form from the organisers.

PREPARATION FOR A NATIONAL

So much for the running of a National, but what about the preparation? When should that begin? Of course, that all depends on how seriously you intend to take the match. For many teams, it is the highlight of the season and they spend months getting ready for this one match. For them, any result apart from promotion is a disaster. Other teams treat Nationals as days out, and enjoy every minute without even thinking about the match beforehand. Practice sessions are avoided and preparations kept to a minimum. For these teams, it is a bonus not to be relegated.

However, if you want to do well, there is no substitute for hard work, and by doing just this several teams have risen to the top division in only a few years, no mean feat when most of the annual matches have taken place on different venues. For a team to do well, you need 12 good anglers who have

nothing less than total commitment. That is something few teams can boast and you can still be reasonably successful without this commitment until you reach the very top and compete against teams whose captains and sponsors expect nothing less than total professionalism. But what about most teams preparing for a National? Even if the commitment is there, few teams, especially those in the lower divisions, will have 12 very good anglers. They might have eight, or even 10, but in a points match like a National Championships, no team looking to mount a serious challenge can afford to 'carry' anyone. This is where practice comes in, because even a mediocre team can still perform well in a National Championship by putting in the time and effort required to succeed.

Preparations should begin as soon as you know where you will be fishing, usually one year in advance of the match itself. These preparations can take many forms. Any team that really means business should visit the venue at least once during the season before their National. This way they can start to familiarise themselves with the place. The fishing might be very different from what it will be on National day, but don't worry about that. Getting to grips with the venue is what it's all about, learning its moods, fishing it in different conditions and pooling all this valuable information together. Once you're into the new season, serious practice should begin. Clubs on whose fisheries Nationals are held will almost certainly be running several open events leading up to the big day. Attend as many as you can, either to fish or simply to watch. Really there's no substitute for fishing, but make sure that you follow the weigh-in to assess your performance relative to others in your section. If anyone has beaten you, try to find out how they fished. Regular team meetings are important, and the captain should start to compile a dossier on his team members' performances, not only to gather information about the venue, but also to help with team selection.

It is extremely useful when preparing for a National to acquire some local help. Get in quickly and you can probably obtain the services of a good angler who will be able to pass on hints and tips about the venue and its methods. Listen carefully to what he has to say and adapt his comments to your own findings. Don't make the mistake of taking absolutely everything that he says as gospel, remembering that many local experts fish every match to win as an individual, which could be fatal for a team wanting to do well. A closed-season outing with your local expert can give you a good grounding, especially if he takes you to several different spots along the match length. It would also be a good idea if he took some tackle along with him to demonstrate some of the rigs and methods required, perhaps even plumbing the depth at each spot. Be generous with your tutor and he will look after you as well. Some sort of payment certainly wouldn't go amiss. Try also to ensure that he spends National day with the team, as last-minute advice on the conditions on the day might be important.

Some venues lend themselves to team tactics, others don't, and it's a foolish team captain who tells his team that all must fish in a certain way just like robots. If the team has prepared well enough, the captain won't have to say anything to his team. They should all know what is required and what they have to do. It is far better for a team to learn among themselves and agree a method if one has emerged as the best. This might be the case on a canal, but it's hardly likely on a natural river where different areas of the match length will respond to different methods. On natural venues such as this, the strongest teams in terms of skill and experience will show their true worth, but on canals where much of the match length will be similar, teams who have practised and shown all-round commitment can also put on a good performance.

To give you an idea of the preparation involved in a National, here's a year in the life of a squad intending to do well in the Championships. Let's assume that the match takes place in July.

August (the previous year) – find out the venue and acquire the services of a local expert.

September – visit the venue, preferably for a team competition. Most of the squad should fish, but a few can walk the bank, watching for likely methods and techniques that might work on the big day. However, don't take too much notice of the result as a venue in September can fish differently to one in July.

October to April – contact should be maintained between team captain or manager and the local expert enlisted to help.

March – book tickets for matches leading up to the event. Book time off work for anyone who is able to spend a week practising on the venue. This should be the last available practice week. National venues are closed to competitors for six days before the match.

April – the whole squad should visit the venue some time in the closed season with the local expert. Walk as many sections as you can, with the expert demonstrating techniques and rigs, offering advice and pinpointing good areas. As it is the closed season, he cannot fish, but he can still give you a detailed insight into the venue. If possible, make a video of the day. This is also the time to pay entry fees and pools to the National Federation of Anglers, and a good time to sort out the two stewards that you will need.

May – produce a transcript of the video and discuss this and the day spent with the expert at a team meeting.

June – practice proper begins with the start of the season. With the match in July, there are only a few weeks, so practice will have to be intense. Every member of the squad should fish several matches, and also walk the bank to see what others are doing. Assess every performance and try to see whether a pattern emerges. Those who are spending the week practising should try different and unusual methods to provide contingency plans should the main approach go wrong. Make numerous telephone calls during the week to check everything is going to plan. If any of the squad feel that they are not confident on the venue by now, they should be honest enough to admit it.

July – the week before the match sees the

Left: Even twice-world-champion Bob Nudd has to prepare.

Below: Work hard in match fishing and you could be like Dave Wesson, 1992 world champion at the age of 21!

last and all-important squad meeting where final methods are discussed and agreed. Confidence should be high for any squad that has worked this hard, and anyone who doesn't make the final 12 is bound to be disappointed. However, team fishing isn't just about those anglers fishing the match, and everybody in the squad should feel a part of what, hopefully, will be a successful National Championships on the day.

Index